AF559639

Indian Millennials

Who are they, really?
Indian
Mille
nnials
a.m. gautam

ALEPH

ALEPH BOOK COMPANY
An independent publishing firm
promoted by ***Rupa Publications India***

First published in India in 2024
by Aleph Book Company
7/16 Ansari Road, Daryaganj
New Delhi 110 002

ISBN: 978-81-19635-89-4

1 3 5 7 9 10 8 6 4 2

Printed in India

For Woolf, the cat
and Goosey, the girl

'All generalizations are dangerous, even this one.'

—Alexandre Dumas

CONTENTS

Introduction

WHO ARE THE MILLENNIALS, REALLY?

'Any idea who Millennials are?' I asked Soham, a thirty-year-old from Gokul, the Uttar Pradesh village famous for being the childhood home of Krishna, a Hindu deity.

'That movie? With superheroes?' he guessed.

▪

What is a generation? Simply put, it's a way of collectively referring to the people born in a specific time period.

If that sounds made-up that's because it kind of is, but in the same way that nation-states, religions, weddings, and brands are made-up concepts we use to make sense of the world and our place in it.

But generational cohorts are still more haphazard than these other constructs.

There is no regulatory body that recognizes or ratifies a break between consecutive generations, for instance. We don't know who was the last Boomer baby or the first Gen Z baby. Newspaper headlines don't proclaim stuff like 'People born between 1981 and 1996 to be known henceforth as Millennials!' every twenty years or so. The names of generations are decided not by some official commission or group but via natural selection of sorts. Whatever name sticks the longest becomes the 'formal' name of a generation, and people may continue to use alternatives if they so wish. For example, in the case of my generation, natural selection has favoured the name used by Neil Howe and William Strauss in their book, *Millennials Rising: The Next Generation*. The exact years that define a generational period are also chosen in an arbitrary manner.

For simplicity's sake, I have picked the generally accepted range of 1981–1996 for someone to be called a Millennial.

For all this apparent laxity, however, generations are a fixture in discussions of culture, politics, art, advertising, and product development in all sorts of industries. The concept also figures frequently in our day-to-day conversations when people express hope in the 'new' generation, deride it for slacking off and being too soft, or talk about how their own generation is better or worse off than other generations.

Why?

Well, because generational shifts are 'very real, even as they're also imaginary', as Malcolm Harris puts it in his book *Kids These Days: Human Capital and the Making of Millennials*.

People born in the same time period live through the same large-scale events that shape the zeitgeist in unique ways, and the similarity of this experience can often cut across other divides such as religion, class, caste, and language. These 'events' that characterize a generation and set it apart from others can be anything from war, rapidly increasing prosperity, or economic depression to the rise of nationalism, health crises, and the development of revolutionary new technologies.

Naturally, there is a great deal of variance across a generation's lived experience in different parts of the world.

For example, the Silent Generation, the people born between 1928 and 1945, had radically different lives depending on whether they lived in America or India.

In the US, it was a time of post-war economic growth. Good job prospects and increased purchasing power led to increased consumerism. A pretty good time to be growing up, in effect, with little reason to doubt traditional institutions and hierarchies.

In India, on the other hand, that generation took their first steps in the horrific shadow of Partition, especially in northern and eastern India and their lives were shaped by all the challenges of a newborn nation-state.

Similar comparisons can be drawn for Boomers, born between 1946 to 1960.

In the US this generation lived through the Vietnam War, the counter-cultural movement against that war, the assassination of John F. Kennedy, and Nixon's Watergate Scandal.

In India, the Boomers witnessed two wars (with China in 1965, and with Pakistan in 1971), embraced newfound food security (brought on by the Green Revolution), and had their first brush with authoritarianism when Indira Gandhi imposed an Emergency in 1975. Towards the end of authoritarian excesses like forced sterilization, they also saw what mass movements could do to challenge the government's power in independent India.

Coming to our generation, here's what the Pew Research Center has to say about Millennials in the US.

> Most Millennials were between the ages of 5 and 20 when the 9/11 terrorist attacks shook the nation, and many were old enough to comprehend the historical significance of that moment, while most members of Gen Z have little or no memory of the event. Millennials also grew up in the shadow of the wars in Iraq and Afghanistan, which sharpened broader views of the parties and contributed to the intense political polarization that shapes the current political environment. And most Millennials were between 12 and 27 during the 2008 election, where the force of the youth vote became part of the political conversation and helped elect the first black president. Added to that is the fact that Millennials are the most racially and ethnically diverse adult generation in the nation's history. Yet the next generation—Generation Z—is even more diverse.

While we may be conscious of a few events mentioned here, and they may even have affected our lives in important ways (via Indian immigrants in post-9/11 America, for example), it is difficult to posit that things like the 2008 elections and the US overseas wars defined Indian Millennials in the same way as American Millennials.

In India, we are the first generation in the country to grow up in a non-socialist economy. Colour television came to the country in 1982 and became a coveted family possession for the growing middle class, along with the Maruti 800 car. The country went through the collective trauma of Indira Gandhi's assassination and the anti-Sikh violence that followed it. Engineering, especially in computer science, established itself in the popular imagination as a ticket to prosperity while the US issued thousands of H-1B visas. The 2008 financial crash left many people disillusioned, but digital technology would go on to become a defining force in our lives, much encouraged by low mobile internet data prices in the recent years (fifth lowest in the world, currently).

Millennials are somewhat novel, however, because our differences around the world are much less pronounced than in the case of previous generations.

This is due to a number of factors like the firm establishment of a US-led capitalistic world order after the Soviet Union's disintegration in 1991, the liberalization of the Indian economy in the early 1990s, and of course, the internet. As award-winning author and generational workforce expert Tammy Erickson writes for the *Harvard Business Review* while comparing generations in the US and India, 'globally, Generation Ys' immersion in personal technology enabled this generation to experience many of the same events and, as a result, develop as the most globally similar generation yet.'

These similarities and differences with our Western counterparts overlap to create interesting contradictions in various aspects of culture, ideas, and politics.

Take food, for instance.

Our tastes are more expansive than those of our parents and grandparents. Eating out is commonplace and food delivery apps have 'scaled up' by penetrating Tier II and Tier III cities. One could easily get cherry tomatoes and blueberries in Dehradun today to try out a recipe from Instagram. Just two hours away, however, a Zomato delivery person in Haridwar can be beaten up for delivering non-vegetarian food by the same people who had placed that order.

The video of the beating is then circulated on WhatsApp to score some street cred, make it to TV, or get noticed by someone in the political class. In the 'new India', one has to be careful about what one eats.

At the same time, another, more general fear about food, has captured our imaginations.

Everyone is afraid of eating something or the other, and the quicksand nature of our world is such that the more informed we strive to be, the deeper we sink into chaos. Nutritionism, with its unique strain of reductive science, blossoms on the internet and bears grotesque fruits. We worry about consuming enough protein, we are dead scared of sugar, and we wonder whether the palm oil in our snacks is poisonous for us. Social media nutritionists and food influencers reap this fear for maximum benefit online.

Moreover, what we choose to eat is subject to ideological preferences.

On one side it could be about the entirely unscientific division of food into tamasic, sattvic, and rajasik categories. On the other, it could mean being self-righteously vegan in a country where large-scale animal husbandry is negligible in comparison to the West and a great part of the population struggles to meet their daily protein requirement.

Veganism's promise of saving the planet with our food choices is characteristic of how most concerns about the environment are now framed in consumerist terms—buy this, don't buy that, use this, don't use that. The only power we have in staving off the apocalypse rests in our pockets, we are told. The individualism that is so characteristic of our generation makes us gullible against narratives that shift the blame from corporations and governments to individuals. Naturally, the responsibility for solving the crises rests with those who accept the blame.

The factors that caused Millennials all over the world to have more in common than any other previous generation run through all that we do, feel, or express.

Especially, what we do, feel, or express online.

Consumerism co-opts every single aspect of our life, a phenomenon that many refer to as neo-liberalism, and turns each of them into a capital or commodity of some kind.

Whether it's the latest iPhone as a status symbol or the popular English-speaking 'guru' who turns baroque religion into palatable spirituality, the commodities feed our need for identity and community. The food we eat, the workout regimes we try to follow, the language we use to caption our selfies, our professed ideological and political beliefs are all consumed by capitalism and regurgitated in marketable ways that can help us feel unique. Courtesy of the internet, these apparently unique identities can form niches together and see the world through the lens of their choosing.

This is great for the market, of course, because it provides easier and more accurate ways of targeting customers.

The industries that monetize body issues, for instance, have discovered a whole new market in Millennial men. Beefed-up male bodies are now the norm in everything from Bollywood movies to daily soaps, social media platforms, and underwear advertisements. A great body has also come to represent a form of social capital that helps us create the image of a disciplined, modern, and masculine man ready to take on the world.

Those desirous of perfect bodies can hardly be expected to hold fast food chains like McDonald's in high esteem, which explains their declining popularity among urban Indians. However, good ol' Mac-Dee is still the preferred venue for hanging out and throwing 'cool' birthday parties in Haridwar, my hometown, a decade and a half after it came to town (as part of our first shopping mall) in 2013.

It is even aspirational enough for people to write reviews after their visit. Here is one titled (what else but) 'I am loving it' from someone in 2017.

> I love going to McDonald and ordering hamburger and snacks. Food is amazing and nothing like it. The place is very ambient and presentation is quite impressive. They have great customer service willing to help their customers every way possible. From a price point its a value for money and very reliable in their quality. All in all worth giving a go cause I am lovin' it

Only, McDonald's (and most other restaurants) do not serve hamburgers in India due to our complex relationship with beef-eating.

If I had to guess, I'd say that the reviewer has assumed 'hamburger' to be synonymous with 'burger' due to the word's ubiquity in foreign movies and shows. In a similar manner, 'ambience', a commonly encountered term in restaurant reviews, has become 'ambient'. Clearly, the diner's opinion is trying hard to fit into the standard template of review-writing by using phrases like 'price point', 'value for money', and 'worth giving a go'.

It is a good example of how unwritten rules of online communication can affect language, flattening it out to be fit for purposes of marketing or self-promotion rather than clear articulation. It goes without saying, almost, that the language in question has to be English.

Muscular bodies and English-speaking skills are important social aspirations not only for our self-worth but also to stand apart in a fledgling dating pool.

In any case, dating, as the Western world understands it, has not moved beyond urban centres even for the youngest generations, despite what founders of dating apps may be telling their investors. Smartphones and cheap data plans, however, have resulted in a number of digital-first relationships where the partners can be in constant contact with each other every day even if they only manage to meet a handful of times a year.

Meanwhile, those who did successfully escape to metropolitans from the rest of the country for education or employment have sustained their upward mobility on a steady diet of American media—sitcoms, news articles, Hollywood, music, and everything else they could access. Courtesy of *F.R.I.E.N.D.S* and *How I Met Your Mother*, we keep looking for New York-style meet cutes and cafe or bar pick-ups in cities like Bangalore, Mumbai, Delhi, Chandigarh, Chennai, etc.

Perhaps we have even managed to create some of what we tried to find, and that's progress of sorts, even if we eventually settle for an arranged marriage with someone our parents like in the right caste, religion, and class. We can always buy some nice pre-wedding shoots to create the illusion of a love story coming to its happily-ever-after conclusion.

Like our counterparts in the rest of the world, Millennials in India are quite adept at creating and consuming illusions. Nowhere is this more apparent than in breaks from reality that cause people to become invested in conspiracy theories.

Our generation did not invent misinformation or lies, but we are the first ones to cross over into a post-truth world where all assertions are double-faced, elastic, and subject to wilful misinterpretation.

There are the funny folks in the US who believe that the earth is flat and all birds are surveillance drones, but there are also vile QAnon followers, vaccine-deniers, and anti-immigrant propagandists. Closer home, we can see how a society steeped in misogyny and general distrust turned a young actor's suicide into wide-reaching conspiracy theories about his murder. For all the hue and cry about the twenty-four-hour news cycle and our attention spans, conversations about Sushant Singh Rajput's death are still going strong more than three years after the incident. While so much else, no less tragic, from the same time has gone the way of blissful forgetfulness.

One of the reasons for this endurance is the sense of community that conspiracy theories provide their adherents.

A common set of beliefs, held together with moral righteousness, and notions of having been wronged by the 'system', also create fertile ground for propaganda films like *The Kashmir Files.* It is all the better for them that their benefactors in politics and media do the utmost to promote them with no concerns about the hate being poured into society.

The largest generation in the country may find itself quite receptive to this hate because they are increasingly frustrated with their precarious positions in life.

Consider, for instance, that a majority (about 70 per cent) of young Indians aspire to software engineering positions, and yet a mere fraction (10 per cent, according to some estimates) of engineering graduates are expected to find jobs.

Even that coveted minority, however, is not safe from job insecurity and a work culture that treats employees as resources to be drained for their last minute on the clock.

In the work from home (WFH) set ups necessitated by the pandemic, some employees have resisted the status quo by holding two or more full-time jobs simultaneously. The practice is commonly referred to as moonlighting, and IT employers have come out rather strongly against it. Some companies like Wipro have even fired moonlighting employees, regardless of their performance at work.

In the next few decades, as AI (Artificial Intelligence) solutions become more and more sophisticated, there will be further shifts and more new trends in the labour market.

It should be interesting to see how Millennials, who now make up a major chunk of the workforce in India, will respond to this unprecedented situation.

A key difference between our generation in India and the US, or most of the Western world, is that of ideology. The majority of American Millennials hold liberal positions, and right-wing leaders generally depend on older generations for support.

In India, on the other hand, right-wing Hindu nationalism has been readily accepted by young people. Prime Minister Narendra Modi, in fact, has a segment of his most staunch supporters among Millennials in India. The rise in the popularity of conservatism is explained by some as a failure of liberalism to be relatable for our generation. Those who do call themselves liberal then need to assess their ideas without any dogmatic baggage from elsewhere and ask themselves what liberalism means from their particular place in the social hierarchy.

Sometimes I imagine our generation as a giant toddler with its head in glittery American clouds and its feet that walk on Indian soil, stumbling at potholes even as its eyes follow CGI-saturated technicolour dreams.

As Snigdha Poonam wrote in her book *Dreamers: How Young Indians Are Changing the World*, 'They (the Millennials) are hitting adulthood with the cultural values of their grandparents—socially conservative, sexually timid, god-fearing—but the life goals of American teenagers.' In other words, '86% of them have been found to feel anxious about their future, but they are bent on world domination.'

The toddler's mind tries to think of an app for every need of toddlers everywhere, the mouth gulps down avocado toast and chases it down with craft beer while trying to calculate its total protein intake for the day. The heart, meanwhile, is stuck halfway between the clouds and the earth. It wants desperately to know where it belongs, and what it can call its own. When the child looks down at its feet every once in a while, it is through a fog—that of our metropolitan existence or our aspirations of metropolitan existence—and the sight of worn-out slippers on our dusty feet invokes for us either utter disgust, the famous '90s-kid nostalgia', or a delusional superiority complex about desi feet, desi slippers, desi road, desi potholes, and desi jugaads for circumventing them.

■

Soham, the man from Gokul I asked about Millennials, had been thinking of Avengers, a fictional superhero team created by an American comic book company, when he answered me.

The superheroes have become spectacularly popular in India ever since the comics were adapted into movies. So much so that the last movie in the franchise, *Avengers Infinity War* (2017), was released here a week before its release in America. When I explained the mix-up to Soham and told him that Millennial is the name of a generation to which he and I both belong, he chuckled.

'But I am right—we are like the Avengers of a new India, aren't we?' he said. I could not decide whether to agree or disagree.

1

THE BODIES OF MILLENNIAL MEN

I knew I was a Fat Guy when my T-shirts betrayed me.

As my belly protruded forwards and downwards week by week, the traitorous T-shirts receded up in shame, exposing a thumb-length or two of my flesh to the world, and I kept tugging at them though I knew it was a lost cause. A few months ago, I had given up on formal shirts because tucking them in the trousers gave my belly a sharp definition and did bad things to my delusion of being 'stocky, not fat' like George Costanza in *Seinfeld*.

The casual shirts went next when buttoning-up became almost as uncomfortable as tucking in. Holding my breath and sucking in helped for a little while, but not when I sat down, and too much of the region between my lower back and my ass was visible to the people behind me.

When a helpful colleague tapped me on the shoulder and informed me of this unwanted visibility, I had to hold my breath to resist punching him in the face. I pulled up my jeans, pulled down my T-shirt, and murmured a thank-you instead.

I could buy new clothes in a larger size, of course, but I didn't. That would be tantamount to accepting my predicament as permanent and I desperately wanted it to be temporary. Instead, I made do with workarounds—put on a long vest underneath my T-shirts some days, and donned an oversized office hoodie over them other days. Overshirts and jackets were, and remain, my best friends—they don't need to be buttoned up or tucked in, are generally loose, and prove helpful in covering things up.

But it's not just clothes, of course.

I found myself cupping my chest and wondering if I had

'man-boobs' yet or not. It was probably stuck in my head because I remembered a batchmate who was teased endlessly about his 'boobs' through four years of college.

A friend's bike touched a speed-breaker and produced the sickening sound of metal against gravel when I was riding pillion behind him. I was ashamed because he had gotten it serviced just a week before.

I produced copious amounts of sweat and after climbing a flight of stairs I panted like a husky in Delhi. I thanked the universe for blessing me with the non-smelly kind of sweat. A long romantic walk left me with chaffed thighs, and for the next few days, I had the experience of going about town with sandpaper stuffed between my legs.

In the shower, I sucked in my belly every other day to check if I could still see my toes easily or not. It hurt when I could not any more.

If all of this sounds horrible in a somewhat undignified way, that's because it is. It is quite silly and, at least for me, it has also been scary. I know I have a lot in life to be happy about, and I know that most of our body image issues are not related to health and fitness. I also know that the fitness-wellness industry is a $4.4 trillion ecosystem, run by big businesses that pour money into favourable studies and research papers, or celebrity-entrepreneurs who mould the pop culture in their own image.

I know all the arguments and vocabulary of body positivity.

But I continue to deeply dislike, if not hate, my fat, loose, non-muscular body, as do so many others.

■

I came across the work of Michiel Baas, an anthropologist and a well-respected India scholar while researching men's relationship with their bodies.

In his book *Muscular India: Masculinity, Mobility & the New Middle Class,* published in 2020 to great acclaim, Baas grounds his research of ten years among gym trainers, young corporates, and professional bodybuilders to explore the new male body ideal that enthrals the Indian middle class. After exchanging a few emails and WhatsApp messages, we connected over a video call (Baas was in Sri Lanka at the time for his current project) and began the conversation by talking about various factors that led to a shift in the perception of male bodies in the last couple of decades.

Baas estimates the origins of this shift to be in the 1990s, which links it inextricably to Millennials. It was a time when gyms in the West were reducing their focus on bodybuilding and becoming more lifestyle-oriented.

As this rebranding trickled into India, it challenged the prevalent view of bodybuilding as a competitive sport or the pastime of 'rowdy types'. Helpfully enough, our economy was opening up right around then and multinational companies from the US were looking at India as a great potential market as well as a supplier of skilled workforce. As Indians zealously invested in upgrading their skills, modernization became the primary aspiration, young professionals began moving to the metropolitans in droves, and a newly affluent middle class emerged with enough disposable income to invest in 'self-improvement'. From learning fluent English and eating 'continental' food to looking smart, everything came under the ambit of this improvement. Belly bulge, common enough to be unnoticeable until then, slowly began becoming completely unacceptable.

Alongside, popular culture was also reshaping the image of manliness.

Muscular bodies of actors like Sunny Deol and Sunil Shetty were replacing the paunches that signified affluence for the previous generation's stars, and Salman Khan took off his shirt in *Pyaar Kiya to Darna Kya* (1998) to great public excitement.

According to Baas, these trends finally boiled over with Shah Rukh Khan's chiselled six-pack abs in *Om Shanti Om* (2007), trumped by Amir Khan's eight-packs just a year later in *Ghajini*.

Wide media coverage was given to the body transformations of these superstars and outlets like Men's Health suggested that chiselled bodies were within everyone's reach with a proper diet and workout regime. In combination with deep socio-economic change and the image of a sharp-looking corporate employee (in contrast with the image of a lethargic government employee), this established the new male body ideal.

In the following years, the ideal pervaded all aspects of culture.

All actors, including not just A-list stars but even minor actors in daily soaps, are now expected to have a certain kind of lean, muscular body irrespective of their characters' needs. Going to the gym is a part of young middle-class men's lives not just in metropolitans but also in Tier II and Tier III cities. If you were to eavesdrop on some conversations in these gyms, as I have, you would easily find men droning on and on about creatine and green tea extract.

Social media has had an outsized effect in recent years, of course, because of the way it minimizes the distance between celebrities and their fans.

The diets and workout regimens that would earlier be found in lifestyle magazines are now always just a scroll away on our smartphone screens. Moreover, the concept of 'celebrity' itself has been diluted and we now have a multitude of perfect-bodied influencers who are more relatable than actors or socialites. They are, therefore, also more aspirational—if the literal boy-next-door can have washboard abs, why can I not be disciplined enough to have them too?

While someone could have looked at SRK or Aamir Khan and thought of them as anomalies, looking at regular people on Instagram will convince you that it is actually you, you with the belly fat and the blunt jawline, that's the anomaly.

'People now workout because they want to transform their bodies into something that makes them stand out, that has a kind of uniqueness to it and that's definitely due to social media because we are constantly bombarded with these images (of the perfect male body). Since interaction with images or videos of a particular kind will motivate social-media algorithms to show you more of the same, it's easy to think that there's something wrong with you if you don't have a body like that,' Baas told me during our conversation. 'Since a perfect body demands a lot of investment in terms of money, time, discipline, etc., the body in this situation has just become something to market.'

▪

Despite everything, and no matter how discontented we may be, despising our own bodies can still be a disconcerting experience.

It is, after all, our literal physicality that we are talking about here. We cannot exist without our bodies outside of science fiction; it isn't a meat-suit that can be shed at will (despite what certain religious and spiritual conmen may tell you) for a better alternative.

Funny, considering that for the longest time now I have thought of my body as if it were only a transient thing. A sort of rental house I am settling for while I construct a better-looking home to which I'll shift in the near future. At the same time, whenever I look at any photographs older than a year, I am always surprised to find that I looked better back then, much leaner and fitter. I cannot, however, remember thinking this at the time those pictures were taken.

My body is always better in the past, and it will always be better in the future, but in the present, here and now, it is an object of disgust.

The more I noticed this in my way of thinking, the more I wondered, are we our bodies or are we our consciousness?

Most people would say that we are a combination of both, and that is undoubtedly true, but I wonder about the ratio in this combination. To put it in somewhat wonky terms, if you had to choose between being brain-dead (body without consciousness) and paralysed (consciousness without body), what would you choose? I gave this choice to a bunch of people over a month (only as a thought experiment, to be clear. I did not abduct anyone and threaten to put them in either of these terrible states) and everyone, without exception, chose the latter. When probed about their choice, they always came up with some version of the fact that they'd much rather be aware of their condition at any point in time, even if they were helpless to do anything about it, than sleep through their whole life.

For most of us, it would seem, our consciousness, is who we are, whereas our bodies are what we own.

I believe what Baas says about people working out to market their bodies on social media has a lot to do with how this view of our bodies as our possessions fits in so perfectly with our exhibitionist digital lives. The way we are constantly told by everything around us that we can get a better life by making our bodies 'better' is not so different from being told that we need to upgrade to the latest iPhone model or a shiny new car to be cool and stay relevant.

The other side of that aspiration is, of course, FOMO, the fear of missing out.

You could be judged for having a suboptimal body just as you'd be for having a cheap smartphone or an old car. It would signify that you haven't really 'made it' in life, that you are lazy, lacking in discipline, or just unworthy of attention—deserving of disgust even—from those who have what you don't.

A great part of my conversations with friends, colleagues, and family now revolve around the things that they are doing to avoid this disgust.

I don't think I have spent a day in recent years without hearing something or the other about diets, weight loss, muscle gain, belly fat, or the latest gym in town. No one likes the way their body looks and exists, everyone is well-read on the science behind intermittent fasting, they are always either on a diet or considering going on one as soon as possible, and their personal trainers sound like psychopaths with good intentions.

I participate in these conversations, make jokes all around, and give my own two bits on the effectiveness of weight training versus cardio, but I am jaded about the whole thing.

I have begun to suspect that not the strictest diet, nor the most disciplined workout regimen can cure us of this particular malaise. No matter what milestone we set for our bodies, when we reach it we will find that we are on a journey that has no destination.

When I asked Michiel Baas if he thinks there is a point at which people can grow content with their bodies, he didn't sound too hopeful.

'It's a never-ending cycle because when you do indeed get a great body, put pictures on social media and you're bombarded with admiration about how you've been able to transform yourself, then you face a terrifying question: if I stop transforming myself, does the applause stop?'

He talked about a manager in an IT company who had built a great body with years of hard work. The man earned well, had a young child and a happy marriage, but was still contemplating taking growth hormones and steroids to 'grow' some more. Forget corporate employees, even professional bodybuilders seem to have a hard time coping with successful body transformations.

'An interesting thing I noticed is, when these guys would post on social media a lot of times it'd be with respect to a negative case,' Baas says, 'A typical caption (with the post) would be something like "People said I couldn't, so I did it", or "Never listen to your haters".'

But Baas spent a lot of time researching these comment sections and he rarely saw negative comments. 'Nobody ever says to them "oh man you're so scrawny" or something like that. So, the backlash they are anticipating is actually a reflection of the fear that they are still not good enough to deserve appreciation.'

I can relate to some of this because even when I lost more than 12 kilos in one of my most fitness-enthusiast phases during post-graduation, I had no great feelings of achievement. My only thought was that I must keep doing whatever I was doing to end up looking the way I wanted to look. That didn't happen, predictably enough, because I could not 'keep doing what I was doing' when I returned to Bangalore soon after completing my degree.

Working out regularly and eating responsibly every day is not easy, as anyone with a regular 9 to 7 job knows. This is why easier options are now emerging for us all to get the bodies we believe we deserve.

On my way back from the office, I would pass by one such 'option' every day—an advertisement board with the promise of weight loss without any need for working out. The company had a techie name, WeightPro, to inspire confidence and it talked about a 'European medical treatment for fast weight loss, without hunger and energetic feeling'.

The proposition sounded crafted to attract the young IT professionals in Bangalore who don't have the time for gyms and fitness lifestyles, but who can shell out money for a quick-fix solution. I, personally, while not of the most disciplined and hardworking variety, was too sceptical to believe that this promised weight loss would be without a catch. The idea of walking in felt similar to acting on those 'Earn Rs.15000/ month with a part-time job. Call this number' stickers one always finds in public transport. It felt like an act of desperation for those who know they cannot do any better. Also, in hindsight, I think I was ashamed to admit that I did not have the discipline needed to reduce my weight the way 'normal people' do.

So I kept my distance from the WeightPro building—until I began writing this book and found a legitimate excuse to satisfy my curiosity.

Finally, on a day off from work, I took an elevator to WeightPro's office and met Saloni, the house dietician.

As part of the free consultation, Saloni asked me a bunch of questions about my lifestyle, my 'dream weight', whether I was on a very tight schedule to lose my weight (as I could be while preparing for a wedding or some other important event, she explained), my dietary preferences, and my cooking prowess. After the short interview, we went into the adjoining room where I stood on what looked like a modified weighing machine (it's called a Body Fat Monitor, I learned later). I was required to hold a metal bar attached to the machine, and then lift it by turns in front of my chest and at shoulder length on each side. The machine churned out a piece of paper (the size and shape of an invoice you get from card machines, but much longer) when we were done and we returned with it to Saloni's office.

She took me through each statistic (water weight, muscle weight, visceral body fat, minimum calories needed at current body weight, etc.) that the machine had printed out. Most of them pointed towards a need for me to start losing weight as soon as possible.

We then moved to a presentation deck about how WeightPro could help me.

Basically, the 'program' would put me in a state of ketosis for a few months by making sure that I only consumed ready-to-eat and ready-to-cook food. I would need to pick up this food from WeightPro in nifty little packets every two weeks. Although WeightPro's advertising, as well as that of their Indian and global counterparts, projects their program as a groundbreaking innovation (also 'European invention' and 'cutting-edge procedure'), going into ketosis is widely known as the keto diet. Essentially, it means ensuring that 70 per cent of the total calories you consume are derived from fat, less than 10 per cent from carbs, and less than 20 per cent from protein.

The Keto diet, the latest in the long tradition of fad diets, has been around since the 1920s, but it gained traction as a means to lose weight about five years ago when celebrities like Halle Berry, Alicia Vikander, and Vanessa Hudgens, in addition to Silicon Valley enthusiasts, gave it the credit for their lean-and-mean red carpet bodies. Closer home, it has the endorsement of Bollywood bigwigs like Karan Johar, Arjun Kapoor, and many others.

Big money is involved, of course, with some estimates putting the ketogenic diet industry's value at a whopping $8.8 billion. It is expected to rise to more than $12 billion by 2028.

'WeightPro's method is basically the same thing as going on a keto diet by yourself,' Saloni admitted when I confronted her about it, 'but we'll help you stay motivated to follow the lifestyle via daily checks on you and the bi-monthly visits to the centre.'

I asked her about the Keto diet's side effects such as headaches, high cholesterol, and bad breath (due to the acetone produced in the body as a result of ketosis), and she assured me that WeightPro's products are meant to minimize most of them. Except for the bad breath—there is no way to prevent that in a state of ketosis, apparently, and you may not be able to afford a mouth freshener because the 'European medical treatment for fast weight loss' sets one back by about 50-60 thousand rupees a month for as long as it takes them to reach their 'dream weight'.

Saloni's clientele is a mix of men and women, including high-earning graduates from top engineering colleges whose mothers consider their bulging bellies an impediment to impressing potential life partners. In Bangalore alone, WeightPro has dozens of competitors and that indicates a healthy demand for the services they offer, which may include anything from drastic diets to cosmetic procedures and surgeries.

I felt my cynicism grow as I climbed down the stairs after thanking Saloni for her time.

Would I also reach a point of desperation where I can make my peace with bad breath and constant headaches to make my body lean, attractive, or—to cut the bullshit—acceptable?

Sometimes my cynicism about all this—various diets, the 'perfect body', the most effective workouts—can make me feel like an idiot. It can make me feel as though I am just another sucker, falling for the con perpetuated by those who benefit from making people feel ashamed about themselves, especially when there is so much else that is more deserving of my attention. I could try to make my peace with my size, I suppose, but I know that getting on the positivity-and-acceptance bandwagon, or saying that I love my body will not actually make me love it—simply because it's not true.

As the comedian and writer Samantha Irby said in an interview, 'The tyranny around loving yourself is bonkers to me. You don't have to! What is this thing where you have to be publicly celebrating your body? The people who do—great! I wish that

I could—(but) no, I don't. I don't think we all have to love our bodies. It flattens the experience of having one, because they don't all work the same. The world is stacked against you. It's not made for you. It's OK if you want to hate your body.'

You can count me in on that, Irby, you can count me in.

■

Instead of sticking to the binary of fat-are-beautiful and fat-people-are-lazy-crybabies, maybe it would be better if we tried to understand what lies at the root of our opinions.

Human beings, after all, have always had a strange relationship with fat, whether we consider it as an adjective (a person being fat) or a noun (fat as a basic building block of all organic life, or fat as an essential component in food along with carbohydrates and proteins).

In sixteenth-century Europe, for instance, they seem to have liked fat outside of their bodies even as they despised it on, or inside, themselves. At that especially intelligent epoch of Western civilization, you could walk into an apothecary's shop with a complaint about arthritis, bone pain, toothache, or gout and come out with a bottle of human fat in your pocket, to be applied on the affected area of your body.

You could also buy candles and soaps made with human fat.

Neither was this limited to a small set of connoisseurs trading in gothic curiosities, as one might expect.

The market for human fat (called 'axungia hominis' and referred to as the poor sinner's fat) in the sixteenth and seventeenth centuries was so lucrative it led butchers during the French Revolution to offer freshly executed 'graisse de guillotiné' as a specialty to the masses. Trust the French to make revolting things sound fine as hell. Meanwhile, popular European folklore extensively featured witches and werewolves using ointments containing baby fat.

Imagine someone telling their kids these horrifying bedtime tales by the light of the special new candle after giving them a bath with the special new soap!

Making soap with human fat appears to be quite a sticky idea, anyway. The Germans were accused of doing so with the corpses of dead soldiers during World War I. Come World War II and the Nazis too were accused of using the prisoners killed in the concentration camps in soap production (though the claim is hotly debated among holocaust experts).

As recently as 2009, a gang was arrested in Peru whose members confessed to killing five people (the authorities suspected their involvement in as many as sixty disappearances) for extracting human fat. Two of the suspects, according to a report in *The Guardian*, were arrested at a bus station, carrying bottles of liquid fat which they claimed were worth up to £36,000 a gallon. While the story was later contradicted by several Peruvian politicians, I was not too shocked to learn that the purported end goal had been to export the precious liquid to Europe, where it would have been used to manufacture anti-wrinkle cream. As gross as it sounds, there is a poetic symmetry of sorts here about an object of human disgust passing through abductions and murders to end up as a means of satisfaction for human vanity.

The context of how we perceive fat is important because our relationship with it goes deeper than our issues with appearance and social media's beauty standards.

Our current obsession with muscular male bodies, everything they represent for us (masculine strength, for instance, or a disciplined life), what we do to get such a body, and how we feel when we are successful or unsuccessful, are all things that are connected to each other by our age-old relationship with fat.

The phenomenologist Aurel Kolnai can be of help here when he explains in his book *On Disgust,* that bodies that are considered 'too much' (by being fat) are disgusting to us because we perceive them as 'life in the wrong place'. It is as if the excess fat was a sign of an overflowing vitality that predicates death and decay, like an overripe fruit about to fall from the branch, or a swollen corpse. Fat, itself, according to Kolnai is a reminder of mortality for humans, and fat people become objects of disgust by association.

In his incredibly insightful paper 'Fat and Disgust' the anthropologist Christopher Forth references Kolnai's views and talks about how the 'feel of flabby body' in our mind invokes revulsion because of its negative association with everything 'soft' or 'weak'.

Any experience with our culture and society should indicate that for men this weakness or softness would translate to feelings of emasculation and trigger in us a disgust for our bodies.

It explains the discord between discourse and reality wherein what we want from our bodies (a particular aesthetic) is quite different from what we say we want (fitness). The pursuit of fitness would not cause us to worry about our body fat percentage the way we do, and it would certainly not lead us to WeightPro, or make us buy into the keto diet. All of this can only be explained by our need to circumvent self-disgust. However, we must hide our 'dream-weight goals' behind our 'fitness goals' because, after decades of chest-thumping about being hunter-gatherers and alpha males, it would not look good for us to admit our insecurities about feeling soft and weak.

Male insecurities bring us, inevitably, to women.

Until quite recently, by the good graces of patriarchy, women were the only ones to face unreal body standards in our society. Paunches on men may have been acceptable on the silver screen for previous generations, but one struggles to find plump leading ladies in films, no matter which generation we talk about. Institutions like arranged marriage, in particular, made a clear division between what was expected from men (financial stability) and women (beautiful bodies and housekeeping). While men may have now started looking at their bodies as some sort of capital, women's bodies have always been held as an important—perhaps the most important—part of their worth. They have always carried the burden of meeting absurd expectations that objectified each part of their body.

The post-90s middle-class demographic that experienced a shift in the male body image, however, has also seen women get more and more independent with easier access to education and employment. Expectedly, this has upended certain social contracts like that of arranged marriages—if women can also bring financial stability to the table then it stands to reason that men must now also satisfy the standards of beautiful bodies and housekeeping capabilities.

'Do not judge, or you too will be judged. For in the same way you judge others, you will be judged, and with the measure you use, it will be measured to you', the Bible says. Well, we have judged, and how can we now expect to be loved and accepted for the bodies we have, when we have always judged women on their bodies and pressured them into drastic measures to meet our expectations? It does not really matter whether women are interested in this updated dynamic or not because men already believe it to be the new reality.

Resentment against it is widely prevalent and can easily be observed on social media platforms.

Young men, especially those exposed to the global incel culture and its infamous icons like Andrew Tate, the American-British media personality, and promoter of an 'ultra-masculine, ultra-luxurious lifestyle', ignore all nuance and place the blame for their low self-esteem or lack of romantic prospects squarely on modern women's high expectations about money and ideal male bodies. Even among my friends, none of whom are young or stupid enough to fall for incel-flavoured nihilism, it is taken for granted that one's dating prospects become exponentially better with washboard abs and bulging biceps.

Men, it would appear, have fallen for the same con they pulled on women—to be deserving of love, we need to have a certain kind of popularly-approved bodies.

▪

Michiel Baas reckons that body standards can roll back sometimes and there's already a mild counter-cultural trend shaping up in the Indian film industry against overly chiselled male bodies. That may very well be true—and for entirely selfish reasons, I hope it is—but in the meantime I have finally ordered larger T-shirts.

I am also trying to goad myself into working out regularly by remembering that my father died of a heart attack when he was in his early fifties and I don't want to be a literal example of Kolnai's 'life in the wrong place'.

In the meantime, there is a lot of chatter in the Western media about miracle drugs like Ozempic, Wegovy, and Mounjaro that can help people quickly shed weight with minimal side effects. The anti-obesity gold rush has just begun, says a *New York Times* essay called 'Ozempic Can't Fix What Our Culture Has Broken'.

Sooner or later, these medications will make their way to India, as all American favourites eventually do. They may have already, according to some reports.

Now, we know how easy it is to get prescriptions in our country and the drugs' high price (about ₹20,000 for Ozempic and ₹60,000-70,000 per injection for Mounjaro) may be the only deterrent against their wholesale use. This means that we should prepare ourselves, if we had not already with the high cost of healthy food and gym subscriptions, to experience lean bodies as commodities. You can get one if you can afford it, and good luck fitting in the world if you can't.

2

MILLENNIALS VS THE APOCALYPSE

It has been a longstanding belief in my family that Baby-di, the oldest of us siblings, sucks at confrontations of all sorts, and will go to absurd lengths to avoid them. When calling her out on this trait, real or imaginary, my mother, refers to an old fable, and calls Baby-didi a kabootar—a pigeon (never to her face though, which indicates that non-confrontation may be an inherited trait).

According to the fable, a scared pigeon, when facing a cat, closes its eyes instead of flying away. If it cannot see the cat any more, the pigeon reasons, the cat cannot see it either, and in a flight-or-fight situation, it chooses the third option: suicide by delusional inaction.

My mother's choice of expression notwithstanding, I always end up thinking of pigeons and cats when I think about humanity's response to climate change and other environmental crises. It appears that, to a greater or lesser extent, many of us have averted our eyes from the fate waiting for us at the end of the slippery slope down which we have been galloping for a while now.

I do not assume for myself an outside-arbiter position to judge our eye-shutting and gaze aversion. I cannot, because

a) I am as much a part of the problem as anyone else (except industrialists, perhaps, and politicians, soldiers, scientists, pilgrims, sailors, poachers, et cetera, et cetera), and
b) I understand that Nature as an antagonist, comprising everything from rising sea levels, to wildfires, to nameless diseases lying dormant (for now) in the rapidly melting polar ice caps, is truly a Lovecraftian horror.

The problems we face are so huge, so terribly existential, they are enough to drive insane any individual who dares to contemplate them in their entirety. We close our eyes to save our minds. We go through our lives as if things were nice and peachy with the planet not because we want to contribute to its imminent destruction (though that may often be what it amounts to) but simply to avoid breaking down in the middle of the street, our office, or the family dinner.

It follows from the second reason that for older people being shut-eyed pigeons does make a practical, if arguably selfish, sense.

They are probably going to drop dead before the cat pounces on them, so why should they waste their time trying to save themselves? They have already seen their fill of the clear skies and had all the fun they could by pooping on important statues and shiny bald heads, so they can choose to go gentle into the good night. Ignorance is bliss, after all, as the cliché goes.

The rest of us close our eyes at our peril because, to make the analogy more accurate, we are facing not one but dozens of cats, and our wings cannot bear us far enough. Despite tacky promises of mass migration to other planets from tech wunderkinds like Bezos and Musk, we only have this one planet, and it doesn't seem to be very fond of us any more.

▪

But what exactly happens if the pigeon keeps its eyes peeled? Well, it sees the cat in all its terrible, deadly, and hopelessly enormous proportions.

It is difficult, for instance, to have grown up in Haridwar and remain unworried about river pollution.

Haridwar is where the river Ganga enters the plains and where millions of tourists come every year to wash away their accumulated sins. On the Ganga ghats, they enact various other rituals that may improve their standing with the gods.

The river flows faster in Haridwar, and is relatively much cleaner, in comparison to its condition during the rest of its course.

This cleanliness and speed are much appreciated by the people who use it to dispose of their damaged idols, diyas, flowers, and other miscellaneous paraphernalia along with the ashes of their dead, water bottles, plastic bags, chips packets, ice cream sticks, cigarette butts, soaps, shampoos, slippers, and used underwear.

As appalling as it sounds, this is only a fraction of what is dumped into the river by factories and sewage treatment plants.

A 2019 Reuters report estimates that 42 million litres of wastewater is dumped into the Ganga every day in the region around Haridwar alone. Other cities on its banks make their own contributions.

Tanneries in Kanpur, corpses in Varanasi, sewage everywhere. Each place it passes through gives the Ganga something to remember it by, and by the time it merges into the Bay of Bengal, the river has had 6 billion litres of waste dumped into it each day.

We generally find it difficult to visualize exorbitant statistics—as evidenced by the continued existence of the Really Existing Capitalism (REC) driven world order—so get this, 6 billion litres is enough wastewater that, if we put it in half-litre soda bottles, we could stack them up to the moon and back four times over. A bit easier to imagine, right? More distressing too, I expect.

Apart from difficult visualization, exorbitant statistics share another important feature—they seem immune to change. The total number of vehicles on the road in metropolitan cities, the wealth of the world's ten wealthiest people (I say people, but they are all men at the time of this writing), the number of children that die of preventable diseases each year. Countable nouns, all of them, but too large for us to expect any real change in them—just like 6 billion litres of wastewater being dumped into a river at hundreds of discharge points spread over a route of about 2,525 kilometres in the country.

Every time I go home, I worry about the Ganga and do not know how to cope with it. The obvious answer, the one at the tip of your tongue right now perhaps, is to 'do something about it' but do what, honestly?

Isn't that the quintessential Millennial condition, to care about big causes and be completely clueless as to what should be done about them?

I have picked up litter from the ghats, told people off for using detergent while washing their clothes in the river, and never let my family put so much as a marigold flower into it. But if I am to be truthful to myself and look beyond platitudes, I have to wonder, what difference does it make? It appears impossible for an individual, however well-intentioned, to make a significant change.

What about the government, then?

Successive governments have been focussing on the polluted state of the Ganga since the 1980s.

The Modi government launched the Namami Gange Programme with much fanfare when it first came to power in 2014. Uma Bharati, of Babri Masjid demolition fame, was chosen to lead the initiative as the minister for Water Resources, River Development and Ganga Rejuvenation because, we may assume, she had extensive experience in river water management. However, when she stepped down from the position in 2017 only a fraction of the ₹20,000 crores allotted for the programme had been spent and a majority of the planned projects languished in dusty files, never even started, let alone completed.

The government, it would appear, is just as ineffective (or unwilling) as anyone else in bringing about real change. It is better at creating a mess, however.

On a 2021 trip to Varanasi, Vishu, my boatman, told me during an early morning ride on the Ganga that motorboats and large-scale construction near the river have made things worse than ever for those who depend upon it for their livelihoods.

The motorboats can seat more people than the traditional boats, are cheaper, and move faster. They also leak diesel into the waters and the noise produced by their engines is believed to have played a significant part in scaring away the Ganges dolphins, our national aquatic animal, from the region. It'd have been embarrassing to tell him that I had taken a motorboat ride just the previous night to see Dev Deepawali celebrations, so I held my tongue.

I took consolation in the fact that it was my hotel that had arranged a bunch of motorboats for the guests and I shared mine with a couple from Tamil Nadu and a Bengali family. It had been an interesting night.

The ghats were lit with a hundred thousand diyas, to the excitement of national news media and tourists alike. I considered sharing a little nugget of trivia I had dug up that afternoon with the rest of the boat. The beautiful diyas we were admiring had been arranged one by one by teachers from Varanasi's government schools, who presumably had a lot of free time left after their professional duties, but I chose not to mar the evening with political comments.

At the Ganga aarti's conclusion, the Bengali patriarch scooped up some Gangajal in his palms, mumbled a quick prayer, drank the water, and wiped his hands on his hair. His little daughter, six to seven years old, copied him. I turned my face away and thought of the numbers I had looked at just before leaving for Varanasi. The water my companions drank had a 22000 MPN/100ml concentration of faecal coliform bacteria.

The permissible limit is 50 MPN/100ml for drinking water and 500 MPN/100ml for bathing.

The aarti was followed by a fireworks display that went on for about an hour. From our boat, we watched the sky light up and held our phones to it with due obsequiousness. A girl on the motorboat next to mine kept her phone close to the river and captured the fireworks in the water as well as the sky; I imitated her and got an amazing video.

I told myself that maybe it's not such a bad thing to forage for beauty wherever we can find it, and yet was unable to forget the acrid air I had left behind in Noida after boarding the train to Varanasi.

Dev Deepawali, you see, is celebrated two weeks after Diwali, a time of the year that's recognizable for me, and many others, by the dismal condition of the air in Delhi-NCR. Just before my trip, the Air Quality Index (AQI) had been above 450, significantly above the 301 mark that categorizes conditions as 'hazardous'. The main contributor to this air pollution is believed to be stubble-burning by farmers in Delhi's neighbouring states, along with increased activity at brick kilns during winters, but ever since the 2017 Supreme Court ban on firecracker sales in Delhi, popular discourse has been occupied by debates about the importance of religious customs versus the importance of non-poisonous air. In Varanasi and other Tier II cities even this debate does not exist and watching aatishbaazi (playing with fire) remains a folk pleasure.

Unlike in Haridwar, the river floats at an unhurried pace in Varanasi, and human discharge doesn't flow out of sight so soon.

Half-burnt fragments of bright wrappers and shells, debris of the previous night's crackers, still floated on the river the next morning, along with dozens of white paper cups in which the tourists had enjoyed lemon tea. Vishu saw the look on my face, perhaps, and told me how he and his brother would lug bucketloads of Gangajal home for household needs when they were kids. Now, their mother has forced them to get a water connection from the municipality because his brother has a year-old son and Gangajal is no longer clean enough for them to even wash their utensils.

The sun was up high when I stepped down on the ghat from his boat and went looking for a breakfast of kachori-jalebi. On the way, I wondered about the quality of tap water in the city.

Can Vishu's family trust it to be better than Gangajal? I still don't know, but I do know that worryingly high levels of arsenic have been detected in groundwater in parts of eastern UP and Bihar. I hope someone is doing something about it, but how can I be sure? But if it worries me so much then shouldn't I 'do something about it' myself?

It has become a pattern. Each new thing I learn about the environment leads me down the rabbit hole of a hundred new nightmares, thousands of nuanced problems, and the reality of my personal impotence against it all. And this too when I pride myself on not giving in to cynicism easily!

As I talk to more and more people about it, I find my experience and feelings reinforced and mirrored.

Hopeless grief pervades conversations about the environment; it is as if the 'information age' has frozen us into a state of shock by showing us too much of what's wrong with the world, all at once.

Chhavi, a media professional from Kanpur who now lives in Gurugram, tells me that she has no memories of the Ganga from her childhood and doesn't think that the river's condition is ever going to improve. The tanneries are not going anywhere, she says. Neha and her brother Akshay from Patna find it absurd that so many people in her city still take a dip in the brown, smelly waters on Chhath Puja. Soumya in Kolkata is hopeless about the future on all counts, including the environment.

The pigeon looks and the pigeon worries. So it goes, as Vonnegut said.

Add to this the pertinent problem that we live in a time where facts are always slippery and second in line to ideology.

Even an expectedly objective truth such as the state of a water body has subjective interpretations that vary according to the political leanings of the interpreters.

On one hand, there are various reports from international publications dubbing Ganga as the world's most polluted river, on the other hand, the United Nations put Namami Gange among the world's top ten restoration projects in 2022.

Does it mean that things were exceptionally bad, but are getting better? Not necessarily.

Various media outlets reported Yogi Adityanath's pronouncement that 'Ganga is clean now' in January 2023, and yet in its December 2022 report to the National Green Tribunal the Uttar Pradesh government admitted that 66.8 per cent of the drains that ended up in the Ganga were untapped or operating without any treatment capacity. So, which of these contradictory positions do you believe? It's up to you, you can choose, and make a poignant observation that choice is not always a good thing. If you think others will be impressed by the poignancy, you can put it up on X (formerly Twitter) or Instagram.

I talk of the Ganga only as an example, of course, because the way I think about it is characteristic of my relationship with environmental issues in general.

I could have just as well talked about the absence of a jackfruit tree in the orchard behind my childhood home.

Plucking an unripe jackfruit or two for breakfast from its branches made up for a fun Sunday morning when I was in school, and it could be because of nostalgia, but I have never had jackfruits as good. At some point, our neighbours started dumping their trash, polythene bags and all, at its roots and the tree died over a couple of years. It turned into a leafless, fruitless, dry wood skeleton, and the akhada that owned the orchard had it chopped down. Eventually, it ended up as firewood during Kumbh Mela. Fifteen years later, I still feel guilty when I look down at that empty patch of land from my terrace. We enjoyed its fruits, and we should have done more than politely ask our neighbours to stop.

Or maybe it's an overreaction to mourn a single tree when so much else is wrong with the world. The loss of trees is a common enough thing in Haridwar, where they are often the first casualty of 'beautification' drives and road expansion projects. Ever since I left for college, I find the town a bit dustier, and a bit less green, every time I return to it. The locals I meet, my neighbours, general store owners, and family friends, don't seem to mind any of it.

I don't judge them terribly because while I do love trees, I am not much of a naturalist myself. There are only a few species—mango, peepul, eucalyptus, banyan, and deodar—that I can name without relying on the internet and I've never planted any trees though I have donated money sometimes to those who promise to do it on my behalf.

That could be why I don't need to know about wide swathes of forest land being cleared to expand the Dehradun airport. A pair of earbuds on my desk is enough to produce a sinking feeling in my gut. As innocent as they look in their minimalistic charging cases, earbuds are a classic example of products forced upon us by businesses in the name of innovation. In the case of earbuds, their need and demand were most notably created by Apple in 2016 when it did away with the 3.5mm jack in iPhones. Wired headphones, such as the ones usually owned by people until a few years ago, became obsolete trash almost overnight.

Most other mobile companies have followed Apple's lead. It looks profitable to do so—by 2020, Apple was making more money from AirPods alone than Spotify, X, and Shopify make with their entire businesses.

Most earbuds come with irreplaceable batteries and are generally irreparable (iFixit gives AirPods, arguably the most popular earbuds in the world today, a 0 repairability score), ensuring that we need to buy a new pair when the batteries die out or the earbuds stop working for some other reason. Since batteries in most units begin to show a decline after about two years of use, people *have* to regularly buy new earbuds while the old ones end up in landfills.

Giant rivers and childhood trees may be beyond saving but this, at least, sounds like we can do something about it.

We could stop using earbuds, but how can we do that when our phones don't have a 3.5mm jack? Recycling defunct earbuds should be a good, middle-ground kind of an idea. It should be, right?

Right?

Well, I wouldn't be so sure.

Recycling electronic waste was, and remains, a profit-driven nightmare in which the trash is shipped out of wealthy countries to poor countries. Valuable items are then extracted there with little regard for environmental impact. Gold used in electronic circuits, for example, is taken out by freely dousing the waste in nitric and hydrochloric acid, leading to polluted waterways and landscapes.

Only 20 per cent of the world's electronic waste is, in fact, recycled through proper channels, according to a 2019 UN report. All the hype around the virtue of recycling then appears merely to be the market's way of letting us dispose of any guilt we may feel for buying new things and discarding old things. So it goes.

Anyway, Ganga, jackfruit trees, earbuds, what else? Why, pick anything else.

Take streaming.

YouTube's annual CO_2 emissions are the same as that of a city such as Glasgow or Frankfurt. Watching a month of Netflix's top ten global TV hits has the same emissions as a car travelling the distance from Earth to Saturn. Must be a nice car, I suppose. But does that mean we should uninstall all our streaming apps?

Aditya S. Sahadevan, a twenty-three-year-old student from Kerala, who has had anxiety attacks over the condition of our planet, admitted to doing just that. He stopped watching anything on OTT (streaming) platforms when he learned that an hour of streaming releases 0.6g of CO_2.

It sounds like a noble thing to do, except for the fact that the same article in *The Guardian* that provides us with the data about Netflix and YouTube ends with Daniel Schien, inventor of a carbon modelling tool used by Netflix, the BBC, and the Carbon Trust among others, cautioning us against worrying too much about these numbers.

'I'm not saying we don't need to care about it,' he says, 'but something as innocent as muesli, with milk, has a higher carbon footprint than one hour of streaming.'

Make of this what you will. Stop eating muesli with milk, or keep watching Netflix, I really am in no position to tell you, and I doubt anyone else is either.

What's next? How about transportation?

Several people I know have already made a switch to electronic vehicles or EVs, especially in metropolitans such as Bangalore and Delhi. Charging stations are not so common yet, and there are the occasional mechanical issues in two-wheelers, but these hiccups seem to be worth the emission-less futuristic EVs. The government is also offering attractive subsidies and tax rebates to support a switch to EVs.

But, as with everything that starts out looking nice and peachy for the environment, people are now beginning to spot worms in the woodwork.

Here's one: since EVs run on electricity, how 'green' they are ultimately depends on how green is a country's power grid.

So, for some of the Western countries that have decreased their reliance on coal for electricity in favour of nuclear and solar power, switching over to EVs could make a lot more sense than it would for countries such as ours that continue to rely upon fossil fuels for electricity.

Try another one on for size—the production of batteries that power EVs relies on lithium, cobalt, and some rare earth elements. Procuring these raw materials can often be a disastrous enterprise.

Most of the world's cobalt, for example, comes from the Democratic Republic of Congo where it's not unusual for 'mine workers' to be children chipping away at mineral deposits with hand tools. The local communities at large also incur great risk in the process because cobalt mining releases hazardous tailings and slags into the environment, and smelting (the process of extracting a metal from its ore) produces harmful gases such as sulphur oxide. Automakers envision a future in which they would not have to source cobalt from unregulated 'artisanal' mines, or would not have to use cobalt in battery production. But this is still a distant future.

For now, we seem to be faced with that old choice—let the miserable child remain chained in the basement, or forego the utopian Omelas.

Rivers, trees, earbuds, electric vehicles, video streaming. We could keep listing down similar stuff and it would never get over. It feels like our generation was handed down the world with all its 'System Failure!' buttons flashing, and no instructions on how to make things better.

It would be understandable if we were to avert our eyes, as I said in the beginning, but we have done better than that.

Various studies suggest that Millennials are more aware of environmental issues than any previous generation, and are willing to make lifestyle changes they deem better for the environment. Yet, our outlook is far from optimistic and hopeful, and the broad objective of these 'lifestyle changes' is limited to a desire of achieving non-complicity in the planet's destruction.

It follows, of course, that many—perhaps most—of us who did not choose ignorance have instead accepted the apocalypse as inevitable.

The pigeon sees the cat, appraises its options, and judges that it can neither take flight nor put up a fight.

So it goes. It goes nowhere.

▪

In a 2021 survey of 10,000 young people by Lancet, more than half of the respondents expressed the belief that 'humanity is doomed'.

This cynicism is commonplace now, and it is having profound effects on us.

Many in our generation have gone far enough to seriously consider the idea of anti-natalism because it seems futile—even cruel and irresponsible—to welcome new life in an irreparably damaged world. Terms like eco-anxiety, eco-distress, and eco-grief are already becoming common parlance among psychiatrists in the West, and will soon start leaking into our part of the world, if they have not already.

Personally, I have begun to experience an overhanging sense of grief and guilt about the environment, and it stays somewhere in my gut, no matter where I go or what I am doing. It's not the kind of grief that cripples you and doesn't let you get out of your bed in the morning, but the quieter kind that settles like a filter over your vision and makes sure that even the bright and happy things in life turn hazy, look dimmer, a little less happy.

And the question hangs over us still—what can we do about it all? If we ignore the option of making a complete break from reality, we are left with a very small set of choices:

1. Become an environmental activist
2. Buy certain things
3. Don't buy certain other things

If we leave out (1) for being too radical or impractical, as we generally do, we are left with the only thing our consumerist culture wants us to be left with—our buying choices. The only real power we have in staving off the apocalypse, we have been conditioned to believe, is the money in our pockets.

At the root of our anxiety about the planet is the fact that being 'more aware' or 'more responsible' has been cast as a duty to be carried out by subscribing in newer, and purportedly better, ways to the same old system. In this way, the individualism that defines so much of our generation has been manipulated to turn our better instincts profitable. Call it neoliberalism, late-stage capitalism, really existing capitalism, or just capitalism, but the truth remains that our imagination has been arrested by a narrative in which the accountability for saving the planet flows downwards in the power pyramid.

We inhabit a reality in which more responsibility lies with the governed than governments, with consumers than businesses, with individuals than organizations.

Kirana store owners who use polythene bags can be severely reprimanded by the authorities, but big businesses like Coke, PepsiCo, and Nestlé can extensively use plastic and aluminium packaging to produce the products we carry in these plastic bags. Mid- and lower-income groups are perceived as being least sensitive to environmental concerns, and they are encouraged to use expensive alternatives to common products with debatable advantages. The crème de la crème of our society, the billionaires, and the political elite, meanwhile are allowed to live in bubbles of unaccountability.

Need some exorbitant statistics to let the contradiction sink in? Well, according to Oxfam International, a billionaire emits a million times more greenhouse gases than the average person. To put that another way, the wealthiest 1 per cent of humanity is responsible for twice as much carbon emissions as the poorest 50 per cent of the world's population.

But we have to admit that the game is good for those who control it.

They convince us of our guilt in ruining the planet, and then they sell us the solutions to assuage it.

Read somewhere that fast fashion is bad for the environment? No problem, because H&M has got a 'sustainable' range of clothes. You can stuff your wardrobe to your heart's content and still go to sleep with a clear conscience.

Plastic in the oceans is choking up marine life? Get a couple of metal straws that you can carry to cafes and restaurants.

Books are made out of paper and paper production causes deforestation? Buy a Kindle.

Is meat production heating up the planet? No worries because Burger King and McDonald's are coming up with vegan options on their menu. Drink a glass of warm oat milk before bed to reduce animal suffering. Only, if it's from Oatly, remember that one of their investors is Blackstone, a private equity firm accused of driving deforestation in the Amazon rainforest, led by a CEO who contributed massive amounts of money to the election campaign of Donald Trump, the US President who did not even believe that climate change is real.

Interestingly enough, the majority of ways in which industries shift the burden of responsibility to individuals—buy new vehicles, use less water, practise responsible eating, and whatever else—rely on the concept of 'carbon footprint'. It can be a letdown for many people to know that even though it *sounds* scientific, the term 'carbon footprint' was popularized by Ogilvy & Mather, a marketing agency and PR firm, working for British Petroleum (BP).

If that sounds like a familiar name, it's because British

Petroleum was responsible for the Gulf of Mexico oil spill in 2010—the largest spill in all of human history.

Fossil fuel companies, however, had already begun to acquire a bad name for their role in environmental damage much before the infamous oil spill, and as part of its efforts to subvert the narrative, BP unveiled a 'carbon footprint calculator' in 2004. The calculator and the campaign around it encouraged people to measure the carbon footprint of everyday activities like driving to work and getting a shower. Apart from the creativity of the folks at BP and their marketing partners, the reason this campaign penetrated the public imagination so deeply, and why it continues to wield so much influence today, is something I pointed out earlier—the challenging nature of exorbitant statistics.

The numbers related to environmental damage are too large for us to fully grasp, and carbon footprints provide us a simplistic, albeit deeply flawed, way to measure it individual by individual.

It is easy to manipulate us into looking at ourselves, and those around us, as culprits by making us forget that 70 per cent of the global carbon emissions since 1988 are courtesy of just 100 companies, with the top twenty among these (including Saudi Aramco, ExxonMobil, BP, and Coal India) responsible for more than a third of emissions. Since we don't see these companies poisoning the planet with our own eyes, the way we see a person carrying his groceries in a polythene bag, it is easier to blame him, instead of them, for ruining the environment.

The greatest con of our times has been pulled by making us feel guilty about the environment when we should instead be furious.

I do not mean to propose that we relinquish all individual responsibility.

By all means, we must discourage littering in Haridwar and avoid taking motorboat rides in Varanasi, but we also need to admit that it's not going to make much of a difference until the government stops those 6 billion litres of wastewater from being dumped into the river.

We have to dial down our self-absorption, no matter how

well-intentioned it is, and accept that none of us alone is going to be the Messiah that saves the world.

When multi-billion-dollar businesses try to guilt us into buying their planet-saving products, we have to be less gullible. When a study talks about how we can all start using Kindle to save the trees chopped down for publishing physical books, we may wonder why Amazon's CO2 emissions grew by as much as 18 per cent in 2021 compared to 2020 when it's so concerned about saving the environment.

More importantly, however, we cannot hold Amazon answerable by switching to Flipkart and we cannot punish British Petroleum by giving up fuel-based vehicles. If we take that approach, we still remain part of the same capitalistic game that needs to end if we are to survive as a species.

We need to understand that we are more than consumers and customers.

We are citizens and our social contract with those we put in power—our elected representatives—entitles us to demand that they work in our interest rather than that of a wealthy and powerful minority.

The alternative is absurd. If the onus of averting existential threats is not on the government, then what is the government good for, really? If our purchasing behaviour can really stave off environmental crises, then why can't we also use it to defend our borders or decide the national budget individually? Why do we even need to *purchase* the government's services with our taxes?

Until we accept in all humility that we need to organize in better ways and use our votes instead of our pockets to drive systemic change, I agree with the respondents of Lancet's survey—humanity is doomed. Until we hold our elected representatives accountable and force them to talk about the E.Coli concentration in Varanasi's waters instead of the Gyanvapi mosque's legitimacy, all our individual efforts will be like that of a man who tries to stop an avalanche by peeing on the snow coming his way.

If that sounds too difficult a thing to do, especially compared to just picking up more 'conscious' products on your favourite e-commerce site, don't worry.

Kurt Vonnegut has helped us by writing, well in advance, the message we can leave behind, carved on a Grand Canyon wall, or the Himalaya, for future dwellers of planet Earth.

> WE PROBABLY COULD HAVE SAVED OURSELVES, BUT WERE TOO DAMNED LAZY TO TRY VERY HARD.
> AND TOO DAMN CHEAP.

3

ABOUT *THE KASHMIR FILES*

As most writers would tell you, we write not so much to provide answers to our readers as to figure things out for ourselves. In the course of writing this particular essay, I hope to know some of the things I have been wondering about *The Kashmir Files* (2022).

It would be better to clarify at the outset that this is not a movie review or a critique. The term that comes to mind rather easily is 'dissection', because when talking about this film I imagine myself cutting open a plague-ridden rat to shine a light on its anatomy. The dissection may help us better understand the disease, identify similarly infected rodents, and prepare ourselves for the swarm coming our way. In doing so, however, I do not mean to undermine the very real tragedy of the Kashmiri Pandit exodus in any way.

Before beginning to write this, I spent a good amount of time asking myself what makes me qualified to write about this particular subject. I am, after all, neither a Kashmir expert nor a film critic. I know a few Kashmiris, but none of them closely enough to claim friendship or gain an understanding of their very unique issues, and I have never been to Kashmir myself. My ideas about the various forces at play there leave much to be desired in terms of nuance, I am sure, having mostly been absorbed off paper and screens.

But, ironically enough, it is precisely this ignorance that makes me, the average Indian (and Hindu) citizen, best suited to write about *TKF*. It has been made for my demographic cohort, not for those who have expertise in Kashmiri matters or love movies an inordinate amount, and it certainly has not been made for Kashmiris themselves. In any case, I will refrain from commenting on the movie's cinematic quality here and will limit my comments on Kashmir to the movie's context.

To understand exactly what I think of *TKF*, and why, I will start by setting up the context of how other movies affected my perception of Kashmir. On the way, we will also stop by a few other propaganda movies from recent years to see why this one has been so much more successful.

▪

By 1994, the year I was born, Kashmiri Pandits had already spent four years in exile and Kashmir had been under the Armed Forces Special Powers Act (AFSPA) since September 1990. In Haridwar, some 650-odd kilometres away, all this may have been happening on a different planet for all I knew about it growing up.

My first interaction with the region, as an object in the public imagination, was at age seven via, what else, a movie.

Doodh mangoge toh kheer denge, Kashmir mangoge toh cheer denge (Ask for milk, we will give you kheer, but you'll be dead if you ask for Kashmir), a classmate of mine kept repeating gleefully in response to everything for two whole days, having picked it up from Sunny Deol's *Maa Tujhhe Salaam* (2002). I didn't get to watch the film, probably because my parents judged it to be the same sort of thing as *Gadar* (which also featured Sunny Deol and had been very popular just six months ago), though I did get my mother to prepare kheer as a result of hearing about it incessantly from the aforementioned classmate.

Movies and news, however, soon became the painters of Kashmir's picture for me, as they did for so many others who did not have the maturity, time, resources, or any reason to dig deeper.

The news from Kashmir, generally, was about soldiers killing militants and militants killing soldiers, followed by politicians meeting other politicians and talking in politician-speak. A routine like that gets old pretty fast for kids who are used to seeing ample amounts of violence on their screens, and they cannot really distinguish the death of a character in *Border* (1997) from a death being reported in the news. But movies have an emotional heft to them that news lacks, and for better or worse the characters in *Border* are more memorable than a list of names read out by some lady on Doordarshan. The long and short of it was that fact and fiction all mixed up together in my head to establish an image of Kashmir as a 'disturbed region'.

When the protagonists in *Roja* (1992) visit Kashmir for the first time and A. R. Rehman croons in the background, 'Yeh haseen vadiyaan, yeh khula aasman. Aa gaye hum kahan, ae mere jaane jaan? (These beautiful valleys, this open sky. What is this place we have come to, my love?)' I was as awestruck as the newlywed couple by the scenic beauty. Like them, I too was scared when a van full of militants kidnapped the hero and zoomed off to their labyrinthian ghetto of hovels and hidey-holes.

Dil Se (1998) informed me that militants had their own stories to tell and it was possible to empathize with them even as we understood the futility of using violence to avenge violence (to date *Dil Se* remains the only mainstream movie I know that mentions the Kunan-Poshpora mass rapes allegedly perpetrated by the Indian Army on Kashmiri villagers). Around the same time, I also remember thinking that the journalist played by Preity Zinta in *Lakshya* (2004) was being unnecessarily obtuse when she bothered the army men (including the protagonist, played by Hrithik Roshan) with questions about such frivolities as human rights and collateral damage.

I mention these films and their effect on me because so many others of my age, from a similar socioeconomic background as me, watched them too, danced to *Chaiyaa Chaiyaa*, dreamt of enlisting in the armed forces after watching *Lakshya*, and worried about the fate of Roja's patriotic husband. These were the movies that defined Kashmir as the 'Beautiful Place, Dangerous Place' for my generation. When I look back at these movies now, I see them with eyes that are better equipped to differentiate fact from fiction, but the impact of films on shaping public perception cannot be underestimated.

Its ability to shape new realities, especially insofar as it involves a reconstruction of the past, is why so many regimes throughout history have used cinema as a tool of propaganda. It happens to other mediums of entertainment too, but as Siegfried Kracauer, the German film theorist, has explained in his analysis of Weimar Germany's cinema, movies are unique among the arts because they do not ask for any intellect as a prerequisite from their audience.

The finances involved in filmmaking are enough to guarantee that most films are made, first and foremost, to appeal to the masses, not for posterity or some lofty ideals. They are, more than any other art form, a product of our time, made to satisfy and please the people of our times. This is why, in addition to affecting the beliefs of a society, films can also tell us what that society wants to believe.

But, if films exercise so much influence over us then does it follow that all movies are propaganda in their own way? And if that is true then why do movies like *TKF* deserve special examination?

▪

In 1941, George Orwell published a collection of essays with a striking title—*All Art Is Propaganda*. What the phrase intends to convey (but doesn't say, probably because it isn't dramatic and catchy enough), I believe, is that all art is 'persuasion'. All artists want to persuade their audiences and hope to reconcile everyone with their personal worldview, which also includes their social and political views.

Bollywood movies from before the 60s and 70s that used Kashmir as a pristine background for their plots (Switzerland replaced it in the 90s, courtesy (mostly) of Yash Chopra) were persuasive as well. Think of *Junglee* (1961) and Shammi Kapoor's famous 'Yahoo' song. Maybe it reinforced the stereotype of beautiful and naive Kashmiri women, or maybe it convinced people that class boundaries could sometimes turn porous. Think again of movies like *Gadar, Roja, Lakshya, Dil Se, Haider* (2014), *Mission Kashmir* (2000), or *Zameen* (2003). They are, all of them, trying to reconcile your worldview with that of the filmmaker but that they feature the Indian Army, Muslim militants, or disputed territory doesn't automatically make them propaganda films.

These elements and their use impress upon us the filmmaker's perspective on a particular place, a particular people, but only in service to the film's plot, not some overarching ideological goals. Propaganda films, in contrast, give their plots secondary importance, and each narrative element exists only in service to an ideology.

We can consider the line between persuasion and propaganda with *URI: The Surgical Strike* (2019). A successful movie, commercially and critically, *URI* is a reasonably well-made film, not so different from the machismo-fuelled war-and-soldier films that come out regularly from Hollywood, and it was defended against allegations of being a propaganda piece by prominent commentators, including contemporary Bollywood icons like Anurag Kashyap.

Does the defence hold?

Glorification of the Indian Army and villainization of Pakistan-based terrorists are not grounds enough for calling the film propaganda, I agree, but only by wilful avoidance can we ignore the obsequious portrayal of Ajit Doval, the National Security Advisor, and Narendra Modi. References to a 'new India' that is more proactive with armed retaliation, the film's release only a few months before the 2019 general elections, and the lapping up of government endorsements by the filmmaker and actors are also difficult to ignore. As for taking its cinematic value as proof of innocence, the naive defence probably originates from a typical underestimation of right-wing creativity.

It would be better for us all to remember that *Triumph of the Will* (1935) is believed to be one of the best documentaries of its time, and *Birth of a Nation* (1915) broke new ground in movie-making. The former was commissioned by Adolf Hitler himself to cover the infamous Nuremberg Rally, and the latter was a retelling of the US Civil War that glorified the idea of white supremacy. Both these 'well-made' movies have long ago been exposed as propaganda pieces (no one ever doubted the intentions behind *Birth of a Nation*, and Susan Sontag took care of Leni Riefenstahl's oeuvre in a 1977 essay titled 'Fascinating Fascism').

In any case, while *URI* may be a little shy about its ideological anchor, there has been no shortage of films that enthusiastically embrace the principles of propaganda since the Hindu right's ascent in 2014.

Take, for example, the 'biopics' that either lampoon an important figure (think *The Accidental Prime Minister* (2019)) or lionize another (*PM Narendra Modi* (2019), *Thackeray* (2019)) to appease their audience and political masters.

Or, the 'social-message films' that, while advocating worthy causes (think *Pad Man* (2018) *or Toilet: Ek Prem Katha* (2017)), link their lessons with government initiatives and policies.

Neither of these two templates has mustered up the kind of mass appeal that marks a propaganda film's success.

'Historical' fiction films such as *Panipat* (2019), *Tanhaji* (2020), and *Kesari* (2019) have fared a little better in their revivalist splendour. The formula is simple enough—brave, righteous, well-mannered Hindus are pitted against conniving, greedy, uncouth, kohl-eyed, long-bearded Muslims to defend their women, land, community, or honour. The Hindus may either come out the victors or die as martyrs and the Muslims are established as forever-villains.

But fictional histories and retellings still fall short of the benchmarks set by *TKF* due to a variety of reasons, which we will explore shortly.

■

As I write this essay, it has been more than sixteen months since *TKF* released in theatres to nationwide excitement. It has enjoyed immense success at the box office, raking in more than

₹300 crores at a small budget of about ₹20 crores, courtesy, in part, of a tax-free run in most BJP-ruled states. The best political promotion, of course, came as a personal endorsement from the prime minister, who lauded it for showing the 'truth' and said that it had rattled the 'jamaat' that usually supports freedom of speech and expression (the use of a word commonly used for Muslim congregations is, obviously, not accidental). There has been some silliness involved, like Vivek Agnihotri tweeting, falsely, about the movie being shortlisted for the Oscars, or Nadav Lapid, an Israeli filmmaker, calling it vulgar propaganda only for Israeli diplomats to try and discredit him in a bid to please their Indian counterparts, but all evidence points towards the film being the most successful propaganda piece to have ever come out of Bollywood.

So, at last, we come to the heart of the matter. I compared the film to a plague-ridden rat at the beginning of this essay; now we spread it out in front of us and bend over it with a scalpel.

Once we peel off the wrapper-plot—a coming-of-age story in which Krishna, a naive young Kashmiri Pandit, studying at ANU (read JNU) gets disillusioned with the 'liberal narrative' about Kashmir—the film begins to exhibit an altogether different nature. After watching it multiple times I realized that for all its grandstanding about truth telling, *TKF* is, in essence, a horror film that uses porno-violence (a term I borrow from Stephen King) to glamorize its propaganda. It exploits the same aspects of human nature that cause regular people to relish the news coverage of violent crimes, (especially when the crimes have sexual overtones), with their morning chai.

The film's horror works so well because it builds upon a larger body of half-truths and lies that its target audience has already subscribed to in the Hindu right-wing ecosystem of WhatsApp forwards and historic resentment.

In the world of Vivek Agnihotri, the Muslim is a Monster who can barge in at any moment to destroy your life. It is Legion with many faces, many ages, many voices, and it is always out to get poor Hindus. The Monster is manifest in a Muslim child who bullies a child for supporting India's cricket team (or classmates who smack him in the head simply for being Hindu), in the women who will throw away bags full of groceries to prevent Hindu women from buying rations, and friends who would sell you to the butcher in the blink of an eye to get at your property and possessions.

Agnitori's familiarity with sleazy tropes, apparent in his previous movies like *Chocolate* (2005), *Hate Story* (2012), and *Zidd* (2014) serves him quite well. There are gory scenes galore for everyone.

Pandits hang from trees by the dozen and a woman is made to eat rice soaked in her husband's blood. Later, she is roughed up by a militant, and then cleaved in two from head to toe on farm equipment (there is a strong sexual subtext in this scene built by the context that she has already been pestered with marriage proposals by a leering local maulvi).

Between grittiness and lascivious horror, Agnihotri chooses the latter and benefits from it because of our peculiar zeitgeist.

As Stephen King theorizes in *Danse Macabre*, his book on the nature of horror fiction and its appeal, the genre becomes particularly attractive to people during difficult times. The major part of this appeal, apart from the obvious escapism it offers, comes from the fact that horror movies personify the world's larger-than-life, vague problems into a visible monster, giving the audience a sense of control over the difficulties they are facing in real life.

It may be difficult for a young man in Uttar Pradesh to understand why the government he voted to power cannot provide him a job, could not provide his parents with oxygen when they got Covid, and cannot control the prices of home essentials such as cooking oil and tomatoes. It scares him, confuses him, and he doesn't want to blame the government led by the Hindu Hriday Samrat, but there is no one else he *could* blame. Along comes a film like *TKF* and the young man, purged of his confusion, becomes part of something larger than his own petty problems for three hours.

By the time he walks out of the theatre, he knows the monster that is to be blamed for his misfortunes.

The very real tragedy of the terrible violence perpetrated against Kashmiri Pandits is only a backdrop here—a plot setting in service to propaganda—despite Agnihotri's oft-repeated claim of making the movie to raise awareness about the Pandit exodus. If that were the case, the film would spend more time exploring the various forces at play in the Kashmir of the late 80s and 90s. Instead, the film acknowledges the tastes and demands of its target audience and actively avoids nuance on all fronts. It picks up the old 'tolerant' centrist claim that 'not all Muslims are bad' and pummels it to death. In every scene the message is clear—all Muslims are bad whether they are young or old, men or women, educated or illiterate, Indian or Pakistani. Your next-door Muslim neighbour would betray you in a heartbeat, we are told, and might as well rape your women after murdering you. To drive this point home with the subtlety of a sledgehammer, the characters claim again and again that the violence against Kashmiri Pandits was carried out by ordinary Kashmiri Muslims, not by any foreign insurgents and terrorists.

TKF works better than historical-fiction films (or biopics and social-message films) because fear is the most effective tool of propaganda.

Understandably enough, we are not as afraid of a dummy prime minister in *The Accidental Prime Minister* or the horde in *Kesari* as we are of the ordinary Muslims in *TKF* who can easily take away our everyday life from us. We encounter them in our daily lives, we work with them and interact with them every now and then. Pushkar Nath Pandit's house is not a palace out of our imagination. It is a simple house that could be our house, his family could be our family, and they are much easier to relate with than politicians or kings from hundreds of years ago. Similarly, it sounds more convincing to support the BJP because they would protect us from the monsters rather than because they built public toilets in some villages we know nothing about.

To safeguard his cause Agnihotri goes a step further and uses another popular horror trope that I call the 'Side Monster'.

The Side Monster is that traitorous (and annoying) character in horror stories who, for one reason or another, always betrays their own kind (the heroes) and supports the Monster. In *TKF*, Agnihotri casts a character called Radhika Menon as the Side Monster to convince his audience that anyone who doesn't share their ideological beliefs is a traitor to the country, or to use his term, an 'anti-national'.

Professor Radhika Menon brainwashes impressionable young people like Krishna under the guise of teaching at ANU. She plays songs written by Faiz Ahmed Faiz on the harmonium, talks about the 'hierarchy of suffering', encourages her students to take college politics more seriously than anything else, smiles when anti-India slogans are raised on the campus, and has intimate connections with Kashmiri militants.

At one point, in a scene that could put a James Bond villain to shame, she admits her immense dark-liberal power to Krishna. 'The Government might be theirs,' she says with a sly smile, 'but the system is still ours.' The 'system' seems to be a reference to some sort of Liberal Deep State, a big bad liberal–Muslim nexus, that works against the Hindu-nationalist government's noble aims. It is a smart trick. By making Radhika Menon a conniving, lying liberal, Agnihotri discredits everything the character says. Since she downplays the suffering of Kashmiri Pandits, the film seems to insist, she must be exaggerating the violence meted out to the Kashmiri people by the Indian Army and the Indian government. Since she is a heartless ideological fanatic herself, it must mean that the people she calls fanatics are brave heroes.

As one would expect, Vivek Agnihotri is not the first to discover the appeal of these tropes and put them to use in propaganda.

A year before Orwell published *All Art Is Propaganda*, a film called *Jud Süß* (1940) released in Germany. It received rave reviews at the Venice Film Festival and won the top award. Supported and enthusiastically promoted by Joseph Goebbels, the Nazi minister of propaganda, it was a huge box-office success in Germany and was watched by more than 20 million people, almost a third of Germany's total population at the time.

The film tells the story of Süß, a scheming Jew, who works his way into a German duke's court and begins to fill his own pockets at the expense of the poor citizens. As the plot progresses, Süß (the Monster) uses the duke (the Side Monster) to torture the masses with impossible taxes, allows his dirty Jew brethren to move into the otherwise clean state, and rapes a Christian woman (a nice dash of porno-violence!). The film ends with the good German people uniting against Süß the Jew and hanging him for his crimes. As the other Jews leave the state, one of the characters gives a piece of advice for the benefit of the movie's audience: 'May the citizens of other states never forget this lesson.'

Jud Süß's screenings elicited violence in many places, and young people were most prone to the film's antisemitism.

The Nazis were overjoyed. On Himmler's orders, the SS units about to be sent to slaughter Jews were compulsorily made to watch the movie, as were concentration camp guards. Veit Harlan, the director of *Jud Süß*, reached the peak of his career under the Nazi regime as one of Goebbels's favourite directors.

TKF has elicited a similar response in India.

Screenings of the film were punctuated by riled-up audiences raising slogans of 'desh ke gaddaron ko, goli maaron saalon ko (shoot the nation's traitors)' with impunity in theatres. In Bijnor, after watching the movie a group of people raised calls of mass murder with chants of 'jab mulle kaate jaayenge, ram-ram chillayenge (when the Muslims are butchered, they'll shout Ram-Ram)'. The hate it brought to the fore may have played a part in the anti-Muslim violence that erupted in different parts of the country on Ram Navami, less than a month after the film was released.

It would be a stretch to suggest that any movie can change a country's political trajectory, but there is enough historical precedent to show that, if made just the right way, to hit the right fault lines, propaganda movies can bitterly exacerbate existing conflicts.

It would be easy for us to dismiss *TKF* as a flash in the pan, unworthy of our attention and serious consideration. Many eminent people have taken a position of silence and it is a reasonable position. Brought out into the light, the film does look childishly incompetent in its ham-handed portrayal of the Other, the Monster, but I am afraid that not enough people have access to light any more. I am afraid for, and of, the people watching it in the cold darkness of movie theatres, the children for whom it will define their perception of Kashmir and Muslims, the women who will start taking 'love-jihad' seriously, the young men who will turn their frustration on people who are even worse off than themselves.

Meanwhile, *TKF*'s commercial success will ensure—has ensured—that others try to recreate Vivek Agnihotri's perversity. *The Kerala Story* (2023) has already reused the formula and earned profits to the tune of 600 per cent, according to film trade analysts. It dealt with the coercion of Hindu girls into joining ISIS and used similar tropes of violence porn and lasciviousness as *The Kashmir Files*. *Ajmer 92* (2023), similarly, is a movie about a sexual exploitation ring led by Muslim men in Ajmer.

This is still only a trickle out of the floodgates that *TKF* has tried to open, I am sure, and worse is yet to come.

After the Nazis lost the war, and Veit Harlan was tried for crimes against humanity, he shrugged it off, telling the court that he had worked under duress. A helpless artist arm-twisted by Goebbels into directing propaganda movies, he could not be considered complicit in the Holocaust. The money and fame he earned through those movies were, according to him, insignificant side effects. He was acquitted by the court twice and died a free man vacationing in Capri, a beautiful Italian island, unlike the victims of his hate-mongering who had been imprisoned, tortured, and murdered in Nazi concentration camps.

When the Hindutva movement meets its eventual end some

bright day in the future, I suspect Vivek Agnihotri will follow Harlan's lead and swear that he had been forced to make *TKF*. On that day we will have to remember the truth and remind him of it.

For now, we would do well to remember that standing against propaganda is not the same as standing against those it seeks to influence.

If we choose to ignore films like *TKF*, and despise those who are naive enough to be hoodwinked by them, then we leave the impressionable at the mercy of those who wish to exploit them. When I say this, I do not mean to take away people's agency from them and I do not wish to patronize the 'masses'. I say this because I think of the boy in Haridwar whose only impression of Kashmir came from his TV screen for a long time, and who would have carried the same impression with him forever, like many others of his generation still do, if it were not for those who sometimes dared to put out unpopular and uncomfortable truths in their books, movies, newspapers, songs, classrooms, and provided alternatives to the dominant narrative.

It is for the sake of that boy that I believe we need to take propaganda head-on and shout the truth from the rooftops, if needed. We need to write it, tweet it, reel it, TikTok it—do anything except shut up about it.

As Rushdie said months before being stabbed in the eye by a young man who swore by religious propaganda, we are not helpless, we can sing the truth and name the liars. We must tell better stories than the tyrants!

4

TRUTH & LIES. WRITING & IDENTITY

In 2014, Navayana, a publishing house that 'focuses on the issue of caste from an anti-caste perspective', according to their website, came out with a new edition of B. R. Ambedkar's *Annihilation of Caste* (*AoC*).

Originally, *AoC* was written by Dr Ambedkar as a speech at the request of an anti-caste group called the Jat-Pat-Todak Mandal. When the mandal found the speech too radical for their upper-caste Hindu audience and cancelled the event, he had to publish the speech as a book in 1936. Over the years, *AoC* has been published by numerous small presses, it is widely read and revered by Dalits, and is available for free at the University of Columbia's website.

Despite its easy availability, however, Dr Ambedkar's intended audience, the kind of privileged upper-caste 'progressives' whom he was supposed to address at the mandal's conference, have remained woefully unaware of his writing and ideas.

The folks at Navayana sought to mitigate this unawareness by inviting Arundhati Roy to write an introduction for their edition of *AoC*.

As the only resident-Indian author to win the Booker Prize, and then to have spent years in daring activism against the powers-that-be, Roy had the kind of international fame and platform that would make most progressives or liberals in India and elsewhere take note of a book jacket with her name on it. The introduction she wrote, called 'The Doctor and the Saint' has since been published as an independent volume, and Roy has made it clear multiple times that its intended audiences are those who remain blind to caste-based discrimination by virtue of their privilege and lack of exposure to India's ugly realities.

That is why, one may infer, the introduction starts by drawing a contrasting parallel between the assault on Malala Yousafzai, which sparked international outrage, and the brutal murders of the Bhotmange family who have been largely forgotten—insofar as they were ever remembered—by all those who do not live every day with death sentences for surnames.

It is also why the introduction is framed as a comparison between the respective views of Dr Ambedkar and Mahatma Gandhi on caste.

Gandhi, after all, is the 'father of the nation', his photograph is on our currency, and his name is everywhere from the textbooks we read in school to the roads we commute. In the West too, he remains one of the most well-known symbols of India, along with Yoga and chicken tikka masala (snake charmers and blue-skinned gods having become rather unpalatable to updated sensibilities). It's no secret that Gandhi's views on caste were quite different from Dr Ambedkar's and they clashed on multiple occasions. When *AoC* was first published, Gandhi expressed his opinions about it and Ambedkar considered it important to address them. This is why the third edition of *AoC*, published in 1945, was, in fact, titled *Annihilation of Caste with a Reply to Mahatma Gandhi.*

All things considered one may be excused for imagining that Roy would have been applauded for writing the introduction. Criticism and protests could have been predicted from Gandhian liberals and right-wing Hindu nationalists, the usual suspects in outraged protests.

But, something rather unexpected happened.

The book's launch in Hyderabad was cancelled by Navayana for reasons that included an SMS circulating in the city before the event. This is what it said.

> Save Ambedkar writings. Oppose Navayan publication. Annihilation of Caste is our holy book. Arundhati Roy

> and Anand. S contaminated it. Participate in the protest on 9th March at Sundaraiah Vigynana Kendram, Hyderabad.

After some confused initial reports, it soon became clear that some Dalit activists and scholars were upset with Roy for writing the introduction to *AoC*. Articles and reports to that effect appeared in multiple news outlets. A news website called Dalit Camera wrote an open letter to Roy expressing their reservations regarding the new edition and she replied to it via another open letter. Various essays critical of her appeared on Round Table India, an online media portal that aims to be a 'resource, a library of sorts, for young Dalit–Bahujans who seek to gain from the knowledge and experience of intellectuals, writers and activists of a similar background'.

On going through these letters, essays, and other expressions of objection, the central issue appears to be the fact that Arundhati Roy wrote the introduction despite being a non-Dalit herself.

Navayana and Roy wanted to take their edition of *AoC* to a foreign audience; its criticism also followed suit.

In an article published by *The Independent* and entitled 'Arundhati Roy's Book on Caste Rejected by Some Anti-Caste Activists', Murali Shanmugavelan wrote that in his opinion, 'Roy's introduction denies readers the opportunity to understand the nuanced relationships between caste, class, religion, capital, technology and neo-liberal politics in India and among overseas Hindus.'

Towards the conclusion of his piece, Shanmugavelan talks about how Roy opens the introduction with an acknowledgement of her own privilege as the child of a Brahmo Samaji father and a Syrian Christian mother.

Shanmugavelan equates Roy's acknowledgement with that of white privilege and quotes Andrea Smith, a 'feminist scholar':

> Andrea Smith's analysis of white privileges tells us how the confession of privilege is often a ritual without much meaning and is eventually based on the structures of

dominations it was supposed to resist.

Roy's opportunity to learn about Ambedkar and critique on Gandhi, to introduce this book to the world is, I would argue, a clear example of her upper-caste privilege. But like 'white privileges' would want us to believe, Roy presents herself as transcending these structures, as a cosmopolitan subject beyond her caste and class privileges. This is only possible however, as Smith says, as long as Dalits remain 'trapped within identities'.

▪

In 2021, an essay entitled 'The Native Scholar Who Wasn't' was published in the *New York Times* magazine. The scholar in question was Andrea Smith (the same one quoted above by Murali Shanmugavelan), a writer and academic famous for being not merely a firebrand feminist scholar but also 'an icon of Native American feminism'.

The exposé, investigated and written by Sarah Viren, was a detailed analysis of how Smith had created her entire career around fabricated claims of a Native American identity.

Described as the kind of person 'who once commented multiple times on the feelings of shellfish after someone ordered shrimp at lunch' by J. Kehaulani Kauanui, a long-time colleague, friend, and fellow Native American scholar, Andrea 'Andy' Smith shot to fame in the 1990s. Her brand of activism was noticeable for refusing to compromise on identity and for calling out activists she felt were not 'legit' enough to raise the Native American cause.

However, rumours about Smith's own Native American identity began floating around in the early 2000s.

By 2008, the University of Michigan had denied tenure to her for undisclosed reasons, and a Cherokee academic named Steve Russell had written a column entitled 'When Does Ethnic Fraud Matter?' However, few non-Natives appeared to be concerned with the veracity of Smith's identity and she continued to hold positions of authority in Native American academia and activism.

In 2015, an anonymous Tumblr called 'Andrea Smith Is Not Cherokee' appeared with collected stories and documentation disputing Smith's ancestry claims. She responded by writing in her blog that she had always been, and would always be, Cherokee.

While working on her thoroughly researched essay, Sarah Viren travelled across the US to talk to Smith's relatives, finding out in the process that her mother, Helen Jean Wilkinson, was born into a middle-class white family, and her father, Donald R. Smith was a white man from Chicago who had worked as a nuclear physicist with the Pentagon before retiring. In the course of her investigation, Viren sometimes felt that she was becoming a little obsessed, but the issue was important to her as a member of the academia, a fellow subscriber to the same institutions that people like Smith used to appropriate oppressed groups such as Native Americans.

In her own writing, Viren has long been concerned with the nature of truth and its subjectivity for different people involved in a situation.

As it turns out, she has more than enough reason to care so much about truth, lies, and identity.

▪

Once upon a time, Sarah Viren and her wife, Marta Tecedor, taught at Arizona State University.

They were respected members of academia with tenure-track jobs, mothers to two children, and Viren was expected to soon receive a coveted job offer from the University of Michigan. The move to Michigan would fit with their long-time dream to leave behind the Arizona desert for greener pastures, and the UoM had assured Viren that they would keep looking for jobs for Tecedor while confirming her own job offer.

It felt as if both of them were 'beginning to find their place in the world', according to Viren.

The feeling began to dissipate, however, when Tecedor was accused of sexually harassing her students soon after Viren's interview at UoM. The accusations had been made in anonymous Reddit posts and more of them popped up as Viren's offer letter from UoM started getting delayed.

The investigator at ASU told Viren and Tecedor that two complaints from different students, Rebecca James and Jessica P. Newman, had been made and they accused Tecedor of harassing and abusing multiple students. The investigator had found no students, present or past, with those names, but that was no reason to drop the investigation because it is fairly common for victims of sexual misconduct to use aliases.

By the time ASU interviewed her wife for the second time, Viren already had ideas about who was behind the smear campaign. In an essay published in 2020, a year before she would write about Andrea Smith's life of lies, Sarah called this man 'J'.

Their attacker, or the 'villain' of their story as Viren refers to him, was a fellow gay academic. He had been in consideration for the same position at the University of Michigan as Viren, and he was prepared to destroy her family for the job.

Viren's suspicions were confirmed when the phone number used to verify the complainants' email addresses turned out to be J's number. The IP address of the computer used to make the complaints was also from the town where he lived. In a novel or movie that would mean a final takedown of the 'villain', and Viren imagined as much, she admits.

But J knew exactly how he could use his identity as a gay man to his advantage.

As soon as he was named a defendant in the lawsuit and served with a notice, J began spreading rumours that someone was attacking him. This is the timeline Viren provides:

> Four days after he was served, J posted that his university and private email accounts had been hacked. His colleagues started receiving emails from those accounts with messages calling him a faggot.
>
> Five days after he was served, J claimed he received

> an anonymous email from a so-called burner account. In that email, someone claiming to be his stalker wrote that he was in love with J and that being rejected by him had caused 'a mental break i cannot explain'.
>
> 'i began trolling you online, sent death threats, broke into your house when you were gone', the person wrote. 'i tried to [expletive] up your job applications by getting into your [work] email, i trolled a friend of yours in Arizona....'
>
> A week after J was served, he emailed the police at his university to say that his stalker had thrown a rock through his car window. He attached a photo of the shattered glass, along with a handwritten note that read 'STOP TRYING TO FIND ME'.

If Viren and Tecedor went ahead with the lawsuit they would have to spend tens of thousands of dollars, their lawyer told them, and having already paid $10,000 in legal fees by then, they decided that they were not willing to pay more for truth. They settled the lawsuit and retained the right to tell their story.

Since then, Viren has made the story a part of her book *To Name the Bigger Lie: A Memoir in Two Stories*, which deals with what 'truth' really is, and how 'we never really know who is behind anything we read'.

▪

As a writer, I regularly grapple with the question of who gets to tell whose story and how.

In effect, as in all of the three instances I have outlined above, it is a question of identity and its effect on the authenticity (or veracity, or truthfulness) of a writer and their writing. Increasingly, however, it is also a question of how well a piece of writing can navigate and avoid the various definitions of being 'problematic'.

In the first case, Arundhati Roy's identity made her introduction to *AoC* problematic because she was writing about Dalits without being a Dalit. Making her non-Dalit status clear right at the beginning did not absolve her, but enabled her critics to paint her as conniving and manipulative.

Much of this criticism, especially the one that came from fellow non-Dalit intellectuals, was all-encompassing and unforgiving.

G. Sampath, for example, in an article published in *Mint*, refuses to deal with the contents of the introduction at all because of restrictions on the length of his column. He chooses, instead to dedicate the available length to explaining why no non-Dalit, and especially not one as famous or popular as Roy, can ever write about Dr Ambedkar without being guilty of appropriation.

Akshay Pathak, another savarna like G. Sampath, begins an essay called 'The Judge, the Jury and the Goddess' by admitting how much he appreciated Arundhati Roy as an adolescent. He writes that he read excerpts of the introduction to *AoC* in magazines and got excited about reading it but changed his mind once he engaged with all the criticism coming its way. He admits to being a Brahmin himself, but even as he proceeds to point out issues with the introduction's contents he defends himself with a disclaimer, saying 'a more intelligent and intellectual interrogation of her essay will surely follow. I am neither an expert nor the right person to do it'.

Why do it then, one is tempted to ask.

Karthik Navayan, in his article 'Introducing Arundhati Roy and Friends', says that 'this spiced up text produced by these elite leftists is meant to be consumed by savarnas and white people, who are not aware of caste'. A few paragraphs down, however, he is of the opinion that 'actually the book *Annihilation of Caste* is directly addressed to all savarnas to change their caste mindsets'. The contradictory nature of this reasoning does not appear to have impressed itself upon the esteemed writer.

Some critics even resorted to pointing snidely at HarperCollins (one of Roy's publishers) being owned by Rupert Murdoch and attacking Roy's choice to continue using her father's surname.

They forget, we must assume, that HarperCollins is one of the five biggest publishers in the world. If we were to avoid writers who publish with them our literature would be much poorer without Aatish Taseer, Amitav Ghosh, Vinod Kumar Shukla, and so many others. Or, could it be the case that it's unacceptable for Roy to publish with HarperCollins because she wrote the introduction in question? There is no apparent way out of the surname quagmire either, because if she had indeed dropped it then she could just as easily have been accused of trying to erase her privilege or being caste-blind herself.

The accusation would actually surface in 2020 when, while promoting a different book altogether, Roy said that she is not a Brahmin. *The Print* published an article entitled 'Arundhati Roy Joins Shashi Tharoor, Kangana Ranaut in List of "Casteless" Upper-Caste Indians'.

Before that, the conversation had already been weaponized in 2016 when Roy faced a criminal trial for contempt of court in India.

In an article published by *The Guardian*, author Pankaj Mishra talked about how 'the Hindu nationalists have also learned how to manipulate the new media, and shape instant opinion'.

> Last week, as the novelist Arundhati Roy abruptly faced criminal trial for 'contempt of court' that could result in imprisonment, a circulating text message claimed that the writer was part of a conspiracy by Christian missionaries to murder Vemula and break up India. It wasn't easy to dismiss this farrago of paranoid nonsense. And then the indifferent, if not hostile, reports in India's mainstream media could have made anyone think that Roy had a case to answer.

One can imagine the difficulty in dismissing the nonsense if one takes into account the context of the discourse around Roy and *AoC*'s introduction from just two years ago and adds to it the fact that Rohith Vemula was driven to suicide by brutal caste-based discrimination.

Writing 'problematic' things can have severe consequences for writers.

I was introduced to Andrea Smith via Murali Shanmugavelan's criticism of Roy in his article for *The Independent* (incidentally, *The Independent* was sold to a company owned by the family of Russian oligarch Alexander Lebedev in 2010, which is a fact I rather enjoy putting together with Rupert Murdoch's proprietorship of HarperCollins).

When I read Sarah Viren's essay about Smith's identity, I reflected on how Shanmugavelan's quoting of Smith's views, while referring to her as a 'feminist scholar', may not sit well with actual Native American feminist scholars. Especially if they paused to consider the irony that the part he quoted from a white woman pretending to be Native American talks specifically about why white women should not be allowed in Native American feminist discourse.

In Smith's case, it appears that one can get away with telling other people's stories, or even leading that storytelling, if one pretends to be that 'other' and keeps sticking to it.

A major reason why Smith got away with fudging her identity for so long, despite a lot of people expressing their doubts, was that non-native scholars and writers did not want to give up their 'one Native American colleague'. Lenape scholar Joanne Barker, who signed an open letter describing Smith's lies years before Viren's essay, predicted as much on her blog. Most people, she said, would 'dismiss the sources and documentation of Smith's fraud as crass or too-complicated identity politics'.

In other words, calling out Smith was more problematic than addressing her problematic behaviour.

Finally, we must look again at Viren's own experience with truth and identity.

While reading about the ordeal her family went through, one of the most striking parts of her essay for me was where, at a point when the university's investigation was still ongoing, she imagined how things would look from an outsider's perspective.

> A true story written about Marta and me at this point could easily include all the facts we know right now: that

> complaints were made about Marta, that Reddit posts appeared and that an investigation was opened. And if I were to read a story like that—without knowing Marta or me or any other facts that came to light later—I would conclude either that Marta had done it or, at the very least, that she was the kind of professor who crossed the line, and that her actions had been misconstrued. I would assume, that is, that even if some of the facts were wrong, the truth lay somewhere in the middle.

I know that if I had read such a story, I would have assumed what Viren imagines.

I may have been a little sceptical because the story involved a couple of reputed lesbian professors. I also know I'd be less sceptical in the case of a hypothetical story, with the same facts, about gay male professors. Less sceptical still if it was about a straight academic couple. What if the couple happened to be white and straight, and 'J' had written his complaints as a young black woman? I don't think I could have been bothered to look for any follow-up news stories on the subject.

For that matter, would anyone have written the follow-up stories?

Or, could a hypothetical straight white woman in Viren's place have published an essay in the *New York Times* defending her husband on sexual harassment allegations, even if they had actually been made as a result of professional animosity?

It is an uncomfortable question, and I squirm as I frame it, but I believe it is becoming more important than ever to ask ourselves some uncomfortable questions.

■

Growing up with four sisters, I was always fairly clued in on how much women worry about their bodies as a result of our society's beauty standards.

My oldest sister would roll up the parathas in her breakfast and throw them behind a wardrobe because she had read somewhere that parathas make people fat. She would also not wear glasses despite being severely short-sighted because she thought it made her look like a geek. Another sister was called less by her name and more by supposedly harmless monikers like 'moti' and 'fatso'. It made her so self-conscious, she told us years later, that she didn't talk to a single boy in school.

In one of the first short stories I ever wrote, I superimposed certain surreal-speculative elements on the experience of my sisters. The shadow of a young girl in that story gains sentience when the girl's conservative parents put her on a strict diet to make her slimmer. The girl becomes slim and submissive, the shadow remains fat and grows rebellious.

Now, did I, as a male, fully understand what women—and teenage girls at that—go through with their bodies? I did not, of course, but this was the story I *had* to write. I talked at length to a close friend who, I knew, had faced subtle harassment from her family about her body and did a whole lot of research on the subject. Then I did that one weird thing that writers still insist on doing, I imagined, thought of King and *Carrie,* and wrote out the damn thing, enjoying and agonizing every minute of it.

Fortunately, it was accepted for publication by a literary magazine whose contents I had appreciated in the past.

But, there was a bit of a snag.

'I would love to feature the story in our upcoming September issue', the magazine's editor wrote to me in an email, 'if you are okay with making a minor edit to the story. I would suggest changing the part where Rinky loses weight because her mother tells her fat girls make no friends. I just don't want to upset or offend readers who might struggle with their weight. Perhaps we could find a different motivation/cause behind Rinky's shadow not matching her current form?'

The shadow's sentience was never the point of that story, and giving it a reason other than body image issues would have turned the whole thing meaningless for me.

But I was a teeny tiny babe in the dark forest of literature back then and I did not want to pass on a publishing opportunity.

'I appreciate your interest in publishing "The Shadow Teacher",' I wrote back, 'the central theme of the story, for me, is the opinion of other people on an individual's body and the pressure associated with that opinion. I understand it might be somewhat uncomfortable for people who are struggling with their weight, but the story is against body shaming, not in support of it.

In India, to this day our society continues to torture young girls into fitting its idea of the perfect woman, and in parts of the country girls as young as Rinky are married off by the time they hit puberty. Since I am also a part of this society, it is important for me as a writer to portray it honestly, without any comfortable whitewashing, even when I am writing speculative fiction or a quasi-fairytale. Not doing so would be a betrayal of my heritage.'

I did not have great hopes of hearing from the editor again after channelling my inner Manto to express lofty goals of presenting the societal condition as it is, but she replied again, and with good news.

'I reread your piece,' the editor now said, 'and I think you are absolutely correct—it is good to explore uncomfortable ideas, especially in a way that is insightful and culturally sensitive. We can go ahead and publish the piece as it is, with your original intentions intact. Thank you for taking the time to explain your thoughts and intentions to me. I appreciate it, and I look forward to seeing your piece in our September issue!'

It may be interesting to note that this exchange of emails took place in the course of a few hours.

I received the first email at 7.50 p.m., responded at 10.19 p.m., and received the final acceptance at 10.33 p.m. It means that it took the editor less than fifteen minutes to reverse her position on aspects she had found problematic only a couple of hours ago. If I were to guess, I would say that it was the mention of child marriage, regressive Indian society, and my 'heritage' that expedited the editor's decision.

In a way, my Indian-ness or brown-person-ness won over-sanitized American body-positivity. Instead of a decision based on the story's quality, two identities went head-to-head, and mine came out the winner in this round.

Calls for celebration, bring out a drum, sing, and dance.

How do other writers deal with questions of identity in terms of authenticity and appropriation? I wondered about that while reading Tanuj Solanki's *Manjhi's Mayhem*, a noir drama whose protagonist, Sewaram Manjhi, is a Dalit immigrant living in Mumbai. Solanki was awarded the prestigious Sahitya Akademi Yuva Puraskar in 2019 and, as the founder editor of the *Bombay Literary Magazine*, he also has a fairly informed perspective on the work of other young writers in India.

I asked him recently if he was concerned about charges of cultural appropriation while writing a character like Manjhi, and how he offset those concerns.

'I regard the matter as a technical one—in other words, the ethical issues here are solvable almost entirely through solving for aesthetics,' Solanki said, 'and I offset these concerns by adopting just one rule: Manjhi must be believable. Believability carries the possibility of an enigma in it; authenticity does not. As a fiction writer, I find authenticity a limiting, and largely useless, construct for my purposes. I aim only for believability, only for a minima wherein my rendering adds to, and doesn't impede, the reader's joy, knowing fully well that this joy is a product of many things—story, language, narrative voice, event, and so on.'

It is possible to discern two slightly contradictory demands in criticisms related to diverse identities in literature.

First, that all writers, especially the ones who are more privileged than others, should aim to include characters from a range of different backgrounds and identities.

It sounds reasonable at first glance, but diktats are not generally famous for leading to a rich body of literature. As Solanki put it rather bluntly, 'There is no "should" when it comes to creative work. Writers should do whatever the hell they feel like doing.'

Second, that privileged writers should leave the representation of characters from different backgrounds and identities to the writers who actually possess these backgrounds and identities. To not do that would be an act of opportunism or 'appropriation'.

Apart from the obvious contradiction with the first approach, it is a self-defeating solution as Solanki points out. 'Going by this line of thought strictly, we reach an untenable, even contradictory, juncture, wherein the life of an oppressed person from the poorest district of India shall find no mention in Indian fiction till someone like them picks up the pen. But picking up the pen is itself an act of some privilege.'

Moreover, most of us can be seen through the lens of multiple identities.

For the white editor of an American literary magazine, I am an Indian and a BIPOC writer (Black, Indigenous, People of Colour writer). But I know that I am also a relapsed Hindu born in a Brahmin family. That means I sit at the top of the Hindu caste hierarchy. Combine that with the fact that I'm also a straight middle-class man and my identity ticks all the checkboxes which establish me as the asshole archetype in the Indian context.

That can have consequences of its own, if taken into account while writing.

My first serious girlfriend, at twenty-one, was from a conservative Baniya family in Haridwar.

By the time we passed out of college, she had made it clear to me that though we may continue to date, the relationship's future was doomed by default. Her parents would get her married in a year or two, and even if I could somehow manage to become marriage-material in that short amount of time, they would never marry out of their caste.

Nothing could be done to change their mind, she assured me, because they would only marry her to a nice and respectable Baniya boy. It was frustrating beyond reason, like slowly driving towards a cliff-edge in a car with no brakes. When we finally broke up, I was left with a sense of my utter individual impotence in the face of an unbudging social norm.

Recently, in an essay about the millennial dating culture, I wanted to write about this period of my life. Halfway through, however, I began worrying about the optics.

An upper-caste boy whining about caste because of a collegiate romance's failure? It could, perhaps, be seen as hijacking the caste-critical space from those who have experienced it in monstrous ways. Could I, not being a Dalit, quote Dr Ambedkar on the curious interplay of caste endogamy and gotra exogamy? If I did, would it be respectable enough?

As in the case of my short story, I ended up putting these reservations aside in favour of what I felt was much more important—telling things in ways I found honest and uncruel. Yet, I could not help wondering whether the reservations were coming from that writerly place inside me where self-doubt grows in parallel with curiosity, or from some external rulebook that stamps writing as problematic and unproblematic.

▪

In 2020, 153 prominent journalists, authors, and writers including Margaret Atwood, Noam Chomsky, Sarah Haider, J. K. Rowling, and Salman Rushdie published an open letter in *Harper's* magazine.

'A Letter on Justice and Open Debate' posed some uncomfortable questions about the current state of cultural discourse. It raised concerns that a spirit of censorship is becoming widespread in our culture, 'an intolerance of opposing views, a vogue for public shaming and ostracism, and the tendency to dissolve complex policy issues in a blinding moral certainty'.

While such censoriousness was traditionally expected from the radical right quarters, the signatories worried that in our times it was becoming increasingly common from those who seek greater equality and inclusion in society.

The results looked catastrophic to them: 'We are already paying the price in greater risk aversion among writers, artists, and journalists who fear for their livelihoods if they depart from the consensus, or even lack sufficient zeal in agreement.'

The backlash was swift and vicious.

Three days after its publication, more than 150 journalists, academics, and writers signed a counter-letter. X exploded in outrage. Major outlets such as the *Los Angeles Times* and *HuffPost* decried Harper's Letter (as it came to be called), and an article in the *Daily Beast* called the people who signed it 'assorted rich fools'.

The actual contents of the letter were mostly ignored in favour of targeting the signatories for their fame and popularity. The counter-letter began by saying that 'the signatories, many of them white, wealthy, and endowed with massive platforms, argue that they are afraid of being silenced'.

It did not matter that the letter was, in fact, spearheaded by Thomas Chatterton Williams, a Black writer who has written extensively on race.

It also did not matter that the 'rich fools' who had signed the letter included Reginald Betts, an African-American poet and memoirist who spent eight years in prison for stealing a car at age sixteen; Orlando Patterson, a Jamaican-born Harvard sociologist known for his work on issues of race; and Kian Tajbakhsh, an Iranian–American professor of urban studies at Columbia, who was held for years in an Iranian prison before returning to the United States.

These things did not matter, I believe, because they did not fit the David vs Goliath narrative that so much of our fashionable moral righteousness depends upon.

It helps to lump together anyone who speaks against leftist censoriousness as 'privileged cis-white writers' because it will be difficult for many people to imagine Margaret Atwood or Noam Chomsky wringing their hands to protect their elitism. For similar reasons, it was better to single out J. K. Rowling while referring to the letter instead of Thomas Chatterton Williams because Rowling is famous enough and controversial enough with her views on gender politics. The headline of the *Daily Beast* article, actually, was 'J.K. Rowling and Other Assorted Rich Fools Want to Cancel "Cancel Culture"'.

The cultural trend that the letter was concerned about, which the *Daily Beast* refers to as 'cancel culture' and which is sometimes associated with the broader label of 'woke culture' depends upon the assumption that in any given scenario it is always better to believe the powerless over the powerful (or the famous).

It is not an altogether bad generalization either, some would argue, and it works reasonably well when applied to institutions with histories of systemic biases. But, applying it to individuals, especially to writers (or any other artists, for that matter) and academics can produce grotesque results.

The equation of powerless and powerful itself is upended when you have a writer, however famous and wealthy, facing a faceless mob that is interested not in debate but in meting out swift punishment.

The writer and their work can be dissected in hair-splitting detail to arrive at any conclusions (If you 'just don't see' the anti-Semitism, fatphobia, and racism in the HP (Harry Potter) books then I can't help you, writes a Twitter user called Samantha Puc) and their most intimate experiences can be dismissed as posturing (when Rowling talks about her history of domestic abuse it is merely 'a ploy to gain sympathy', and Arundhati Roy's activism is like that of 'a poverty baron who flies around the world offering her services to reduce poverty').

A mob on the internet itself, however, is shielded from repercussions because of its collective identity and anonymity (several writers who signed the counter to Harper's Letter chose to remain anonymous, not noticing the irony of an anonymous open letter). Even if someone takes the time to look at its individual members, they are beyond criticism because of their irreproachable identities (the LinkedIn profile of Samantha Puc, who cannot help us with our Harry Potter ignorance, tells us that she 'is a fat, disabled, lesbian writer and streamer'. In her X bio, she calls herself a 'fat witch'. Yet, in none of her introductions on websites like *CBR* and *Polygon* does she mention that she is also 'white'.

It also looks like some of us on the liberal side of culture have become so obsessed with the glamour of speaking truth to power that the emphasis has shifted entirely from 'truth' to 'speaking' and 'power'.

That is not altogether surprising, admittedly.

The platforms on which we express our opinions are driven by shadowy, all-powerful algorithms whose job it is to keep us engaged with the platforms for as long as possible. They are well-known for incentivizing outrage, aggression, and quick response. But others understand the rules of digital engagement just as well as we do, and to be heard through the cacophony of everyone speaking over everyone else we must craft ever more unique identities for ourselves.

In leftist-intellectual spaces, the more 'oppressed' or 'weaker' an identity, the more it matters. For example, fat-disabled-lesbian-writer-and-streamer wins out against white-woman-successful-writer.

At some point, however, despite the fear of being attacked by our own, we are going to have to admit that belonging to any particular group should not be proof of 'pure intentions'. We are going to have to recognize that going after people for ideological transgressions could be an attempt to gain the online version of street cred *at least* just as often as it is a critique in good faith.

As Sarah Viren found out after going through her ordeal, 'we never really know who is behind anything we read'.

In a 2022 essay, the Nigerian writer Chimamanda Ngozi Adichie meant to say as much when she pointed out the 'social-media-savvy people who are choking on sanctimony and lacking in compassion, who can fluidly pontificate on Twitter about kindness but are unable to actually show kindness'. Or, when she talked about the 'people who claim to love literature—the messy stories of our humanity—but are also monomaniacally obsessed with whatever is the prevailing ideological orthodoxy'.

■

What a writer chooses to write about is an intimate, personal decision that cannot be guided by dogma, irrespective of where that dogma comes from and how righteous its upholders are.

Many of us seem to somehow forget that if a writer is dishonest, if they resort to perpetuating tired old tropes and lazy stereotypes, then they will end up writing boring things and will face the worst possible punishment—people will not read them.

Regardless of anyone's intentions, there is no shortcut around this, no way by which a group of people can decide what should or should not be written, that does not lead to a perpetually afraid, stifling cultural atmosphere. As the famous Harper's Letter pointed out, 'The way to defeat bad ideas is by exposure, argument, and persuasion, not by trying to silence or wish them away.'

Perhaps we would all do much better, generally, if we were a little slower in jumping to conclusions, and realized that good-bad binaries are as flawed as they are easy to adopt.

There are already enough of the book-burning and book-banning kind of people on one side of the ideological spectrum; it may not be possible to have them on both sides and still produce things worth reading.

The 'identity trap' is attractive because it gives us a way of neatly slotting people into categories that deserve different responses. However, like all systems that divide people based on the assumption that a group's characteristics are more relevant than the personalities of individuals that comprise it, it is a system of classes and hierarchy. As the German–American political scientist Yascha Mounk points out in his book *The Identity Trap: A Story of Ideas and Power in Our Time*, the ideas of identity synthesis are pernicious and inimical to a functioning society—they should not be allowed to take precedence over free speech and expression promised by liberal universalism.

5

EAT YOUR FEARS

'Tell me what you eat, and I shall tell you what you are', the French lawyer and politician Jean Anthelme Brillat-Savarin wrote in *The Physiology of Taste,* his 1825 magnum opus.

The claim is true enough because what we choose to eat and reject, the tastes we like and pretend to like, and the food we find revolting or frightening all form an integral part of our identity. What would Brillat-Savarin have said, I wonder, if I had told him that I was a vegetarian for the first seventeen years of my life? A 'pure' vegetarian at that, who had never consumed an egg, or so much as dined with someone who was not a vegetarian.

Provided with some more information, familiarity with Indian society, and an unusually long lifespan, maybe he would have correctly deduced that I was born into a vegetarian family and grew up in a city like Haridwar.

As a result of its religious importance to Hindus, Haridwar is one of the handful of cities in India where the sale and consumption of meat are legally prohibited. Eggs can be bought by asking for 'potatoes' at certain bakeries, but they will come wrapped in more layers of newspaper than sanitary pads or prophylactics at the pharmacy. Living in this environment during my formative years gave me an early, and unique, experience of what it means to be afraid of food.

The uniqueness came from the fact that while I may still have been a vegetarian in another city because of my family, in Haridwar vegetarianism was more a natural fact than a decision. An alternative diet, or taste, was not just inaccessible but invisible.

The first time I saw meat, I was fourteen.

We were visiting Meerut for a wedding, and I was shaken by the sight of goat and chicken carcasses hanging at butcher shops in a crowded market. They were dead animals to me, not food, and the thought of someone taking these *things* home and eating them was frightening.

Another early experience, unrelated to social or religious conventions, with what it meant to be afraid of food came when my father died of cardiac arrest at fifty-three.

I was in the 6th standard and I remember how terms such as 'cholesterol', 'vascular congestion', and 'obesity' became common points of conversation at home overnight. These were the forces, it seemed, that had suddenly upended our lives.

My mother was diagnosed with diabetes and hypertension in the aftermath of that stressful time, and we decided to pay more attention to what we ate.

The wheat flour we used to use every day was replaced by a multi-grain mixture of wheat, ragi, jowar, and barley. Pulao, my mother's favourite lunch, was rationed because rice was not good for her diabetes, according to her doctor. The casual intake of jalebis and samosas in the evening stopped, and paneer salad replaced paratha-sabzi in our breakfast. Poori, pakode, and other deep-fried food items that had featured frequently in our meals were relegated to the sidelines, only allowed to make ceremonious appearances on special occasions.

At one point, my sisters became so paranoid about Mummy's health that we considered completely giving up on salt (bad for hypertension), sugar (bad for diabetes), and fried food (bad for the heart). I am glad the suggestion was vetoed by my mother herself.

It was natural, perhaps. We only had one parent left, and she had to be protected. Papa's death had been so unexpected, and we held ourselves responsible in some way, I think, for not being more aware of healthy lifestyle choices.

This was in 2004, a time before smartphones and social media platforms, so we updated our diet based on the advice of Mummy's doctor and newspaper columns.

The newspaper columns contradicted themselves several times and the fluctuation was reflected in what we ate. For instance, I remember that at one point ghee was vilified as a cholesterol-raising saturated fat by a Hindi-language daily and we started having rotis without smearing ghee on them. Just a week later, the same newspaper praised ghee as a healthy homegrown alternative to refined oils. We went back to having ghee-smeared rotis.

I can only imagine how much more anxious and afraid we would have been to find ourselves in a similar situation today. The internet is a sinkhole for the paranoid, and there is a seemingly endless supply of dietary advice available on social media platforms.

Being concerned about what we consume is perfectly natural and food choices have always been important to the trajectory of our evolution as a species. Or rather, evolution has played a major role in determining what we eat today.

In *Delicious: The Evolution of Flavor and How It Made Us Human*, the ecologist Rob Dunn and medical anthropologist Monica Sanchez expand upon this idea by connecting survival with taste.

It can be observed in the way we perceive the five tastes—sweet, sour, salty, bitter, and umami.

Sweet, salty, and umami 'evolved to point animals, through deliciousness, to what otherwise might be missing from their diet'. In other words, we needed food that would give us more energy and fill us up for a longer time, so we developed a taste for high-calorie, nutrient-rich food. Sour and bitter, on the other hand, 'serve the opposite purpose; they can point animals away from danger. They do so through feelings of displeasure.'

Evolution is, of course, a slow process. Much too slow for the immediacy and consumption frenzy that marks the twenty-first century.

▪

A study undertaken by Sodexo to map the eating habits of Millennials in India found that we are much more experimental with our food choices than previous generations.

'Millennials are not only ready to taste food from across the world, but also to cook the same at home', the report said. 'The availability of a variety of ingredients at grocery stores, unheard of even a decade back, is proof of the growing inclination of Millennials to experiment in the kitchen.'

Certainly, there is more than enough scope for experimentation and our perception of food has come to be defined, first and foremost, by an exponential increase in choice, that godly virtue of the free market.

At the time of writing this essay, if I decide that I am in the mood for avocado (the global stereotype of Millennial food), a search on Zomato tells me that I can get my food from The Avocado Cafe, Avoke the Avocado Cafe, Avocado Kitchen, Avocado Gallery, or any of a dozen more places around my neighbourhood in Bangalore. I can further choose exactly what I want done to the avocado from a list of more than fifty options. It includes Pepperoni-Avocado Toast, Avocado Salad, Avocado Seekh Kebab, Avocado Toast with Egg, and Avo Summer Roll Salads.

If I decide to be less of a yuppie and choose to have biryani, the choice of restaurants expands to hundreds. Courtesy of a recently added option called 'Intercity Legends' in Zomato, I don't even have to restrict myself to the city where I live. For my pleasure, I can have the biryani flown down from legendary eateries in other cities like Kolkata, Lucknow, and Delhi.

If I do not decide to have either avocados or biryani, chances are that push notifications from Zomato (or one of the other food delivery apps) will soon make a wittily-worded suggestion to me based on my purchase history or active discounts.

The enthusiastic interest of Millennials in food is hardly an India-specific trend.

In her 2015 book, *A Taste of Generation Yum*, Eve Turow Paul points out that in the US, Millennials spend fourteen times more money on food than an average middle-class family and

87 per cent of them said that they will indulge in a meal even when 'money is tight'.

As for the reason behind this obsession, this is what Paul said in an interview with *The Atlantic*.

> I really think it comes down to technology, for a few reasons. One, is sensory deprivation. We have formed into a society that's so accustomed to sitting in front of a screen and typing, for the vast majority of the day. And the truth of the matter is that it's not exciting all of our senses. Through interviews over and over again, I kept hearing that people want something that's tangible, that they can see and feel and smell and taste and that we're the guinea pigs of growing up in that [digital] world.
>
> At the same time, it's also making us more isolated. We're craving community. And food is also allowing us to access the globe, so we can find out what harissa is made with and how to prepare something with it, in two seconds on our phones.

My personal experience supports Paul's view and I can clearly see that our relationship with food underwent a big change after the successful launch of Instagram in 2014–15.

There had been social media platforms before that, of course, but Instagram was more focused on visuals than any of them. The app spread like wildfire in my college. Soon, every other person started calling themselves a 'foodie' (the word's usage jumped by more than 800 per cent between 2000 and 2019) and posting pictures of their food with hashtags such as #foodporn, #foodstagram, #foodgasm, #foodphotography, etc. Smartphones with decent cameras were starting to become affordable at around the same time. It meant that decent-quality images for Instagram did not require sophisticated camera equipment and anyone could be a (food) photographer.

Since the popularity of these images could be measured by the number of 'likes' they got, it turned our food into a kind of social currency. In the post-Instagram era, Brillat-Savarin would not have needed to say 'tell me what you eat', because he could have just checked out everyone's tastes for himself on his phone.

It is business as usual to neatly fit contemporary culture within the confines of technological development, but there are limits to how the internet and co. have changed our world.

Apart from Instagram and smartphones, there are broader social and economic factors that have contributed to the development of the millennial palate.

As per *The Changing Culture of Eating in India*, a report published by IndianRetailer.com in 2013, a significant number of people in India were already dining out two to three times a week.

It signalled a major change in Indian food habits and most of the diners leading this change were in their twenties and early thirties. The survey, motivated by the interest of restaurant owners, only looked at the country's bustling cities that had restaurants, leaving out most of rural India as well as smaller cities and towns. It took into account, therefore, the urban India where a rising middle class (much of it made up of migrants from the aforementioned villages and small towns) could trade in the typical restrictions of religion and caste for some social currency.

I too belonged to this group.

I doubt I would have ever had biryani if I had not moved out of Haridwar for college. In all probability, I'd have continued to find non-vegetarian food frightening.

As it turned out, I moved to Chennai for college, a friend convinced me to try chicken-popcorn at McDonald's, and I followed the clichéd arc of going from 'gravy-only' to 'boneless-only' to 'chicken-only', and finally to 'anything-that-tastes-good'.

In small towns such as Mathura, Aligarh, and Yercaud also the young people I meet are generally excited to try out new (and sometimes forbidden) tastes.

A second cousin from a very orthodox and 'pure' vegetarian family in Meerut, for example, recently confided in me that for years he has been eating boiled eggs at a friend's house after working out. Do you think that's bad? he asked me. I assured him that it was perfectly all right as long as he was confiding in me, but perhaps he should take some time before telling his parents.

That was OK, he said, because he would soon leave for Delhi to attend college.

Increased travel, especially the kind undertaken for pleasure, has made us less particular about what we may eat, and food delivery apps have brought extensive menus to our doorsteps. My parents and grandparents knew nothing about litti-chokha or medu vada or mutton biryani—food that I now consume regularly—not because they chose not to have it but simply because they never had access to any of it.

There is however an interesting contradiction at play here.

For all of our interest in trying out more food, we are all too ready to pigeonhole our identities based on what we eat, even as social and religious identities that define what we eat are melting away.

The quintessential Millennial need to stand apart and build a unique identity has necessitated a further division of the 'foodie' label as soon as it became commonplace. A bunch of implication-laden tags are up for grabs. We have done Brillat-Savarin's work for him—there is no need to ask us what we eat and then figure out who we are; we are all too ready to do all that ourselves.

Preferring chai over coffee, for example, can make someone a chai-lover and confer upon them a salt-of-the-earth, no-frills identity. The coffee drinker, on the other hand, especially if they drink it black, can revel in appearing more sophisticated or intellectual. Further depth, of course, can always be added to an identity by pontificating on the 'authenticity' or 'correctness' of particular recipes and flavours.

Since outrage and fear sell better than anything else on the internet it should not be surprising that being a food expert, or someone who points out dangers in different food items, is an increasingly popular choice.

Most studies and surveys on Millennial eating habits agree

that as a generation we are more inclined to engage with the scientific and ethical aspects of our food choices. This inclination, when combined with our identity synthesis and the overabundance of food choices available to us, can often cause situations where our first reaction to food is distrust, suspicion, and outright fear.

These emotions—distrust, suspicion, fear—mark the way we think about food, and they are quite different from the evolutionary 'concern' mentioned by Dunn and Sanchez.

▪

To better understand how our identities, anxieties, and societal change affect our food culture, I spoke to Krish Ashok, a food science expert and the author of the bestselling book *Masala Lab: The Science of Indian Cooking*.

Ashok is an internet sensation in his own right with an Instagram following of more than 8 lakh. Generally known for detailed takes on food and busting puritanical or unscientific myths, his work is also interesting for its curious exploration of how food choices impact social trends.

Recently, for instance, one of his social media posts went viral for suggesting that the resistance against using refrigerators in India was, at least in part, a result of the patriarchal attitudes that expect women to spend all their time in the kitchen preparing 'fresh food' for the family. Many who objected in the comments section took it upon themselves to play the part of 'food experts' by spouting pseudo-scientific factoids about the dangers of eating refrigerated food.

I asked Ashok what he thinks about the identities we create around our food choices.

'I think as we head to a world where regular human relationships are increasingly complicated and hard, and we don't necessarily identify with the traditional big-picture identities like caste or religion and so on, we need to find micro-identities like coffee-lovers, chai-lovers, biryani-lovers, etc.,' he said. 'It's a natural extension of our culture that people need to find these tribes. Social media, again, makes it easier to posture and sort of celebrate your unique identity. And (unlike caste or religion) people can always grow out of one identity and simply just adopt another, or they are allowed to have multiple identities.'

At the same time, however, the current nature of the internet can also amplify and distort our natural tendency to be wary of what we eat.

During our conversation, Ashok stressed that we 'live in a food culture where our information and education ecosystem is designed not to inform, but to scare'.

As with refrigeration, there are thousands of people on the internet who warn vociferously against all sorts of things like using microwave ovens, consuming refined oil, mixing watermelon and milk, drinking water while standing up, eating brinjals, and having dairy with meat or fish. A lot of this advice contradicts each other, but all of it adds to the general din in the discourse about what we should and should not eat.

'I get hundreds of messages every day, mostly from women, who are just completely scared out of their lives,' Ashok tells me. 'They have to feed their husband and their kids and their in-laws, and they're on Instagram all day, and it's telling them that literally everything and anything that makes their life easier is horrible for health, is killing them, or giving them cancer.'

I asked him if, in his opinion, we are more afraid of food than previous generations.

'Yes, absolutely we are. Yet, in a sense, one cannot really blame people for being scared because they are seeing more people being diagnosed with diabetes, hypertension, and cancer around them. It's a very difficult statistical fallacy to navigate. Even well-educated people are often just as susceptible to fearmongering as anyone else because of what they observe around themselves.'

Broadly, three factors fuel this observational misjudgement.

First, it can be easy to overlook the fact that the average life expectancy in India, just thirty years ago, was less than sixty. So, most people simply never lived long enough to get 'diseases of age' such as Type-2 diabetes or hypertension.

Second, regular health check-ups or even annual physical assessments are a very recent phenomenon. When people had health issues in the recent past, they often went undiagnosed, and that makes it difficult to do an objective analysis of whether modern eating habits can be blamed for the uptick in health issues.

The third, and perhaps most important, factor is the profound way in which the flow of information has completely changed in our time.

There is so much information available to us online that there is no way to discern whether something is a general trend or a one-off incident. It is profitable to present the latter as the former because it adds a certain amount of shock-and-awe flair to the content. Ashok refers to this as the 'amplification of the trivial'.

It ties up again to Paul's ideas about the causal connection between technology and the millennial obsession with what we eat.

Take, for instance, the broadly correct idea that excessive consumption of sugar (like excessive consumption of most things) is bad for us and the claim that sugar is literal poison due to the use of sulphur in sugar factories.

Due to the traditional system of information flow and news, Ashok points out, that is exactly the kind of trivial misinformation that would never have gone viral twenty years ago. 'Let's say a journalist even found this out to be true for a factory somewhere that was playing fast and loose with the regulations and didn't quite treat the sugar properly. That would probably have been a one-off news item on a local newspaper's third page with no impact on our general perception of sugar.'

The amplification of the trivial taken along with the assumption that our ancestors ate healthier than us can often lead to a misplaced tendency to go for more 'natural' alternatives.

Jaggery, for example, is billed by many as a better alternative to white sugar. Several food influencers on social media go so far as to suggest that it can replace artificial sweeteners for diabetics and people looking to lose weight. The fact that it has a high glycaemic index of 84.4, and no significant health advantages over processed sugar, has done little to check the meteoric rise in its popularity.

When I read about the jaggery-craze, my mind immediately went back to when we were so shaken up by my mother's diabetes diagnosis. Would we have replaced her Sugar Free capsules with jaggery if we bought into such a narrative at the time? It doesn't sound impossible, and I can only imagine how her health would have been damaged.

Choosing uniodized salts (Pink Himalayan Rock Salt, for example) in favour of the usually iodized table salt commonly found in Indian households, is another example of a similarly 'healthy' trend. For a macroscopic (pun intended) view of how an excess of unreliable or undetailed information affects our food choices, we can look at the worldwide craze for protein-rich food and protein supplements.

It is perhaps best summarized by the title of a *Wall Street Journal* article on the subject: 'When the Box Says "Protein", Shoppers Say I'll Take It'.

Sounds true enough, considering the supermarket shelves, physical and digital, filled with protein-rich foods. FMCG companies outshine each other in their efforts to attract us with product categories such as high-protein biscuits, protein bars, protein potato chips, protein smoothie mixes, etc. These products are invariably more expensive than their regular variants, which is not surprising when we consider how 'aware' everyone suddenly is about their protein intake—in 2017 alone, there were 64 million Google searches for 'protein'.

Marketing has been of great help, no doubt.

Whey, for example, used to be a useless by-product of the cheese factories in the US. In the 1970s, however, when restrictions were placed on the amount of dairy waste that could be dumped into rivers, the factories had to find ways to get rid of it somehow. Initially fed to pigs, whey could be produced on an industrial scale for human consumption once the technology had been developed to pre-concentrate it before it dried. Since then, it has been recast as an everyday essential for even the most casual gym-goers. In India, the market size of whey protein is expected to grow from USD 91.78 million in 2023 to USD 120.29 million by 2028.

The trend can be understood in the context of the health supremacy struggle between the other two macros—carbohydrates and fats.

As Bee Wilson, a British food writer and journalist, puts it, 'While the low-fattists and the low-carbists continue to slug it out, protein comes out the winner as the one safe thing that most of the population feel they can still put their faith in, whether for weight loss or general health. We have to eat *something*, after all.'

The terminology and psychology around choosing food according to the amount of protein (or fats and carbs) it possesses suggests an approach rooted in science. An approach, in fact, that is quite similar to Instagram food-influencers who read out ingredient lists of everyday products to caution people against consuming them.

The similarity is not coincidental because both of them are a result of people placing their belief in half-truths and imagining cause-effect relationships where none exist.

Michael Pollan, the celebrated writer of *In Defense of Food*, looks at this as part of a larger phenomenon he calls 'the ideology of nutritionism'.

Essentially, it involves looking at food in terms of its components such as proteins, fats, carbohydrates, vitamins, minerals, lipids, etc., and then attributing the effects of different food items to these components. Nutritionism also has the attractive quality of sounding scientific while operating on a rather reductive form of science.

According to Pollan, nutritionism, like most ideologies, works on the basis of unexamined assumptions. The basic assumption, or the ideological premise, is that 'the key to understanding food is indeed the nutrient' while a deeper assumption is that 'the whole point of eating is to maintain and promote bodily health'. Yet, curiously enough, nutritionism cannot explain why it doesn't lead to the health results it promises while cultures that look at food as food—rather than the sum total of its nutritional components—do much better.

In this respect, Pollan and others mention the 'French Paradox', i.e., the fact that, despite consuming 'unhealthy' nutrients such as saturated fat and dietary cholesterol, French people are typically healthier than people in nutritionism-obsessed societies like the US.

Since the ideology of nutritionism is based on flawed science, it misleads not only the masses but also the scientists whose job it is to inform the said masses.

In an essay entitled 'Unhappy Meals', Pollan quotes nutritionist Marion Nestle pointing out the exact problem when she says that 'it (nutrition science) takes the nutrient out of the context of food, the food out of the context of diet and the diet out of the context of lifestyle'.

Taking information out of context is a common indulgence of our times.

In the case of food, it is slowly ballooning up into an all-encompassing fear that is based less on facts and more on the pursuit of identity, ideology, and influence.

While nutritionism has permeated our culture in the form of 'scientific' approaches that try to evaluate food rather than enjoy it, there is another movement that deserves due attention.

The vegan lifestyle is arguably a defining trend in the Millennial food culture and it may very well form an important part of our legacy. What exactly does it mean? Well, according to the Vegan Society, being a vegan involves 'avoiding all animal foods such as meat (including fish, shellfish, and insects), dairy, eggs and honey—as well as avoiding animal-derived materials, products tested on animals and places that use animals for entertainment'. The stated objective of vegans is to reduce the environmental impact of human eating habits and make food consumption more ethical.

A noble objective indeed.

As should be evident from its popularity, veganism combines

several aspects unique to the zeitgeist.

There is the responsible-consumerism angle to it which characterizes so much of Millennial activism, particularly with regard to the environment.

There is a social-media friendliness to it that comes from the aesthetic appeal of artfully arranged Buddha Bowls and avocado toasts placed next to a glassful of oat milk.

There is also a counter-cultural edginess to it that sells quite well on the internet. It is enviable and aspirational—due to the sheer amount of money and time it requires to switch lifestyles, and the high cost of vegan substitutes for animal products, veganism is a marker of class sophistication.

Most importantly, no rational person could counter the fact that eating more plants and fewer animals is better for our health as well as the environment.

'The fundamental logic of veganism is irrefutable,' says Krish Ashok. 'Large-scale animal husbandry is terrible for the planet. A kilogram of poultry causes about 10 kg of carbon emissions and a kilogram of beef can take up the figure as high as 90 kg. Plants-based food only causes a fraction of these emissions, making their consumption so much better for the environment. But, it is important to understand the problems that arise when this decidedly Western, and undeniably upper-class, movement is imported to a country like India.'

In its current form, veganism, like nutritionism, is also an ideology. As such, it also is unable to appreciate that what people eat has a lot to do with their lifestyles and these lifestyles are not necessarily a version of the average Western lifestyle.

Ashok is all too ready to expand on that.

'The vegan movement started in response to industrial meat production, but the vast majority of people in the third world do not consume industrially-produced meat. The problem is that people are not able to distinguish between large-scale ranches in Texas and a farmer in the village having two goats, a cow, and four chickens running around his house. That is why when I think about vegans looking down on (non-vegan) people in India, whose per capita meat consumption is amongst the lowest in the world, the moral posturing seems ridiculous.'

'For you to eat a balanced vegan meal, you need supplements, you need to eat a bunch of soy, you need to eat a bunch of really processed, hyper-processed substitutes, and so on. So in that sense, if you're able to do it fantastic, but how many people can afford it here in India? I appreciate vegans for their individual drive and their motivation to save the planet. I don't want to question that. I only have a problem when they become activists and they go after meat-eaters in India because this is still a country where only a tiny minority meets their protein requirement and so many have barely any food security as such. Among those who can buy meat, the vast majority only eat meat once a week, probably on a weekend, as a special dish.'

Further problems arise when one pauses to take into account India's social complexity. It is difficult to imagine essentially well-intentioned vegans being sympathetic to the rhetoric of Hindutva extremists, but it is true that in our country people, mostly Muslims, are frequently killed over their food choices.

The moral righteousness of veganism when imported to India is bound to find common ground with the Brahminical demonization of meat-eaters.

Like nutritionism, veganism seeks to change what it does not understand. For instance, it is difficult to imagine anyone making the ethical argument against consuming meat to Dalits who have been traditionally prohibited from agriculture and farming. Beef, the archenemy of vegans, is particularly contentious considering that 'the co-relation between untouchability and the use of the dead cow is so great and so close that the thesis that it is the root of untouchability seems to be incontrovertible,' according to Dr Ambedkar himself.

Other ideological examples include utterly unscientific theories of Ayurveda and the classification of different food items as satvik, rajasik, and tamasik.

They act for traditionalists as veganism does for environmentalists and nutritionism does for the scientific, that is by providing a rigid framework of evaluating food and divorcing the act of eating from pleasure and lifestyle choices.

▪

A lot of Millennial confusion and fear about food stems from overabundance—of food itself and information about food.

More food is accessible to us, more easily, and more information is accessible to us about it, more easily, but most of us are instrumentally rational, which is to say that we make only those choices for which the benefits exceed costs.

It means that since we cannot reasonably invest the sheer amount of time and effort needed to understand something as fantastically complex as food, we are inclined to gobble up all sorts of scientific and unscientific information we find (or that finds us, actually) on social media.

A little learning is a dangerous thing, as Alexander Pope tells us.

Ideally, we should be able to fill up the gaps in our knowledge with even more information but, realistically speaking, that's quite impossible to do unless one decides to dedicate their life to food research. That may be a slippery slope, however, because the example of nutritionism shows us that science can also be corrupted by ideological biases and cultural ignorance. Neither is blind traditionalism a good answer to our dilemmas and anxieties.

What serves us best in this situation of overabundance then may be a philosophy of reduction.

If we reduce how much we try to know and think about our food, as well as how much we consume, we will have to rely on our instincts and common sense. Fortunately for us, these have served us rather well in choosing our food for thousands of years.

Our tastes may be more experimental and extensive than those of our parents and grandparents, and science has certainly served us well in making good food choices to an extent. But, we can benefit enormously, I believe, by going back to appreciating the food on our plates rather than analysing it. Once we do that, we may be able to re-evaluate our food in terms of pleasure, and relieve our eating choices from the entire responsibility of keeping us in states of peak performance.

If we still do want a guiding light on our way to the kitchen, we can refer to Michael Pollan's advice. He keeps it rather short and simple.

'Eat food. Not too much. Mostly plants.'

6

MILLENNIALS IN THE MOONLIGHT

If a Martian were to visit your living room and ask you to describe what is this 'job' thing you keep talking about, you would probably describe it as a set-up in which you put your skills to work for someone and get paid for that. The definition is sound enough, even if it leaves something to be desired in terms of nuance. But hey, you are talking to an alien here and hoping that they don't get irritated by long explanations and shoot you dead with laser beams.

For more than a month, I asked various friends, former colleagues, and acquaintances to imagine themselves in the same situation. Most of them came up with similar descriptions, though many of them insisted on depressing the poor alien.

Someone at my last company, a fintech start-up, referred to 'a bleak journey that can sometimes feel like a countdown, with each task chipping away at precious moments of mortality'. A friend from college called it 'something that pays you to do boring monotonous stuff'. Another ex-colleague put it simply as 'work done for money'.

The Alien Perspective is a thought experiment used by philosophers, scientists, sociologists, writers, and others as a tool of defamiliarization to see the world with new eyes. It can throw relief on absurdities that we take for granted, and it's useful in clearing the clutter around complex concepts.

The 'alien' is beyond our social contracts, which helps in boiling things down to their essential components.

In the case of jobs, and white-collar jobs in particular, these components seem to be skills and money. Also, if our curious alien has access to the latest data, chances are that it chose a Millennial with whom to conduct this interview. Currently, Millennials make up more than a third of the global workforce, and the numbers are higher in younger countries like India.

The IT industry, in particular, has been quite partial to our generation with NASSCOM reporting in 2022 that 68 to 70 per cent of the tech employees in India are Millennials.

Assuming that they started working in their early twenties, Millennials have been at it for about two decades now and our relationship with our jobs has changed in various ways during this time. The 9 to 5 workday is dead in all but theory, as are labour unions. Hustle culture is no longer a fad but a common employer expectation, and 'flexible hours' is often doublespeak for as-many-hours-as-possible. The lack of job security that became apparent after the recession of 2007–2008 has gradually become a fact of life that must be taken into account while making any life decisions.

Various technological tools, sold with the promise that they would help people increase their productivity, have delivered on that promise. But whether that's a good thing or not depends on whether one looks at oneself as a human or a 'human resource'.

Naturally, our work lives do not exist in isolation from the condition of the world at large, despite what capitalism would have us believe.

And what does the world look like in the middle of the twenty-first century's second decade?

We have spent close to four years coping with the Covid-19 pandemic's fallout in various aspects of our lives, including our jobs.

Experts differ on what the immediate economic future will look like for different sections of the workforce in different parts of the world, but the uncertainty itself has sent tremors through the corporate landscape. Since 2022, there have been rumours of another global recession looming over the horizon. Regardless of whether they turn out to be true or not, tech giants such as Meta, Google, and X have already fired employees by the thousands and smaller companies have only been too willing to follow their lead.

In the middle of these serious concerns, a whimsical-sounding word keeps coming up regularly in discussions about the changing nature of jobs and Millennial work culture.

Moonlighting. The practice of a person holding two or more full-time jobs at the same time, generally without the consent of their employers.

While professionals in a few other industries may also be experimenting with it, the limelight mostly falls on the IT industry which has a number of people working from home and offers some of the most lucrative jobs. Looking at the work-from-home set-ups as 'means' and the lucrativeness of these jobs as 'motive', from an employee's perspective one can easily understand why people would choose to moonlight and earn as much as they can, while they still can.

Employers, however, are not fond of the idea, to put it mildly.

Rishad Premji, Wipro's chairman, has called it 'cheating—plain and simple' and Ramachandran Sundararajan, chief people officer at HCL Tech has said, 'We do not approve of that.'

Many of their contemporaries have expressed similar views, including Infosys founder N. R. Narayana Murthy. 'My fervent desire and humble desire to youngsters is please don't fall into this trap of I will moonlight, I will do work from home, I will come to office three days in a week,' Murthy said during an event in early 2023.

In 2022, Infosys also sent a mail to its employees with the subject line 'No two-timing, no moonlighting'. It was made clear that the employees who did not heed this warning, or advice, could be instantly terminated.

A few start-ups (Swiggy, for example) promise to be more benevolent if the employees inform them upfront about any moonlighting ventures.

Curiously enough, while there are legal and performance-related aspects to the matter, most of the criticism against moonlighting is based on concepts like loyalty and ethics. When Premji calls it 'cheating', he sounds like a jilted lover and when Narayana Murthy talks about the 'trap' or 'two-timing', he invokes a worried grandparent advising the 'youngsters' not to stray from the good path.

Nothing wrong with that per se. Loyalty and ethics are appreciable, necessary things in civil society.

But, if you told your Martian interviewer all this and then had it go through the news reports and labour market statistics from the last few years, it may be baffled by the hypocrisy on display.

For instance, while it is unethical and disloyal of employees to work two jobs, directors at any IT firm are allowed to run other businesses and be independent directors in up to seven public firms and more private firms. Elon Musk, the poster boy of toxic work culture, did exactly that when he took over as the CEO at Twitter in 2022 while also being the CEO at Tesla and SpaceX. He also fired 50 per cent of Twitter's employees when he came on board—loyal and ethical employees, presumably, with families to feed, bills to pay, and loans to honour.

Did that attract the same amount of hand-wringing in the IT industry as moonlighting does? Of course not.

People getting fired isn't very much out of the ordinary and our capitalist masters live by simple credos—employees are expendable, businesses are not; all employees are equal, but some are more equal than others.

We don't need to look as far out as Musk for proof, of course.

In 2022, it was widely reported that Wipro, led by Rishad Premji, had cut down its salary offers to engineering freshers.

The candidates who had already received offers of ₹6.5 lakh per year, and were waiting to join the company, received emails asking them if they would like to join at ₹3.5 lakh per year instead.

Many candidates who accepted Wipro's initial offer may have rejected competing offers, only to accept reduced salaries in the end. Does that sound like an example of a relationship where 'loyalty' and 'ethics' are important?

Consider that Wipro is not a loss-making company—it reported a net profit of ₹3,052.9 crore for the quarter that ended December 2022 (Q3FY23)—and the Premji family is worth billions of dollars. It is also quite impossible that the leadership at Wipro did not realize that employees were quite anxious about their jobs in 2022 due to rumours about an incoming recession. Those about to start their careers were especially vulnerable.

We can also consider that IT CEOs' salaries increased by 1500 per cent in the last ten years while freshers' salaries went up by less than 50 per cent at Infosys, Wipro, and TCS, according to *Business Today*.

Yet, it is 'cheating- plain and simple' if employees want to supplement their income with another job.

Benevolent thoughts of saving youngsters from traps such as moonlighting (more money) and WFH (more convenience) must also come rather quickly, we can imagine, when one, like Narayana Murthy, has an estimated net worth of $4.8 billion. Also worth wondering is whether Sudha Murthy, who publishes widely read children's books at a regular frequency, and works as the chairperson of Infosys Foundation, is a moonlighting employee or not.

Moonlighting, which irks employers so much, doesn't exist away from the reality of India's skilled labour market. Motivations for it, and reactions to it, are products of the same underlying conditions that characterize so much of millennial work culture.

■

Daksh, a senior software development engineer (SDE) I consulted for this essay, was ecstatic when he topped the 12th board exams in his village's only English-medium school.

His family's primary source of income was farming and the salary of Daksh's uncle (his father's younger brother), who worked as a police constable in Jaipur. Their financial situation had turned precarious three years before Daksh passed out of school, when the family borrowed ₹30 lakhs from a local moneylender at the going interest rate of 4 per cent per month for his aunt's marriage.

As the eldest son of the house, the responsibility of improving his family's conditions fell on Daksh, and the family was willing to invest in him.

A month after the school results came out, he was enrolled at a coaching centre in Delhi to prepare for engineering entrance exams. Making it to an IIT was the big prize, of course, and even his illiterate mother recognized 'IIT' as a magic word that could change all their lives overnight. In Delhi, Daksh could stay at a relative's place, which made the arrangement cheaper than studying at Kota, a small town in Rajasthan, known as the hub of entrance exam preparation (and student suicides).

Daksh studied nine to ten hours a day that year.

He didn't see anything in Delhi except the route between his relative's place and the coaching centre, never talked to his school friends back in the village, and watched just about an hour of TV on Sundays.

The coaching centre was charging his family ₹85,000, and with other miscellaneous expenses, the cost of his year in Delhi would come close to ₹1 lakh. An amount that would add further strain to his family's already overstrained budget.

There were two batches at the coaching centre. Batch 1 was the 'good batch', whose students consistently scored high marks in fortnightly tests. Not scoring the cut-off marks in two consecutive tests meant being demoted to Batch 2, 'the bad batch', and students rarely climbed back up again.

Daksh stayed in the good batch throughout his stay in Delhi, until a month before the entrance exams when he took some time off from the classes to revise the syllabus on his own.

For almost the entire month, he could not get a good night's sleep.

'I kept thinking about what would happen if I didn't get into IIT,' he told me, 'and even having dinner felt like a waste of time.'

To this day, he cannot clearly remember how he wrote the exams because the memories of that time are all garbled up with extreme anxiety.

The memories of checking the results, however, are clear enough.

Like 98 per cent of the people who sat for the IIT-JEE exam with him, he did not make it to an IIT. Neither was he able to clear any of the so-called 'Tier I' colleges, and he was so confident about his preparation that he had not applied to most of the private 'Tier II' colleges such as SRM and VIT.

He could get into Manipal University, a decent enough private college, but its fees were well beyond his family's budget.

After a lot of tiring deliberation, he enrolled himself at Mahendra Pratap Engineering College in Jaipur, a group of four dilapidated buildings on the Haryana–Rajasthan highway. It was a far cry from the kind of institution he had imagined he would attend, and he could not help but feel like he had lost at life.

Still, he decided to make the most of a bad situation. When he graduated from there four years later, he was one of the twenty-odd people in a 500-student batch to have secured a campus placement. Part of a 4 per cent minority, that is.

The web-development job, at a Jaipur-based marketing company, paid him a starting salary of ₹7,500 per month. It would be bumped up to ₹10,000 once he completed a six-month probation period, the HR manager informed him at the time of his interview.

Daksh worked there for just three months before moving to Bangalore in search of greener pastures.

■

For most Indians, the choice of their career is a family decision.

In case that feels like a dated idea, and popular movies have managed to convince you that young people follow their hearts nowadays, we can refer to a recent LinkedIn study which found that 82 per cent parents in India are still involved in deciding their children's careers.

There is little room for risky decisions.

Government jobs, once looked at as the ultimate guarantee of a stable life, look increasingly difficult to get. Between 2014 and 2022, for instance, out of the 22.05 crore people who applied for central government jobs, only 7.22 lakh were recommended for appointment. That translates to a success rate of 0.3 per cent and makes government jobs unviable for most young people from middle-class families who need to start earning soon after finishing college.

In private jobs, the choice between engineering and medicine is considered choice enough by families that can afford the school-to-graduation pipeline. Between these two, the former has emerged as the far more commonly chosen option.

The preference can be seen clearly in the disparity between the number of medical colleges (about 700) and engineering colleges (more than 4,000) in India. Data also tells us that engineering, and IT in particular, is overwhelmingly the favourite among students.

The NASSCOM-Indeed study published in December 2022, for instance, found that as many as 70 per cent Millennials and Gen Z students want to be engineers. The study also provided an explanation for the preference: 'The younger generation is not only seeking a promising career in tech but is also aspiring to do a desk job while maintaining a work-life balance.'

A perfectly logical aspiration, but not an altogether realistic one, unfortunately.

In *Kids These Days*, Malcolm Harris defines the labour market's supposed deal with the twenty-first century—the population gets more educated, more effective, better skilled, and in return it's rewarded with high-paying post-industrial jobs. In other words, the 'desk jobs with work-life balance' that the majority of Indian students expect out of a career in IT.

It became clear that we had fallen for this pitch hook, line, and sinker almost as soon as the oldest Millennials entered the workforce.

In an essay published in 2000, Manu Joseph provides a window into the ground reality of 178,000 software engineers produced by India that year. 'The dream of upward mobility is more like a nightmare,' he says, and talks about how lower middle-class households ambitiously invested in getting their children an education in computer science. Most of these students enrolled themselves not in the four-year degree programmes that are the norm today, but in months-long courses that taught everything from multimedia to JAVA and web development. Many of them, having invested money to the tune of ₹30,000 to ₹35,000 in these courses, found jobs that paid them anything between ₹700 to ₹1,000 per month.

The craze for IT jobs and its mismatch with reality have both survived the twenty-odd years since Joseph's essay was published.

As of 2022, India has the second-highest number of software engineers in the world, trailing only behind the US, and it is predicted to surpass the US by 2024.

Yet, as many as 95 per cent of engineers in our country are not considered fit for software development jobs. Even among the remaining 5 per cent, too many would have to settle for low-paying jobs, because only 1.4 per cent could write functionally correct and efficient code—a basic requirement for an entry-level software development role.

Due to the sobering picture they paint about the topmost career choice in India, these numbers can be difficult to accept for many. IT veterans like C. P. Gurnani, CEO & MD of Tech Mahindra, however, agree on the overall state of things.

In a 2022, article on the unemployability of engineers in India, Gurnani was quoted in the *Economic Times*: 'The top 10 IT companies take only 6% of the engineering graduates. What happens to the remaining 94%?'

▪

Moving to a new city without a job and only a limited amount of cash can be challenging for a twenty-one-year-old, Daksh discovered soon after shifting to Bangalore in 2016.

If he had known the numbers from up above, Daksh told me that he would probably have held on to his first job in Jaipur and been grateful for it.

For months after the move, Daksh lived in one of the many

Men's PGs that offer bad food and cheap lodgings to bachelors in the city. Every day he devoted most of his time to practising his coding skills. At night, he often stayed up late looking for job openings for freshers.

He interviewed at a bunch of start-ups but failed to get past the personal interview round due to inadequate soft skills. When he left Jaipur, he had hoped to earn ₹5–6 lakh per year. Many rejections and six months later, he had to settle for a ₹2.4 lakh package from a multi-national software consultancy.

₹20,000 was double the salary he would get in Jaipur, but he was sending more than half of it back to his village and the living costs were much higher in Bangalore.

For the next year and a half, Daksh stayed at the same PG and gave his best at work. He went out of his way to get included in projects, updated himself on the latest technology, and stayed away from office politics.

Slowly, he picked up on the how the corporate system worked.

It soon became clear, for instance, that appraisals depended on who was the manager's pet, which in turn was based on who gave the impression of giving maximum time at work. Soft skills carried enormous weight, sometimes more than the skills essential to the job, and the highest paid people never stayed at the same organization for too long.

Staying more than two years at a service company was in fact seen as evidence of mediocrity, a friendly senior told him.

The fastest way to grow his cost to company (CTC), he learned, was by switching companies at regular intervals of a year and a half, preferably a few months after getting an appraisal. It gave him the advantage of getting a hike on a salary already increased by 10-15 per cent, and by leveraging different offer letters against each other he could jump further ahead by 40-50 per cent.

The approach yielded good dividends. By the end of 2019, Daksh was earning ₹18 lakhs per annum, achieving a salary growth rate of about 650 per cent in just four years.

A bunch of his friends and colleagues were following the same method and getting good results. The only hindrance, if it can be called that, was the great amount of hard work, quick learning, and skill development needed to crack multiple interviews each year. Daksh did all this and looked at it as a game. Success gave him a heady rush and the significant amount of debt on his family back in Rajasthan served as motivation to keep playing.

For all his work, however, the rewards still felt disproportionate.

In early 2020, he was considering an executive MBA, but the expensive degree would have meant another loan and he was not keen on the prospect.

▪

The labour market's deal with the twenty-first century—more education and higher skills leading to better and more secure jobs—has not held up.

If anything, a blind acceptance of it has resulted in the characterization of white-collar and blue-collar jobs as 'good jobs' and 'bad jobs' respectively. Obviously, everyone has to have 'good jobs', which means that it's harder to compete for a good job, the bad jobs are worse than they used to be, and all kinds of jobs are less secure.

A 2023 essay by Alex Travelli and Hari Kumar, 'Want One of India's Best Jobs? You and 1,800 Other Applicants', gives a harrowing account of the situation.

It compares government jobs in Patna where almost 2,000 people compete for a single vacancy with well-paying manufacturing jobs that find no takers. Those with engineering degrees hang somewhere in between—they know how difficult it is to get government jobs and they look at non-tech jobs as bad jobs.

Mr Ramesh, an auto parts manufacturer from Coimbatore, for example, needs skilled employees for his thriving business but struggles to find them due to this misalignment. Blinkered by their BTech degrees, the young people in his own state would much rather earn less by working 'in tech' as delivery persons or drivers for app companies like Zomato and Uber, than work with him as skilled labour. It is not their fault; it must be difficult to admit that the comfortable white-collar jobs promised by their college education are never going to be within their grasp.

'The fate of the planet's biggest generation of workers hangs in the balance,' Travelli and Kumar remind us. 'Success could mean a more middle-income future that fulfils the country's world-shaking promise. Failure could leave swaths of India mired in pervasive poverty for decades to come.'

If the alien we conjured at the beginning of this essay was still with us, it would be overwhelmed by the absurdity of our situation.

Here is what things look like in simple terms:

- We have a lot of young people who need employment.
- Most of them want to be engineers and work in IT, the other preferred option is getting a government job, but the odds of getting a government job are so slim as to be non-existent.
- The IT industry has a number of vacancies, but not nearly enough for the millions of engineers who graduate from thousands of colleges.
- The kind of private jobs that *are* available do not attract job seekers.
- Even if enough vacancies were miraculously created in IT, employers and independent commentators agree that most engineers in the country are not at all employable.

One may despair or laugh, but it's clear that a trend like moonlighting could only be a problem of the few. When people cannot even find one white-collar job, especially in IT, who would have multiple jobs?

Who makes up the moonlighting minority?

Well, a fraction of the 1.4 per cent software engineers who can 'write functionally correct and efficient code' and have a fair bit of industry experience. They are among the few who can still leverage their *relative* irreplaceability to negotiate with employers on various fronts, monetary and otherwise.

Moonlighting is the strongest expression of autonomy from these employees yet, and that is why it causes such strong reactions.

Since only a few people can, and are, moonlighting, it is not the security of their trade secrets or the performance of these employees that businesses worry about. No, what truly riles employers, is the message that such an expression of autonomy sends out to the labour market at large—employees own their free time and they can use it to gain financial independence.

Free time, after all, lies at the heart of modern, post-internet work culture. As a by-product of the WFH set-ups necessitated by the pandemic, it is also the primary means for moonlighting.

American art critic and essayist Jonathan Crary writes on the subject with particular precision in his book *24/7: Late Capitalism and the Ends of Sleep*.

'By the last decades of the twentieth century and into the present, with the collapse of controlled or mitigated forms of capitalism in the US and Europe, there has ceased to be any internal necessity for having rest and recuperation as components of economic growth and profitability,' he writes. 'Time for human rest and regeneration is now simply too expensive to be structurally possible within contemporary capitalism.'

The 24/7-alert lifestyle may be exhausting for the Millennials living it, but it is ideal for employers.

When the majority of the workforce has the same degrees and similar skills how do employers keep the workers on their toes? By rating them based on how much time they dedicate to their jobs, as Daksh discovered at his very first job. It is no longer a matter of working all the time, which is a practical impossibility, but of being available for work all the time. Technology has helped, of course, because for how long can an employee leave a text from their boss unread, and how many times can they avoid picking up calls with excuses of a bad mobile network?

It is easy to suggest that people should set their own boundaries, but these people then have to compete with peers who are willing to compromise.

'A competitive childhood environment that encourages each kid to "be all they can be" and "reach their potential" undermines the possibility of solidarity,' Harris writes. 'As long as there is an advantage to be had, Millennials have been taught to reach for it, because if they don't someone else out there will. This kind of thinking produces some real high achievers, but it also puts a generation of workers in a very bad bargaining position.'

In a 2019 article called 'Why Are Young People Pretending to Love Work?' published just a few months before the pandemic hit us, business journalist Erin Griffith wrote about how we have been forced to buy into exploitative lifestyles.

'In the new work culture, enduring or even merely liking one's job is not enough,' she wrote. 'Workers should love what they do, and then promote that love on social media, thus fusing their identities to that of their employers. Why else would LinkedIn build its own version of Snapchat Stories? This is toil glamour, and it is going mainstream.'

Moonlighting subverts this narrative and puts employees in a very good bargaining position. It bears against job insecurity—why would someone worry about losing one of their three jobs as much as they would about losing their only job—and renders ineffective the constant competition produced by this insecurity. Is it any wonder that the employers talk about it as if it were the ultimate sin?

■

As the world ground to a standstill in the spring of 2020, Daksh's company asked all employees to work from home.

Like many others at the time, he suddenly found himself with a lot more time, most of it saved from traffic-heavy commutes, chit-chat with colleagues, and extended coffee breaks. Two months later, as the company extended the WFH set-up indefinitely, he realized that it was pointless to keep paying rent in Bangalore, and moved to his uncle's house in Jaipur.

This freed up even more of his time because his aunt now took care of all the housework he had been doing for himself in Bangalore. He and his uncle divided the daily grocery runs between them.

How could he derive maximum profit from all this time?

In March, his girlfriend had received an offer from a London-based software company to work for one of their clients. The company would bill the client hourly according to UK rates, pay her slightly more than the going hourly rates in India, and reap the sweet fruits of a globalized labour market. She declined the offer because it felt less secure than her regular job at a software service company in Banglore.

Bored out of his mind in Jaipur, Daksh now asked her to put him in touch with the HR manager she had talked to in London.

By July, he had managed to clear the technical interviews and settled on a fixed annual package of ₹23 lakhs, which came out to be lower than the hour-based compensation his girlfriend had been offered. Daksh didn't mind. Combined with the salary from his regular job, he would get more than ₹3 lakh per month, which felt good enough for the time being.

'I figured out that there were only two problems in working multiple jobs,' he told me, 'obviously, you couldn't do it while working from the office because you'd have to hide the second laptop from other people and do a bunch of other jugaad. Secondly, you could easily get caught if you were on the PF (Provident Fund) records of two companies at the same time. The first problem was solved by work-from-home, and the second by working for overseas companies.'

Both his jobs together required about three hours of solid work, i.e., coding, from him. The rest of the time went into juggling meetings and brainstorming sessions. Only a few months ago, he had been spending close to ten hours every day at the office for half the amount of money.

Predictably enough, he figured there was nothing to stop him from reaching for more.

Between December 2021 and February 2022, Daksh worked as many as four jobs and earned a total of ₹30 lakhs, which comes down to about ₹10 lakhs per month. In March 2022, he repaid the entirety of his family's debt. Six months later, he started financing a project to rebuild their ancestral home that had fallen into disrepair years ago.

Once the construction is finished and his younger brother gets a job, he will go back to working for a single employer, he told me. The current lifestyle, exciting as it has been, is now beginning to affect his physical and mental health.

Did he never feel any moral or ethical dilemmas about lying to his employers? Daksh shook his head and laughed at the naivete of my question.

'Never. See, the relationship has always been simple enough—they try to maximize work and minimize payouts, while we try to minimize work and maximize payouts. Working simultaneous jobs is simply a new development and as long as I am not selling someone's data to someone else, I don't see what is the big deal.'

Daksh also points out a glaring contradiction that is in many ways indicative of the hollowness in corporate culture.

Performance evaluation is a regular activity in most companies, and all of them assure their employees that this evaluation is crucial to job safety as well as growth (salary hikes or promotions).

But, what does it tell us if companies cannot judge, from their supposedly sophisticated appraisal exercises, if the employees are dividing their time between two (or four, in Daksh's case) companies?

The implication here is that either the employers are not as good at judging the performance of their employees as they would have us believe, or that decisions about whether a company fires its employees or doubles their salary are dependent on factors quite different from their performance.

For Daksh, the fact that he can play the system so easily

indicates that the system is not the meritocratic capitalist utopia it says it is.

He knows that he can lose his job at any time to the spectre of recession. After spending so much time and money on his education, the only way he can cope with the anxiety of failing once again is by making as much money as he can while the WFH set-up is still available at software companies.

▪

Employers do not really need to hide the power dynamics of their relationship with the employees, and unnecessary politeness must get frustrating at times.

Recently, several instances of this frustration have become apparent to us via outbursts on social media platforms and news media.

Shantanu Deshpande, founder of Bombay Shaving Company, for instance, wrote in a 2022 LinkedIn post that for the first four to five years of their careers, employees should put in eighteen hours per day into their jobs. He dismissed 'work-life balance, time with family, rejuvenation, bla bla' as unimportant.

Healthtech unicorn Pristyn Care's co-founder Harsimarbir Singh went a step further and shared how his team looked for the perfect employee. His 'hacks' included contacting job seekers at 8 a.m. and 11 p.m. to find early risers and late sleepers, taking interviews on Sundays to find 'extraordinary commitment', and asking candidates from other cities to show up for an interview the very next day to check for 'hustle'.

Deshpande and Singh received bitter backlash on social media, and many people cautioned others against joining the respective organizations. Based on the market situation, however, it is difficult to imagine that the majority of employees can afford to reject prospective employers. Moreover, Deshpande and Singh have merely chosen to express what the post-internet system demands—employees must surrender all their waking hours in return for their monthly salaries.

Those who consider this to be an issue among start-ups and new-age leaders must refer to the views of undisputed titans in the IT industry.

In a 2023 interview, Narayana Murthy expressed his belief that young people must work at least seventy hours a week (which translates to fourteen-hour workdays) to ensure the country's progress. For inspiration, he spoke about countries like Japan and Germany.

We must assume that Murthy is unaware that a fourteen-hour workday would be illegal under Indian law. It may also be better to assume that he is unaware of the global outcry against Japan's work culture, which often drives employees to early deaths. The phenomenon is, in fact, prevalent enough that the Japanese have a word for 'death from overwork'—karoshi. Germany, of course, is known worldwide for its incredible efficiency-based culture and a noteworthy expression of this culture was played out under the Nazi regime when the Jews and other prisoners were used as slave labour for companies like Audi, BMW, and many others. The slaves must have put in seventy-hour workweeks without complaint.

In any case, it is no surprise that moonlighting, and the work-from-home set-ups that enable it, must sound like 'cheating' and 'traps' to businesses.

In the post-pandemic work culture, there are a few other terms that have garnered attention from employees and employers alike. Like moonlighting, they are also associated mostly with the better-paid variety of white-collar jobs in IT and IT-adjacent industries.

The 'Great Resign', for instance, refers to a trend in which a large number of people have resigned from their jobs either to switch to jobs with better salaries and work environments or to drop out of the workforce altogether.

'Quiet quitting' is the practice of doing the bare minimum at a job to better manage employer expectations and maintain work-life balance.

'Quiet firing' is where an employer makes the workplace so

unrewarding or monotonous for an employee that they quit of their own volition.

Like moonlighting, these trends also define a growing disillusionment with the narrative about jobs that we have been fed since we were children. Ambition's place as a grand human virtue is becoming questionable and hustle culture is on the decline, at least among those for whom it is not a matter of survival.

Latest studies, such as HP's Work Relation Index published in 2023, point out similar trends.

As many as 96 per cent of Millennial and Gen Z knowledge workers, for instance, 'are ready to sacrifice a portion of their salary for a more fulfilling work relationship' and 75 per cent of all the workers surveyed think it's important to choose where they work. Recent surveys also suggest that Gen Z is not afraid to turn down work that doesn't align with their values or break sacred corporate rules such as not discussing salaries with colleagues.

It is also important to note we are at a singularly important juncture in our relationship with labour right now where, for the first time in history, Artificial Intelligence (AI) is being looked at as a viable alternative for jobs that require intelligent creativity. The tiny percentage of the workforce that is currently moonlighting or renegotiating the status quo between employers and employees will also need to grapple with the overarching changes in the human relationship with work.

As more and more Millennials move into mid and senior-level management, it remains to be seen whether they will perpetuate the con pulled on them or come up with processes and systems that can help us reach a point where employees are looked at as humans first, and resources later.

Until then, I wish the best of luck to those who walk in the moonlight.

7

AT THIRTY, AM I STILL A LIBERAL?

When I went to college for my bachelor's degree, I was only too glad to tell my friends that I was a liberal. They didn't really care—we were at a private engineering college, after all—and it was just as well, perhaps, because I would have been hard-pressed to explain myself. Liberalism was a new concept for me. It was cool and suitably rebellious.

That second part was the most important at nineteen, I suppose—being liberal, to me, meant rebelling against society's hypocrisy, and a distrust or rejection of authority figures.

From where did this disdain for the old and typical come?

A part of it was driven home by our relatives in Aligarh, the city where my father was born, and from where he ran away as a teenager to pursue an engineering degree in Roorkee. Visits to his extended family often threw into relief the differences between their way of life and ours. One of my uncles, for example, sent his sons to a posh private school and his daughter to a run-down government school. My grandfather and his brothers did not approve of girls who wore jeans. Accepting and giving away large dowries in arranged marriages was a matter of pride for them. Religion was extremely important.

My own family in Haridwar had a different way of going about things, to say the least.

All my sisters studied in English-medium co-ed schools, could wear what they preferred, and talk to who they wanted. We celebrated all festivals and visited temples on occasion, but religion was not a big part of our lives. My father had also forbidden, much before I was born, any affiliations to the godmen and ashrams that litter Haridwar.

More of it was absorbed from the copious amounts of literature I consumed from seventh grade onwards.

More than the content of the books (or the ideology of their authors), it was the very act of reading, not all that common in small-town northern India, that set me apart and gave me some degree of individualism. I did not indulge in books with the intention of standing out, of course, but I was (and remain) an introvert, not very good at sports, and quieter than the other boys (especially after my father's death when I was in the sixth standard). Reading was the perfect refuge, albeit one that I entered and exited alone.

Literature made me realize something central to the idea of liberalism—a great variety of outlooks existed in the world, and there were many alternatives to the views we inherited from our family or copied from our immediate company.

Do I mean to argue that a reading habit is essential to developing a liberal worldview? Not necessarily.

But, if the accident of birth has been reasonably fortunate for you (as it was for me), and there is not much in your everyday life that feels profoundly wrong, then you will need some external force to wake you up.

Feel free to draw an analogy with the law of inertia, if you like things to sound scientific. The external force that moves a Privileged Inert Object (PIO) can be books. It can also be other people (teachers, older siblings, friends, etc.), movies, specific incidents reported in the news, or music—but something *has* to be there to make a liberal out of a middle-class Brahmin boy from Haridwar.

However, this raises a rather pertinent question: can this boy, with all that identity baggage, ever really be a liberal?

■

Ideologies, I believe, are like religions in their own right.

They are created at a particular place, for a particular time, and from that epicentre they spread, gathering followers and detractors. They have their scriptures, rituals, gods, and holy places. Devils too, and unpardonable blasphemies. Some of these aspects are constant, others are variable, adopted and discarded as per convenience, just as it is with most religions.

Take communists, for example.

Gods: Marx, Lenin, Stalin; Devils: Capitalists; Sacred Texts: *The Communist Manifesto*.

Or, capitalists.

Gods: Henry Ford, Reagan, Thatcher; Devils: Communists; Sacred Dogma: Free Markets = Free Peoples.

Closer home, we have Seculars/Liberals. Their gods are Gandhi, Nehru, Patel, Bhagat Singh, and Ambedkar, the devils are Hindu nationalists (call them Hindutva nationalists, if you start feeling queasy) and the sacred text is, perhaps, the Indian Constitution.

On the opposite side are the Hindutva nationalists. The gods are Savarkar, Gowalkar, Patel, Godse, Bhagat Singh, and others (having no problem appropriating entirely different ideologies, they are quite good at constantly expanding the ranks of their gods and champions). The devils are Muslims and Seculars/Liberals. The sacred texts are the *Manusmriti* and WhatsApp forwards (but what they lack in reading they more than make up in online trolling and real-world lynching).

All of these are, of course, gross simplifications, and the reality consists almost entirely of entangled nuances and unpalatable contradictions.

Conservative leaders in the US, for example, so recently sworn into Islamophobia by Donald Trump can reach out to Muslim community leaders for support in shared woke-phobia. Liberals who swore by feminism are increasingly given to calling women all sorts of names if they refuse to toe the dogmatic line on issues of gender and sex. Hindu nationalists as well as communists in India have similarly adopted a pendulum-like position on caste issues for decades, and self-proclaimed secular politicians have no trouble making a great show of being devout Hindus to get more votes.

Due to the rather slippery nature of ideologies, before exploring the possibility of liberalism for a middle-class Brahmin boy from Haridwar, it would be prudent to ask another question: what does it mean to be a liberal?

The word itself, like liberty, has its root in the Latin liber, meaning free, and was synonymous with 'generous' or 'tolerant' before the nineteenth century. In socio-political vocabulary, it first appeared in the early 1800s as liberales in Spain and became increasingly popular after the Whigs in Britain evolved into the Liberal Party in the 1840s. Before then, the concept's origins can be traced back to medieval Europe where it implied a position against religious conformity and in support of increased individual liberty.

Tracing a term's etymology, however, is not the most reliable way of deriving its meaning.

Words divulge from their roots over time, cultural context is in constant flux, and people can infer whatever meaning is more convenient for them.

Freedom, for instance, can mean the freedom to oppress others, and it can mean the freedom to rise against oppression. Freedom of speech can be used to indicate the freedom to speak the truth to the power without fear of reprisal, and it can also be used to advocate for the freedom to spew hate without fear of repercussions.

Perhaps we can understand liberalism better by considering it as a reaction to conservatism.

It includes enough nuance to make up several encyclopaedic volumes but, simply put, being a conservative means that you wish to resist change, want to keep the social order as it is, or want to revert it to an older, 'purer' stage. Who would want to resist change and maintain the status quo? The ones who benefit from the currently prevailing conditions, expectedly, or the ones who currently hold power in the form of political, financial, social, cultural, or sexual capital.

A liberal, therefore, must be someone who wants to bring

about change, who wants to reset the status quo and drive a more equitable distribution of different kinds of capital.

Who would want to take up this challenge? Someone who has been at a disadvantage in the prevailing conditions, we might assume, someone who feels like they got the shorter end of the straw.

Most young people, for example, can relate to feeling disadvantaged in a world that runs on grown-up rules. The desire to subvert prevailing conditions is also generally attractive to raging hormones. Does that mean most young people are liberals, by default? Of course not, and the example should illustrate the fact that feeling disadvantaged or wanting to change the existing system cannot be the primary metric for liberalism.

A Brahmin is as likely to believe that they are at a disadvantage as a Dalit, just like those who subscribed to the Nazi ideology believed themselves to be at a disadvantage in comparison to the money-controlling Jews. Just like young men all over the world are increasingly fond of online rants about feminism taking away men's rights. Just like many middle-class people in India believe that they are the only ones paying taxes, and resent those they imagine to be benefitting from those taxes.

Almost no one, it appears, would prefer to believe that they are the ones holding the longer end of the straw.

■

Rajat, one of my oldest friends from school, belongs to the Pasi caste, which makes him a Dalit in the Indian caste system.

In the 1970s, when his grandfather secured a government job as a lineman in the electricity department, the family migrated to Haridwar from their native village near Lucknow.

As teenagers, Rajat and I hung out at each other's homes virtually every day after school, watched the same movies, and cribbed together about the unfairness of various things, the way school friends do. We knew what girls each of us fancied, what teachers we hated, how our families drove us mad, and exactly what we would do when we got uber-rich after graduating from an IIT.

Yet, it took Rajat more than seven years of friendship to confide in me the fact of his caste.

Both of us were in different private engineering colleges by then. My first reaction, after scrambling for an appropriate reaction, was to call him an absolute idiot for not using reservations to get into a good government college. He was smart enough to make it, and I knew that I would have done it in a heartbeat if I had the chance, so I could not understand why he had chosen a mediocre private college in Roorkee instead.

Rajat laughed it off and said something about not wanting to move too far away from home.

When the placement season came a year later, both of us found ourselves worried about the future. The software consultancy companies that recruited the bulk of students at my college were paying peanuts, and they were not even going to visit Rajat's college. During a late-night conversation after a day of unsuccessful interviews, I asked him why did he not consider using his quota to take a shot at government jobs.

Once again, he shrugged off the suggestion and I could not comprehend why he would be reluctant about using such an 'advantage'.

I would understand a little, a couple of years later when, while visiting Rajat at his home, I met his father who had fractured his leg in a minor accident. Even after submitting all the necessary proofs, he failed to get a medical leave at work.

It had always been that way at his office, he told us between sips of tea, because his immediate senior was a Baniya who never missed a chance to humiliate those he considered undeserving of their jobs.

In any case, the fact that I looked at caste-based reservations as an advantage at one point speaks volumes about the liberalism of a middle-class Brahmin boy, doesn't it?

■

If I took a 100-metre walk to the right from my house in Haridwar and took another right, I would find myself in a locality officially known as Ravidas Mohalla.

Each morning, on the way to school, my auto picked up two siblings from there and I would hold my breath to avoid the stench that rose from a mound of rotting garbage beside their street.

Ravidas Mohalla has many such mounds and empty plots of land where pigs roam around, shitting and chewing through plastic bags full of more garbage.

It is named after Sant Ravidas, the fifteenth-century spiritual leader revered by many Dalits all over the country, but the area is better known in Haridwar as Bhangi-khaana, the place of Bhangis. Most of its population consists of middle-class and lower-middle-class Dalits.

Ravidas Mohalla is one of the several caste-based ghettos in Haridwar. There is a similar ghettoization of Muslims too, in an area called Jwalapur, which explains why I had never seen a mosque until I visited Delhi, and why I only had a single Muslim classmate through twelve years of school in three different schools (this classmate's father was a minister in the state government which, I assume, would have given him certain leeway with crossing boundaries).

When I proclaimed myself a liberal at nineteen, I was blissfully ignorant of this segregation and everything it entailed. To understand my idiocy and blindness I must revisit the two things I credited earlier for providing me with an intuitive grasp of liberal principles: my family and the literature I read growing up.

I would not say that my family was overtly casteist or religiously biased.

There was no separation of cutlery for the owner of a garage below my house, a Bhangi and a resident of Ravidas Mohalla, my friends who belonged to castes 'lower' than ours, or anyone else who visited us. My mother did not hire upper-caste maids exclusively, as I have seen many other families do over the years, and I was never taught that we were superior to anyone else.

Yet, old prejudices are difficult to shake off. Biases creep into language, unnoticed by those who are too young or too careless to know any better.

I grew up with a condescending upper-caste vocabulary: gaudy things like neon-coloured clothes or glittery bicycle accessories were 'chamaaru' and if someone did not take a bath they could be called 'mallichh'. 'Kanjar' was a moniker thrown around casually to refer to a miserly neighbour.

All these words, so common in our everyday conversations at home were, of course, casteist slurs.

Maybe I would have known this, the way I knew that 'negro' was a bad word, if my reading had included Indian authors (and Indian languages). Unfortunately, it did not.

My school was no different from many private schools in India that buy into what has been called by Geetanjali Shree the 'classic colonial condition'—the assumed merit of English over Indian languages. The fiction shelves in the school library were stacked with English books and this library happened to be my only source of reading material because Haridwar had no bookstores (and still doesn't, unless one counts the religious shops that sell scriptural texts along with other spiritual paraphernalia).

The only things I could read in Hindi were the subject's school textbooks and children's magazines like *Champak* and *Nandan*.

So while all my early reading may have instilled in me certain fundamental values like an appreciation for diverse perspectives and a distaste for discrimination, it gave me little understanding of the world around me.

In any case, like anyone else, I picked up something every now and then from the air around me. Like the perception of Kashmir as a dangerous place that Pakistan wanted to wrest from India's rightful ownership. My mother's frequent refrain that 'BJP always comes to power with a wave of riots, and goes from power with a wave of riots.' Her rather strange belief that Muslim tradesmen were inherently more honest than Hindu tradesmen. My father's opinion about all godmen being sanctimonious conmen.

Things of a different variety as well.

Resentment against caste-based reservations in education and jobs, for example, was widespread. At home, school, and coaching classes, remarks were frequently made about the need for 'merit-based' selections, at least in technical disciplines such as engineering and medicine (which just so happen to provide the most financially rewarding jobs).

It can be astonishingly easy to harbour such resentment when you have been blind to caste discrimination as a result of what Arundhati Roy refers to as the 'project of unseeing'.

The main argument for meritocracy, I remember, often went on to suggest a replacement of caste-based reservations with income-based reservations. It sounds reasonable enough when someone comes from 'a place of such rarefied privilege that caste has not been stumbled upon, not even in the dark, and therefore it is presumed to have been eradicated, like smallpox', to quote Roy again.

I had grown up in such a place and I also saw income-based reservations as a better alternative back then, and would retain that position until I stumbled upon a YouTube video of Kanhaiya Kumar talking about Rohith Vemula. It became the external force to move a PIO such as myself. That one video sent me down a rabbit hole, and in the darkness below the sunlit lands, I was stripped of my blindness.

The manner in which someone as bright as Vemula was driven to give up on his life, and ignored even after he died by our country at large, was obscene, and ugly, and it ripped apart any illusions I had entertained about 'merit-based' education and employment.

It also forced me to take a deep look at liberalism as it applied to my personal life, rather than as a theoretical ideal. Over time, I have grown to think of caste first and foremost when I think about my liberalism.

Due to its European origins, the ideology is not equipped to deal with caste as it does with race, religion, class, or sex.

Yet, for someone to challenge any kind of status quo in India, it would be dim-witted to not tackle caste, first and foremost. As Dr Ambedkar said, 'Turn in any direction you like, caste is the monster that crosses your path. You cannot have political reform, you cannot have economic reform unless you kill this monster.'

This is why, I believe, various reformist movements led by caste-blind liberals (I think of myself at nineteen) have failed to make any lasting change. We pick up these West-certified liberal causes, bounce them around in our upper-caste bubbles, become giddy on our moral righteousness, and pick up new causes when the old one fizzles out just outside the bubble's walls.

Take gender equality or feminism.

The discourse is currently dominated by conversations about reducing the wage gap, making women financially independent, or raising awareness about domestic violence. Few people want to come out in the open and state the truth that there can be no equality for the wide majority of women in India until the caste-based institution of arranged marriage is rooted out.

But we cannot get rid of arranged marriage until people can marry out of love, and that cannot happen until caste is abolished. It follows that we cannot get rid of dowry until we get rid of arranged marriages, and we cannot get rid of female infanticide until we get rid of dowry.

Since problems like these can also become invisible or outdated in 'places of rarefied privilege' where liberals like me dwell, it might be helpful to point out that there were more than 35,000 'dowry deaths' between 2017–21 in India. Moreover, there is a ton of research-based evidence to suggest that the burden of dowry is the topmost reason behind the undesirability of a girl child and the resulting femicide epidemic.

Talking to people in my socio-economic circle also revealed such contradictions between liberalism and the reality of our society.

All my friends and colleagues, for instance, swear by typical liberal positions—women's rights, gay rights, class abolition, the whole package—and yet most of them agree that it would be problematic for them to marry someone from a different caste, especially a Dalit.

Of course, I have only mentioned women's rights as an example.

In a similar fashion, one could pick up a cause like class struggle or anti-capitalism and explore why it would not work in India because we have here not only a division of labour, to paraphrase Dr Ambedkar, but also a division of labourers.

Often, the odious bargain a liberal must make with themselves to ignore caste as normal or unimportant while pursuing other liberal goals leaks into everything else, causing a moral-ethical failure, and making hypocrites of us all.

Or, perhaps, hypocrisy is a feature of liberals everywhere, going back to the term being associated with those who were 'tolerant' or 'gentle', which are nice ways of describing people who couldn't care less about things until their individual liberty was infringed upon. When people talk about how India was so much more liberal before BJP came to power in 2014, it seems that we are concerned about liberal values only when ugly things happen right on our doorsteps and there is a threat of violence spilling directly into our lives.

This is a rather disheartening view of things because an ideology that allows lesser evils to survive in the interest of a 'greater good' will always end up corrupting itself.

Those who calmly reasoned the necessity for Armed Forces (Special Powers) Act (AFSPA) in Kashmir are, at least for me, not so different from those who defend the necessity of caste as the adhesive glue of Indian society. Neither of them should express any horror when a Muslim is lynched or when a Dalit woman is raped and burnt alive in the 'new India' that has a deep disregard for liberalism.

To give a recent example, it feels ironic in 2023 for the Aam Aadmi Party, whose leaders cultivate a liberal and secular image, to be so offended by the parliamentary passage of the Delhi Services Bill (which shifts away most administrative powers from Delhi's elected government to a centre-appointed lieutenant governor) when AAP supported the abrogation of Article 370 in the same parliament in 2019. The abrogation, in addition to its various other effects, shifted the power from elected representatives of the people in Kashmir to the central government, just like the Delhi Services Bill. Logically, if someone was opposed to one on account of their liberal principles they would also be opposed to the other, but ideology can evidently be bent in most convenient ways.

Incidentally, the Mayawati-led Bahujan Samaj Party, believed by many to be India's only 'mainstream' Dalit party, had also extended its support to the BJP on the scrapping of Article 370 and the bifurcation of J&K in 2019. Should the oppressed groups that trust BSP to fight for their rights continue to do so considering that BSP does not really care about the rights of the oppressed in Kashmir? It is for them to decide.

▪

Opponents of liberalism would have us believe that such contradictions and hypocrisies make liberalism an essentially corrupt ideology.

In ideologies, as in religions, it is difficult to embrace an evolution of views. Even considering that change is possible may be perceived as blasphemous.

As we have seen, liberalism suffers from various problems in the Indian context.

Its origins are Western and its agendas are still formulated mostly in the West. The heroes and gods are also imported, at least when one is first introduced to the concept, courtesy of the Western cultural hegemony and the English language. This distance, or foreignness, ensures that those who are introduced to liberal ideas belong to the classes, castes, and religions that have access to a globalized reality.

The charge of elitism made against liberals is true, therefore, insofar as its selective accessibility is concerned.

I freely admit that it has been true in my case.

Would I have grown up in a relatively open-minded family if

my father had not left Aligarh to pursue an engineering degree? Would he have been able to do that if he had no caste privileges of his own? Would I have discovered literature if I was enrolled in a government school with no library? Would I have had the time to research, think, and write anything if I were not privileged in a myriad ways and needed to spend my days worrying about the source of my next meal?

Some of these things are possible, of course, but not very probable, and certainly not easy.

However, the charges of elitism ring much less true for those who did not have these privileges—the Dalits, the poor, the women, the farmers, the Adivasis, and so many others of our country—and still managed to defeat the conditioning that their current situation is their natural state of being.

Though they may adopt the language of liberalism, and some of its Western heroes, their understanding of their own issues can hardly be dismissed as being derived from a foreign source. When conservative critics use terms like 'decoloniality' to attack liberalism as a foreign import, or when they talk about the Hindu civilization-state as opposed to a liberal Indian nation-state, they very conveniently forget this.

The so-called liberal values like individualism, freedom to practise one's faith, or the instinct against suffering indignity, after all, are fundamental to human nature. They were not invented a few centuries ago in Europe.

Indian politician and public intellectual Shashi Tharoor has elucidated as much while countering the arguments that favour civilization states over universal ideas of liberalism.

> There is room for debate on how far the supposedly universal principles advanced by advocates of liberalism are truly universal, but none on the standards most human beings seek to apply to themselves. When one hears of the unsuitability or ethnocentrism of liberal norms, what are the human rights that someone in a 'civilization state' can do without? The

> right to life? Freedom from torture? The right not to be enslaved, not to be physically assaulted, not to be arbitrarily arrested, imprisoned or executed? No one actually advocates the abridgment of any of these rights for themselves.
>
> Moreover, if liberalism is to be discarded because it came from the West, then why should exceptions be made for modern medicine, clothes, food, etc.? We have not abandoned our railway infrastructure just because it was once used to transport British soldiers and fill British granaries, so why must we do it to an ideology? Ideas, we must understand, are not subject to anyone's monopoly, and we don't need to impose the biases of inventors upon their inventions.

Even Dr Ambedkar, who symbolizes the best of Indian liberalism in my humble opinion, honed his beliefs at prestigious institutions like Columbia University and the London School of Economics. He frequently referred to ideas of thinkers like John Dewey and expanded them in the Indian context, he also made use of examples from early Roman society to elucidate his points, and intentionally invoked the French Revolution's slogan when he said, 'My ideal would be a society based on liberty, equality, and fraternity.'

The ones who need to give serious thought to the imported nature of liberalism are those like me, the PIOs. We are the ones who have to constantly check our motives for embracing liberal principles, and we have to contend with the fact that we will be frequently disappointed not only by other privileged liberal heroes in the West, but also closer home.

■

So finally, can a middle-class Brahmin boy from Haridwar be a liberal?

Yes and no.

'Easily' and 'Perhaps, but only with great difficulty'.

Yes, and easily, if he accepts the liberal values that have managed to reach him in our deeply conservative society, and freezes this acceptance at a particular point in time.

Being middle class and upper caste, he will have access to liberal spaces and institutions in which he can passionately debate his frozen ideals. The conservatives will always be there to provide him an ideological punching bag. He can be all the more heroic because he doesn't *need* to be a liberal, he is doing it by choice, out of the goodness of his heart. The oppressed masses will also always be there to work for, and he will not lack in self-righteousness.

No, but perhaps with great difficulty, if he refuses to accept any positions for which he does not have personal convictions and in-depth understanding. These personal reasons need not be selfish, and they don't need an explanation of the status quo.

A Brahmin may want to see the caste system destroyed simply because he wants to live in a society where everyone has a shot at equality. A Hindu may want to prevent violence against Muslims simply because that is the decent and humane thing to do. But, the Brahmin must then be ready to accept that he may need to renounce his religion itself, if that is essential for the destruction of caste. The Hindu will need to accept that Muslims are not a homogenous mass, and the rights of those in Kashmir or anywhere else are no less important than of those in the rest of the country.

Even so, he will need to constantly question and update his beliefs without freezing them at any point in time. Most difficult of all, he will have to accept that he can neither set agendas for those less fortunate than him nor try to lead them like a messiah. We have enough precedents by now to see how that works out.

It may be reasoned that if he does manage to carry out all this in practice, he cannot be described as a 'liberal' any more, and I am inclined not to protest. It is why I now call myself a liberal only when I absolutely have to place myself under an ideological label, which is not very often. At the same time, however, I have made my peace with being labelled a 'liberandu', 'libtard', 'sickular', etc., by those who hold the ideological majority in our country today.

They intend these terms to represent their opposite in all matters, and that much is perfectly acceptable to me.

8

THE AWAARAGARDI OF MILLENNIAL HEARTS

Awaaragardi is a Hindustani word that translates, roughly, to loafing around.

In my house, however, it was a blanket term and euphemism for everything from casual dating to teen pregnancies and adultery. It was something done by young people predicted to not do very well in life and by grown-ups who were not quite as respectable as grown-ups should be.

Creepy middle-aged men were awaara, and so was a kid at school who asked the biology teacher how babies are made.

Invoking this conceptual bogeyman was not entirely consistent with the general behaviour of my parents who were reasonably liberal by Indian small-town upper-caste middle-class standards. Not very high standards perhaps, but high enough for me to be grateful about the birth lottery's outcome. When my eldest sister, Baby-di, was put in a co-ed convent school it was commented upon by relatives and family friends as an extravagance. In response, my parents went on to put the rest of us in English-medium private schools as well.

I, being a boy, was expected to get some freedom, but regarding my sisters, an aunt once wondered if my father was trying to raise the next Indira Gandhi in our house. He replied that he would only be too glad if that happened.

Romantic relationships, however, continued to have immoral connotations as we grew up.

The Indira Gandhi-hating aunt had a told-you-so moment

during one of her visits when one of Baby-di's classmates died in the 9th standard. Everyone in the city knew that the girl had either committed suicide or been poisoned by her parents. She was pregnant when she died, the rumours went, and were lent credibility by the househelps fired soon after the incident.

I heard about this when I was in the 9th standard myself and Baby-di was visiting us with her daughter. We were looking at old photo albums and a school picture got them talking about the classmate who had died so tragically young. My mother placed the blame squarely on the girl's stepmother who, apparently, had been too busy doing 'awaaragardi' with the staff at their shop to spare any attention for the poor child.

There it was again. Awaaragardi. The one thing out of which no good could ever come.

It was there when a neighbour's daughter ran with the PTE teacher from her school, and when a group of teenagers were caught watching blue films in a cyber-cafe. Also there when a random guy started giving blank calls on the landline phone to impress one of my sisters.

In *The God of Small Things*, Arundhati Roy defines Love Laws as 'the laws that lay down who should be loved, and how, and how much.' In the early 2000s Haridwar where I grew up, the Laws had declared all romance taboo, the concept of 'dating' did not exist, and awaaragardi carried an unmistakably sleazy connotation.

What was I doing in the 9th standard, about the same age at which Baby-di's classmate had allegedly died of awaaragardi?

Papa had died three years earlier, and I was busy throwing myself head first into fiction. I had started noticing girls a couple of years ago, I believe, but when that happened, they suddenly turned into creatures of mystery and sharp laughter. They were unapproachable for most of us boys, except a select few who seemed to have received some kind of special training in how not to cut themselves on the sharp laughter, and how to keep talking even when the girls appeared to have lost all interest in the conversation.

We were beginning to discover the pleasures of ribald humour at school even as the science teachers were skipping chapters on human reproduction. Completely innocent remarks could suddenly be mined for sexual innuendos and sniggered at on the last benches.

Yet, sex was only a dream subject, present only on the periphery of our thoughts and conversations because no one knew what it entailed. Porn was not so readily available back then, the internet being rather slow and expensive, and erotica magazines, like the famous *Manohar Kahaniyan*, were difficult to procure unless one had a suitably colourful older brother or young uncle.

My perception of sex was that of a forbidden and pleasurable thing that other people did; I was separated from these people by much more than age.

■

A 2006–07 survey called 'Youth in India: Situation and Needs' took into consideration the views of 50,000 young people from six states across India.

It found that only 19 per cent and 9 per cent of young men and women respectively had been in pre-marital romantic partnerships. Even these few relationships or 'partnerships' were usually hidden from parents. Moreover, just 8 per cent of young men and 7 per cent of young women reported that they would prefer to have a 'love marriage'. Rural–urban differences were negligible and most people preferred getting married soon after they turned twenty.

Also from 2007, the Face of Global Sex report published by the Durex Network informs us that the average Indian 'lost' their virginity at around twenty-three years of age.

Incidentally, I was in the 9th standard in 2007, and these numbers look as if the term 'awaaragardi' has been put in statistical confines. They might surprise those of us who grew up in urban centres, but they seem perfectly natural to me. Looking at both studies, it is safe to infer that most of these twenty-three-year-olds having sex (cis-het penetrative sex, that is) for the first time were doing so within the socially approved construct of arranged marriage.

But today, nearly two decades later, what is the first thing that comes up in conversations about matters of the Millennial hearts or the 'Millennial dating culture'?

Dating apps, of course, with their promise of instant gratification for empty hearts and beds. There are options for all sexualities, we are told, and ever more sophisticated algorithms that can help us find a better love life. Even without these dedicated apps, we have novel ways of connecting with perfect strangers over social media platforms, and we can easily look people up online (or stalk them) to form ideas about their personal and professional lives before approaching them.

Going by this popular discourse, or looking at mainstream movies and social media, it appears that the times, which were already beginning to change when the first Millennials reached adulthood, have completely shifted as the last Millennials reach their mid-twenties.

Techno-solutionism aside, societal changes have also been favourable to romance, according to this optimistic view.

In the last couple of decades, it has become more and more common for young people to move away from home for higher studies and work. It increases their chances of finding someone beyond the small puddle in which they were born, and lifts the burden of parental control from their day to day lives. Moreover, the increasing financial independence among women, and their presence in white-collar jobs, have given them more freedom to choose their partners. This freedom translates to more romantic opportunities for everyone.

Love marriages are on the rise, we are informed by recent surveys, with arranged marriages seeing a steep drop of 24 per cent from 2020 to 2023. Our ideas about sex may also be evolving: nearly a third of Millennials are likely to agree with premarital sexual intimacy, according to recent surveys.

The credit for these developments is attributed to increasingly progressive views of families and more individualism among Millennials.

Yet, evidence of growing loneliness, particularly among younger generations, casts a shadow on this pleasant picture. Major publications have expressed beliefs that we are in the grip of a 'loneliness pandemic' and Millennials come up in various studies as the loneliest generation ever.

The same things that should have provided better ways of pursuing love are also credited with exacerbating loneliness.

Social media is believed to socially isolate us, dating apps make us anxious with hours of unfruitful swiping, and looking up potential partners is often an enigma-killer. Financial independence may not be all its hyped to be either because we are poorer than previous generations on various metrics even though we work longer hours and switch organizations frequently.

Data can also present a contradictory picture of changing attitudes.

A BBC article about love and marriage in India, for example, talks about a 2018 survey of more than 160,000 households which revealed that '93% of married Indians said that theirs was an arranged marriage. Just 3% had a love marriage and another 2% described theirs as a love-cum-arranged marriage, which usually indicates that the relationship was set up by the families, and then the couple agreed to get married.'

Around myself, in people my age, I see a growing cynicism about romantic relationships. Friends who have tasted metropolitan freedom, dated multiple people, and been in serious relationships are increasingly getting tired of the whole 'independence thing' and choosing arranged marriages as an inevitable part of growing up. Arranged marriages, for their part, have undergone a makeover and now provide the option of becoming almost-love marriages.

Elaborate pre-wedding shoots mimic, and try to manufacture, Bollywood-esque love stories, while grooms often go down on their knees to 'propose' *after* the wedding is well underway.

Dating apps often give way to wedding apps that are little more than digitized (and therefore, glorified) versions of the old matrimonial newspaper supplements commonly used to arrange marriages. These apps do involve more participation of the prospective bride and groom, but the final approval still comes from their parents.

The newfound progressivism in most of our families, such as there is, applies only within limits prescribed by the Love Laws.

It is as if our hearts inhabit multiple realities. One of slick apps, pick-up lines, blind dates, and romantic vacations. Another in which 'i-love-you' texts have to be deleted as soon as they are sent, marriages are strictly transactional, and most relationships are doomed from the start.

▪

Tinder was the first dating app to launch in India in 2016, the year I graduated from an engineering college.

Also in 2016, I gave Karishma, my first-ever girlfriend, a peck on the cheek and she told me we would have to break up if I ever pulled something like that again. I was twenty-one, she was twenty-two, and we had been playing long-distance-boyfriend-girlfriend for about two years.

I was visiting her in Dehradun, where she was in college, when I offended her with a kiss in an auto speeding along the brightly-lit Rajpur Road.

The next day, before I left to resume my internship in Bangalore, she explained the reason for her restraint: she wanted the guy she married to be the first person to kiss her. That wasn't going to be me, obviously, because I was not a Baniya like her.

I could not blame her. Both of us had lived most of our lives in Haridwar, in the same socio-economic class, and I understood how important caste was to most people there. I also knew that if she did muster the courage to tell her parents about us, the good daughter would immediately transform into a garden-variety slut, and the twin spectres of samaj (society) and biradari (caste-family) would come to poison her relationship with her family.

It did not matter that my family already knew that I was dating her, or that we had been making sincere admissions of love for more than a year by then.

It also did not matter that she was pursuing a post-graduate degree that would soon make her financially independent. Like my sisters, she had studied in a co-ed, English-medium private school, and her parents trusted her enough to send her to live by herself in Dehradun. In many ways, she was freer than she would have been if, say, she were born thirty years ago in Haridwar. But all these other freedoms accorded to her, it appeared to me, were on the condition that she would adhere to the Love Laws.

To put it differently, she could do whatever else she wanted, but she could have no sexual agency or choice of romantic partners.

We could keep going on as we were, Karishma told me in Dehradun, but nothing was going to change. Her parents had started looking for boys a month ago and expected to find a suitable match by the time she got her degree.

I could have kept my patience with the platonic nature of our relationship, but I realized that I would be unable to live with an expiry date looming over the horizon.

So, I broke up with her after reaching Bangalore. On the same day, I also resigned from a plush internship that involved pretending to be an IIT graduate to coerce hapless parents into buying overpriced ed-tech solutions. In both cases, I realized that I had been trying to live a life based on lies, which is not something I am very good at.

Karishma would be married two years later, and the company where I was interning would go on to become India's biggest start-up. I too would go on to do a few things that would not have been possible if I had been less decisive. Happy endings for everyone, I suppose.

But back then, a week after coming from Dehradun, I boarded a bus back to my college in Chennai, jobless and heartbroken.

It took me a considerable amount of time to realize that

despite our similar roots, Karishma and I had moved into worlds with very different ideas of love. Or rather, I had moved, and she remained in the same one where we grew up.

On my first night in college, for instance, I remember my roommates discussing the best way to go about getting a girlfriend. If it sounds desperate, that's because it was.

But it was also hopeful. There was no resentment towards girls, and most of the 'ways' they discussed were typical self-improvement pointers shared by young men all over the country. Buy better clothes, learn better English, get a friend who owns a vehicle, and find ways to stay out of the hostel past curfew.

All of us were fresh-out-of-home adolescents who had been assured (while preparing for engineering exams) that life would be a series of enjoyable events from here on out. Eventually, we would come to realize that we had been duped, but that was still in the future. In the meantime, the move away from our (mostly) small-town homes, the release from 5 a.m. coaching schedules, and the hostel's bristling young-adult energy told us that the old rules no longer applied.

We were free, and so was the Wi-Fi. Everyone binged on everything, but especially on things that could bolster their English-speaking skills, and included some romance.

F.R.I.E.N.D.S, most notably perhaps, but also *How I Met Your Mother*, *The Big Bang Theory*, *Modern Family*, the *American Pie* movies, and so much else.

We superimposed the world of these shows and movies on our own, related with the protagonists who were only slightly older than us, and aspired to their mode of life. It became a given that one dated multiple people until a perfect fit was found, those who called or texted first lost the relationship's power game, and being a virgin or not having sex for a long time was a highly undesirable state of things.

Maybe we were trying to prove that we had outgrown the places we came from. Chennai felt impossibly far from Haridwar, and as a result perhaps, New York felt near enough?

We didn't get most of what we wanted, but we aspired to all of it.

In any case, cocooned in our privilege, we did not worry about caste and life partners the way Karishma did. We were kids; we worried about college placements and Valentine's Day gifts. The antagonists in our love lives were not parents who wanted to get us married at twenty-two but wardens and campus guards who patrolled the campus after 6.30 p.m., all too eager to pull up couples sitting in dark corners.

A kiss on the cheek of the sort that had kickstarted my break-up with Karishma was an innocent enough thing in my college.

Less innocent things were difficult to pull off, at least until the last two years when some of us gave up hostel rooms in favour of rented apartments. Even so, physical intimacy remained the exception, not the norm, and making out with someone was generally a big enough event to warrant a minute analysis at a later time.

It was not as if we were completely oblivious to the dissonance between our collegiate ideas and their real-world application, of course.

One of the things I remember discussing with a friend, for instance, was the absurdity of people saying 'I love you' when asking someone out. The blind commitment did not make much sense to us, especially when it came without so much as a first date. The 'proposals' to perfect strangers could often be elaborate affairs involving teddy bears, love letters, chocolates, and the works. More than a young person asking another to have a cup of coffee, the whole thing resembled a marriage being fixed up.

Having spent the better part of our teenage years preparing ourselves for the rat race that defines the Millennial work culture, we did not fully realize that the very act of 'asking someone out for a coffee' was foreign.

The social contract on which dating is based was as non-existent around us as it had been in our provincial hometowns. We were making it all up on the fly by mixing sitcom-ish ideas of love and romance with the reality of a deeply patriarchal, casteist, and classist society. A new set of Love Laws, so to speak.

No wonder 'asking out' looked like a pre-wedding ritual for us, minus religion and relatives.

By the time we left college, our notions about concepts like consent, sexual liberty, or virginal purity were significantly different from those of someone like Karishma. They were definitely different from those of our parents and the generations before them.

Yet, in the years since, even when I did not look for supporting studies and data, I have had a persistent feeling that the bubble of make-believe we created is wearing thin as we grow older.

■

There is a sequence in the movie *Eat, Pray, Love* (based on Elizabeth Gilbert's memoir of the same name), where the protagonist recounts how a psychologist friend of hers, Deborah, was once asked to provide counselling to Cambodian refugees.

Despite her ample qualifications, Deborah worries about how could she possibly relate with, and help, people who had 'suffered the worst of what humans can inflict on each other—genocide, rape, torture, starvation, the murder of their relatives before their eyes, then long years in refugee camps and dangerous boat trips to the West where people died and corpses were fed to sharks'.

But, when she meets the refugees, Deborah is surprised to learn that they want to talk to her less about their trauma and more about their love lives. It was all:

> I met this guy when I was living in the refugee camp, and we fell in love. I thought he really loved me, but then we were separated on different boats, and he took up with my cousin. Now he's married to her, but he says he really loves me, and he keeps calling me, and I know I should tell him to go away, but I still love him and I can't stop thinking about him. And I don't know what to do....
>
> This is what we are like.

This is what we are like. Perhaps. But, of late I have been wondering: are we, really?

I am all for the universality of human nature, but love is perhaps one aspect of it that means wildly different things to each one of us. Especially, in a country as diverse and divisive as India.

What does a cab driver from Meerut think about the fact that his wife will be waiting to serve him dinner after he drops me home at 2 a.m.? Is that in any way similar to the ideas of romance harboured by a kirana store owner in Haridwar? Is either of their 'love' comparable with the Tinder dates of a software developer living in Bangalore?

We can hazard guesses at these questions, or conduct studies to figure out the answers, but I doubt we can ever know for sure. As the poets already know, love is far too slippery a subject for sociology, anthropology, or pop psychology.

For me, love is an idea tied up with where we come from and who we think we are.

About a year ago, Hitesh, an old school friend of mine from Haridwar, told me about a guy he knew who was getting separated from his wife a mere five months after his wedding. As unnoticeable as such an incident may sound on tabloid pages and celebrity gossip sites, divorces in Haridar are still anomalies. They may even be a worse violation of the Love Laws than love marriages (though they are not as bad as intercaste or inter-religion marriages).

I asked Hitesh if this friend, Sanjay, would be willing to talk to me about his experience in the relationship.

Our timings matched up when I was home last summer, and on a particularly balmy evening, we sat at the Ganga ghats with our feet dipping in ice-cold water.

I was expecting that I would have to spend some time building a rapport with Sanjay and slowly get the story out of him, but he dived into detailed accounts of his personal life immediately. Maybe it was because he knew I would be writing about it, but he spoke with the air of someone who has polished his story with many retellings and revisions.

Sanjay Ahuja met his wife-to-be, Aashima, for the first time in September 2021, at her house in Roorkee.

Her family was present, his family was present, and a couple of Aashima's friends were also present at this meeting. Sanjay and Aashima talked alone for about half an hour, at the end of which he asked for her mobile number and she told him that she would pass it on to his mother via her mother.

According to Sanjay, this refusal to immediately share the number should have been sign enough that Aashima and her family were 'bohot tez', extra-cunning. He pointed this out to his mother at the time, but she brushed it off in her excitement about the family's first wedding.

In any case, Aashima's mother shared her number a couple of days after the meeting in Roorkee.

The couple met once in October and twice in November before their engagement in late December. All three 'dates' were in public places and one of Aashmia's friends always accompanied them as a chaperone. Sanjay wanted them to meet more often, but this was progress enough, his mother said, and reminded him that she had not even seen his father properly until the day of their wedding.

Sanjay and Aashima did talk for long hours on the phone. They had minor tiffs, discussed how they wanted to furnish their room in Sanjay's house, and declared their love for each other right after the engagement.

In January, three months after being introduced to each other, they were married.

Everything went well at the wedding and Sanjay did not regret the 5 lakh rupees loan he had taken to bear his family's part of the expenses. By the next day, the last of their guests had left and he was finally free to be alone with his wife.

Sanjay's eyes welled up at this point in the story, in a way that would have been difficult to fake. 'But my first night with her, bhai, it was a total depress(ing) nightmare.'

Aashima suffered from hirsutism, a hormonal disorder that can cause growth spurts in women's facial and body hair. Sanjay only found out about it when they went to bed together and he stroked her body with his hands and felt coarse hair between his fingers. He switched on the light despite her protests and could not speak for the shock when he looked at her naked body. Aashima had tried to get rid of the thick, wiry hair with a course of laser treatments, but Roorkee did not have the best facilities and she was left with discoloration marks all over her back and chest.

She explained this to Sanjay while he sat in silence. When she was done speaking, he went to sleep on the terrace without saying anything.

Now, he told me—someone he had known for barely an hour—that he could have sex with his wife only thrice in the few months they had lived together. He did not feel attracted to her after that first night, could not muster any empathy for her, and felt that she had 'cheated' him by not telling him about her condition beforehand.

I asked him if he had ever had a relationship before his marriage and he told me he had flirted with his neighbour over SMS for a few months before college, but that was it.

He knows about dating apps from movies and shows but has never used any of them. He also considered it immoral to visit the massage parlours in Dehradun that deliver a lot more than 'massages' and are currently quite popular among young men in Haridwar and neighbouring cities.

As for Sanjay, the first woman he ever saw naked outside of porn videos was Aashima.

When he talks about what he found unattractive in her, he inevitably comes across as juvenile and immature. He was repulsed by the fact that the skin of her armpits was dark, for instance, and complained that her breath smelled bad when she kissed him to wake him up. His sense of victimhood is so strong that he is not bothered in the least by this objectification of a woman who is still his wife. A large part of his outrage comes from the fact that despite being a 'good guy', the arranged marriage model had failed him. He subscribed to it because it promised him a woman he would be attracted to, and it did not deliver on that promise.

Things unravelled fast after the fateful first night.

They never went on their honeymoon in Dalhousie and Sanjay gave flimsy excuses of being sick to his family when they asked him why he had suddenly turned so quiet.

Aashima tried to initiate sexual relations between them multiple times and Sanjay also tried his best—by his own account—to make things work. But he couldn't manufacture attraction where it did not exist.

The sexual frustration led to other ugly and unnecessary developments.

Sanjay suspected that his wife was not a virgin, as she was more enthusiastic about sex than he expected women to be. He did not like it when she wore sleeveless clothes on their visits to the market without shaving her arms. He did not find it funny when Aashima borrowed his razor to shave her facial hair and made a joke about it. He felt 'gay' when one night he dreamed of her sleeping next to him with a full beard.

By his own account, this was a deeply disturbing time for both of them. Aashima was miserable and he started staying away from home for as long as possible to avoid her.

He also started having suicidal thoughts. He could not imagine spending a lifetime like this and Aashima's mother had let slip the possibility of filing a dowry case if he did not mend his ways soon.

Unable to deal with it all by himself, and tired of making excuses for sleeping on the terrace, he eventually told his family about Aashima's medical condition. His parents and younger brother were shocked, and they agreed that they had been cheated by Aashima's family, but they advised him to make the marriage work with whatever it took. By way of awkward euphemisms, his mother told him that sex was anyway not all that important for marital happiness.

She also had a word with Aashima and her mother.

Three months of relative quiet followed in which Sanjay tried to play the role of a good husband as he understood it. He showed

Aashima around town (after she had shaved diligently) and brought her flowers. His mother sent them to watch movies every Friday.

They were still not sleeping together, however, and the peaceful period eventually ended up with a huge fight when Aashima told him that she had physical needs that were not being met. The family could not cool things down and the episode ended only when Sanjay fainted and had to be hospitalized. The doctors diagnosed his condition as a breakdown brought on by severe stress.

While he was in the hospital, Aashima's family took her back to Roorkee and told Sanjay's mother that the couple should either start living together as married couples do, or get separated.

That was a month and a half before I met Sanjay.

Since then the two families have met twice.

In the presence of relatives from both sides, it was agreed that the marriage could not be saved and negotiations were ongoing about the compensatory sum that Aashima would be paid for an out-of-court settlement. Her mother had initially quoted 25 lakhs, but Sanjay's maternal uncle assured him that he could bring it down to 10-12 lakhs.

Even that amount of money would stretch their finances to breaking point (Sanjay earns about 20,000 rupees per month from his kirana store), but he doesn't regret the cost all that much.

He would never get married again, he told me with great conviction before we ended the conversation. But his mother has already started looking at young widows in their community, Hitesh told me. No divorcees though, because she doesn't trust them.

I must admit that based on what Hitesh had told me, I was pre-inclined to hold Sanjay at fault even before I had met him. While listening to him, however, I could not help but feel a little sorry for him. At the end of the day, like Aashima he is also the product (and a victim too, therefore) of a rigid social system that recognizes no value in an individual's right to choose their partner.

For me, the story of Sanjay and Aashima's love (or lack thereof) is the story of how the old and new overlap in our time.

The fast-track arranged marriages are an unchanged artefact from the previous generations, yet Aashima as an educated Millennial woman is vocal about her sexual needs.

Sanjay's self-centeredness and his insistence on ending the marriage, on not compromising or empathizing with his wife, is typical of a patriarchal mindset but at the same time, he does not care about society as someone from his father's generation might have done. His behaviour is that of a dissatisfied customer returning something they bought rather impulsively on Amazon.

Dating apps and social media may not be active characters in this story but technology is as present here as it is in all other aspects of our lives.

The families found each other via WhatsApp groups dedicated to matchmaking within specific castes. Sanjay researched his wife's hormonal disorder by looking up the symptoms on Google. Aashima kept an online gratitude journal and towards the end of their marriage, she told Sanjay that she could no longer think of anything to make the daily entries. The idea that his mental health requires therapy sessions also came to Sanjay from social media discourse on the subject.

For exploring out-of-court settlement options, he had got in touch with other men who have had similar experiences on Reddit, and while talking to me he often kept coming back to the 'lack of rights men have in India because of feminism'.

■

More than 90 per cent people on Tinder in India identify as men, according to the latest data.

It means that for a man the odds of just coming across a woman on Tinder, let alone matching with them or going out on a date, are a disheartening 1:10. Even after adjusting for different sexual preferences and multiple apps, it's evident that despite the amount of attention they get, dating apps are no match for the traditional ways of finding companionship in India.

But this is just a minor contradiction in our generation's

perspective on love, which is a perspective that consists almost entirely of contradictions.

Our hearts, caught in the space between expectations and reality, cannot quite make sense of either.

Pop culture, Western as well as Indian, promised us that anyone could find love if they made an effort. Social media platforms opened up the world for us and gave the impression of an infinitely wide dating pool. Those of us who moved to urban centres felt like we had left behind provincial baggage for romantic and sexual liberty. Over the years, however, we have realized that popular culture and urbanization are no match for social structures that have survived for thousands of years.

As we slowly come to terms with how little has changed about the choices we are allowed to make, our dissatisfactions become apparent in odd ways.

Stories of failed marriages are suddenly all around us because we cannot simply 'adjust' blindly like the previous generations were trained to do, and we know enough about love for its absence to feel fundamentally wrong. At the same time, wherever some freedom has been gained, it often finds the vilest opposition from amongst us.

Used to the comfort of arranged marriages, and unable to come to terms with a world in which women can choose their partners, young men are not shy about venting their frustrations on the internet.

Just as we imported other ideas about dating in the West, we are also importing ideas about incels (short for 'involuntary celibates') from their heroes like Andrew Tate, and adapting them to our desi flavour of misogyny. Anti-feminist, anti-woke movements like MGTOW (Men Going Their Own Way) are finding popularity in India by evoking fantastical images of a world in which women persecute men with fake dowry cases, false rape charges, and general mental harassment.

A Facebook page called MGTOW India, for instance, has been noted by the Global Network on Extremism and Technology for routinely publishing misogynist comments. In several posts on the page, dating is compared to a form of slavery for men.

Understandably, therefore, it is difficult to say what the future will look like, whether it will be more awaara or less, or whether the love lives of a cab driver, a shop owner, and a software developer will become ever more similar or diverge completely from one another. I want to be optimistic because I don't think that the growth in women's rights or their sexual agency will be diminished by a few men whining loudly on the internet. The next generation—despite all the romantic cynicism they express so often on social media—also seems to me much surer about what they want to sate their hearts, and how they want it.

However, it is difficult to ignore the general trend of regression or conservatism that has become characteristic of our society in the last couple of decades. Away from urban centres, the cages around our hearts are still as solid as they were for any of the previous generations, while modernity suffers ever more from charges of foreign elitism.

And as obsessed as we are with solutionism, who knows, maybe someone someday soon will make an app to make love and sex altogether obsolete, solving all contradictions in one fell swoop. One (anti)dating app to rule them all, perhaps.

As for Millennials, I expect it would be helpful if, instead of growing up with awaaragardi as something to be reviled, their kids could grow up humming the old Dev Anand song.

Hai apna dil toh awaara...
My heart, it's a free spirit...

9

SPIRITUAL, NOT RELIGIOUS

What does a boy from Haridwar say about religion?

Sounds like the opening to a bad joke. We may as well have another one.

How many boys from Haridwar does it take to say something about religion?

A hundred. One to do the talking, and ninety-nine to assure people that he is not giving a sermon and will not ask them for money at the end.

Better opening; bad joke.

But maybe we are not too off the mark here because what is religion itself, if not a pathetic joke? Old joke, sure, ancient even. Still stinking bad though, always delivering punches instead of punchlines.

Religion offends people, as is expected from bad jokes.

As is also expected, people are offended only by other people's bad jokes. Their own they hold sacrosanct. But good, bad, or something in between, the consensus among the world's clever people is that religion is essential to civilization. It is, they tell us, an important story that keeps societies glued together. An essential bad joke that we keep playing on ourselves to drown out our existential worries in meaningless mirth, that's religion for you. Each generation tells this joke, laughs at it, and gets offended for (or by) it in ways best suited to the zeitgeist.

■

On a cloudy August afternoon, I talked to forty-year-old Sheela Maurya, who was born the oldest of five siblings in Chandauli, a small town in Uttar Pradesh.

When she was sixteen, her grandfather set up an arranged marriage for her. After the wedding she moved to Pune with her husband who ran an electronics store in the city. The young couple had their first son the same year, and two years later Sheela's uterus had to be removed due to complications in the delivery of their second son.

At thirty-five, Sheela had a standard-issue middle-class existence, two sons (seventeen and nineteen years old respectively), and a husband who 'did everything a husband should do', according to her.

Yet, despite having everything that she thought a woman in her position ought to have, Sheela was going through a rough patch she describes as being 'angry all the time at everyone, especially my husband'. She was utterly bored with the life she had led over two decades.

A typical day back then would start with her dragging herself out of bed at eight in the morning to prepare breakfast for the family (it was usually something low-effort, she says with a guilty laugh, like bread-butter-jam or cornflakes). The kids and her husband would leave by ten, and she would get busy with chores for the next few hours.

By afternoon, there would be nothing to do. She would watch TV, chat with her mother on the phone, and soon find herself deeply resenting everything and everyone in her life.

She had always gone through the motions of visiting temples and praying for a few minutes each morning, but it was around this time that she began browsing the internet on her smartphone for the 'correct way' to do puja and 'explanations' behind various religious rituals. It was this online activity, I expect, that caused a video of ISKCON to appear on her YouTube feed.

Sheela went through the twenty-minute-long video while preparing her post-lunch cup of tea and kept watching other videos on the channel until her husband returned from work in the evening.

For the first time in years, I felt a sense of purpose that night, she told me, sounding giddy even now, years later.

The very next day she looked up the ISKCON chapter in Pune and hailed a taxi to visit it in the afternoon. She returned home with the sense that she had finally turned her life around.

What made Sheela's newfound faith better than the religious tradition she had always been following? A big bunch of things, according to her.

As a low-caste woman in her native Uttar Pradesh, she would not have been comfortable interacting with the priests in a mandir, but in ISKCON nobody really cares about 'all those things'. The guru–shishya parampara is also missing in 'normal' mandirs, she says, and nobody knows why they are doing any particular part of the puja. At ISKCON, on the other hand, she has a shiksha–guru who clears all her doubts and helps her go through the different religious books published in-house, and she has the option of choosing a diksha–guru who will be her spiritual guide in helping her refine her bhakti, her devotion.

I asked Sheela if she still considers herself belonging to the Hindu religion, and she sighed. 'Yes, but Hindu, Muslim, all this is too new,' she said, 'in the beginning, there was only Sanatan, and I consider myself a Sanatani spiritual person.'

She has been born again since she discovered her spirituality, she told me twice during our conversation. 'Spirituality or religion?' I asked her.

'Spirituality,' she said decidedly, 'it's older than all this religious stuff.'

▪

It may or may not be older, but it is certainly ubiquitous.

You can easily encounter 'spirituality' everywhere from newspaper columns to YouTube podcasts, self-help books, Instagram reels, political speeches, and follower conventions held by popular English-speaking, sunglasses-sporting gurus. So much so, that on analysing some data from Google's Ngram Viewer, I found the word's usage to have jumped by more than 500 per cent from 1980 to 2019.

We are becoming more spiritual, evidently, or at least more curious and vocal about being spiritual.

What is spirituality, exactly? Well, you would be hard-pressed to arrive at a unified definition even if you (like me) talked to a dozen people who called themselves spiritual.

Instead of working as a weakness, however, this vagueness seems to have made spirituality universally adaptable.

Sheela is spiritual, so is one of my friends who goes for a bi-weekly meditation class, and so is a colleague who believes that the human body is a self-healing machine that never requires medication. Their core beliefs are widely divergent, yet all of them claim to be 'spiritual, not religious'. Generally, they say it with a sense of superiority, establishing their one-upmanship over those who are merely religious.

The increased popularity of spirituality in our time has been ascribed by many to a corresponding decrease in the popularity of traditional or organized religion.

According to an analysis published in the *New York Times* in 2015, 1 out of 4 people, among those born after 1980 in the US, no longer subscribed to any religion. By 2021, the number of US adults with no religious affiliations had jumped to 29 per cent, an increase of 6 percentage points from 2016, with the shift led largely by Millennials. In India, religion has shown similar trends of decline, according to a 2019 survey, even though the percentage of religious people (and of people who pray daily) remains much higher compared to the West.

For me, a disregard for religion is now such a fundamental part of my existence that I struggle to remember a time when it wasn't so.

If I try hard enough, I can remember myself as the five- or six-year-old boy who folded his hands and murmured the Gayatri Mantra at every temple when he went out with his parents. It must have been a busy habit because in Haridwar you cannot walk 100 metres without coming across a temple. But, I did it even when I was riding on the tank of my father's motorbike, and to this day I can recite the Gayatri Mantra in under ten seconds.

I accompanied my mother to the temple during Navratri, whenever she let me because it involved a visit to the market at a festive time of the year.

I also volunteered to visit the nearby Hanuman mandir every week when I was in 7th standard, largely because it gave me a reason to go on walks all by myself.

Every Tuesday I would take twenty rupees from my mother and hop down a kilometre or so to the temple, after making a stop at the nearby sweetshop to buy syrup-filled, crunchy sweet boondis for prasad.

It used to be fun, except for the sticky orange tilak the priest insisted on drawing on my forehead.

None of this stopped suddenly, and there was no major awakening that I can remember, but other things, typical teenage preoccupations, gradually drove out whatever little interest I had in religion. Anyway, are there any religious teenagers in the world outside of cults? I certainly didn't know anyone like that back then, though the extent to which people went along with their parents' wishes varied between families.

A boy, one year my junior, always came to school in slippers during the exams because his father thought his grades would improve if he didn't wear leather shoes. I had no issues eating a tablespoon of sweet yogurt for good luck before leaving home, but that was more superstition than religious belief. No one talked about caste very much. My family loved the dry-fruit-rich sheer that our Muslim milkman brought for us on Eid.

Religion was there, it wasn't there, it wasn't all that important.

I tend to agree with studies on the subject of religiosity, such as those by the Pew Research Center, that suggest that our reliance on religion decreases with a decrease in existential worries.

Political scientists like Pippa Norris and Ronald Inglehart suggest that in countries with greater risks of war, famine, riots, etc., people are more inclined towards religion, compared to people in safer countries. In other words, religious commitment is lower where (and when) life is easier. This could be one of the reasons why younger people in countries with increasing existential stability tend to be less religious than their parents and grandparents.

But what should happen if these younger people with 'increased existential stability' belong to the most individualistic generation yet, which also happens to be the largest adult cohort worldwide?

Religions, as well-established institutions, have rigid rules that are resistant to change. While the larger world may update its views on things like race, caste, gender dynamics, sexual preferences, etc., religion stays—or at least tries its best to stay—the same as it has always been. In fact, this unchanging quality has been one of religion's most effective promises, because it gives people a feeling of stability and provides communal support structures to their shared beliefs and ethics.

I asked Khushi Rajeev, a behavioural psychologist based out of London, to weigh in on this. 'Behaviourally speaking, this "unchanging" quality of religion, with its entrenched traditions, rituals, and established belief systems, becomes a sanctuary for those seeking constancy and support in an ever-changing world,' she said. 'In this sense, religion becomes a *psychological anchor*, a consistent reference point, which can have a grounding effect in the face of life's uncertainties. The communal support structures inherent in religion not only provide constancy but also seem to feed what Maslow referred to as 'belonging needs'.

Also, in the traditional relationship between religion and the individuals who follow it, religion is always more important than the individuals. There is always a greater emphasis on showing due obedience to the institution rather than on getting due value out of it. Priests in mandirs are generally too preoccupied with their duties to worry about 'customer satisfaction'. They don't wear pleasant smiles while going about their work and they don't engage with devotees in the manner of fast-food joint servers or credit-card sellers.

When Sheela talks about her preference for ISKCON, she may as well be pointing out the shortcomings of her original faith in metrics like personalization, updation, and value-for-money or value-for-time. She can do such an evaluation because consumer capitalism has taught us that success on these metrics is necessary for good services and products.

Choice itself is equal to liberty for us. It is held essential to basic human dignity, and the religions decided for us by the accident of our birth offer very little of it.

'Navigating the conflict between one's evolving world-view and the psychological anchor embedded in traditional religious guidelines can birth cognitive dissonance,' Rajeev explains. 'In other words, it can create a mental struggle as individuals strive to reconcile their changing perspectives with the established principles they've internalized. Spirituality, may then seem a more appealing avenue than traditional religion.'

▪

Neoliberalism, of the political and economic ideology espoused by the Austrian–British polymath Friedrich Hayek, and the love child of Margaret Thatcher and Ronald Reagan, is believed to have become the reigning ideology of our time during the early 1990s. Around the same time, Sheela was in her teens, I was, and most of our generation was somewhere between these two stages of existence.

The neoliberal world order we inherited looked at all aspects of a society as quantifiable market resources and religion was not exempted. As economies opened up around the world, the new middle class faced decisions about what traditional beliefs, and how much of them, it wanted to carry forward in its upward journey in the socio-economic class system.

On top of that came the internet, and the world, already being imagined as one giant marketplace, was connected via the World Wide Web.

Religious institutions then faced a double threat.

First, the consumerist (or neoliberal, or globalist) mindset driven by values such as competitiveness, USPs, and consumer-centricity would require them to change, putting them in direct conflict with their commitment to resist all change. Second, the sceptics, rationalists, and atheists who would earlier have been oddballs in their communities, amenable to assimilation with the religious masses, could now find like-minded company on the internet. Together, they could question or mock religion on a larger scale than ever before and rationalism might even come out the winner.

The optimistic mood of that post-Cold War, post-liberalization era, however, was not able to sustain itself for long.

The kids growing up in the 1990s witnessed the dot-com bubble's spectacular crash in 2000 and learned that the IT revolution was not all rainbows and unicorns. Just eight years later, the Great Recession would follow the financial crash originating in the West.

Life, for many, turned increasingly unpredictable from then onwards.

Despite the glamorous and peppy sentiments often associated with the world's largest generation, multiple studies show that Millennials are objectively worse off than previous generations on multiple counts and many in India admit to being anxious about the future.

We are so exhausted that we have no time to meet people and as a result, we are lonely. We are so lonely that it exhausts us. We marry late, or not at all. We cannot afford houses, or cars, or children. We are anxious about climate change; we have already gone through one recession and may be in the middle of another one. Facts are no longer sacrosanct, the news cannot be trusted, previously unknown viruses can bring the world to a standstill, hold us hostage within our homes for the better part of two years, and the geopolitical horrors of the last century seem intent on staging a comeback.

Going by the Norris and Inglehart school of thought, we

should be ripe for religion's appeal right about now. We need something—a metaphysical glue—to keep us from falling apart in a world that demands everything from us and yields next to nothing in return.

Yet, religion doesn't quite fit the bill for those of us privileged enough to be entrenched in consumerism. In India, that implies an upper-middle class, educated, metropolitan existence constantly on the lookout for upgrades and improvements.

Religion requires service *from* us, but we want a service *for* ourselves. We want it to come to us (via the comfort of our screens, preferably) rather than making us go to it (at, say, a designated place of worship). We don't want to belong to a community, we want something that can help us craft a unique identity.

Cue, enter spirituality.

Despite its penchant for staying free of definitions, over the years various people have made attempts to define spirituality, and my favourite one, by far, is by Matthew Hedstrom, professor of US religious history at the University of Virginia.

Spirituality, the good professor says, is what consumer capitalism does to religion.

This 'doing', I believe, is the transformation of an institution into a product.

Products, unlike institutions, can easily be updated, customized, or personalized. They don't come with a set of inviolable rules because we don't belong to our products, we own them, and different varieties of a product are encouraged to compete in a free market.

Just as we choose different flavours of potato chips or ice cream, we can choose different flavours of spirituality and switch to a new one when we get bored with the same old, same old. A spiritual person can subscribe to ISKCON, ISHA, Art of Living Foundation, Sufi mysticism, transcendental meditation, and active positivity all at the same time, or keep moving between each of them, but a religious person will find it difficult to be Hindu and Muslim at the same time.

Sheela, devoted to ISKCON for the last five years, has been sensing a disconnect lately. In part, it had something to do with the repetitive routine she follows every day, but then there was also the news coverage of Virat Kohli and Anushka Sharma visiting Swami Parmanand with their daughter. Sheela was impressed enough to do a quick research on Swamiji and it felt like he was talking directly to her in his sermons.

In the last four months, she has travelled thrice to Vrindavan to see him. For better or worse, ISKCON is out and Parmanand is in, as far as Sheela's spiritual growth is concerned.

The availability of choice is also apparent in the sense that spirituality, unlike religion, has no ideological barriers.

For those with centre-of-left inclinations, there is a whole lot of spirituality that discards outdated orthodox beliefs. Manifestation, for instance, which refers to the practice of achieving your goals by visualizing them day in and day out, does not prefer straight people over homosexuals or Rajputs over Dalits. By placing your faith in Manifestation, you can get back a sense of control over the world's random chaotic machinations—thus getting the benefit of religion's main feature—without needing to compromise on your liberal worldview.

If you lean right of centre, no problem, there are flavours perfect for you as well.

Upper-caste Millennials who want to hold on to their pride-by-birthright but find it incompatible with their modern lifestyles can find solace in English-speaking, bike-riding, sunglasses-sporting gurus. Their religion's bloody history, its baroque trappings, are all cleaned up and legitimized by the new vocabulary of spirituality.

Their resentment against caste-based reservations is justified when caste is explained as a merit-based system that was benevolent to one and all in the glorious past, and only got corrupted by external influences. Burning crackers on Diwali was, following similar narratives, a way of killing mosquitoes and other disease-laden insects that got active during that particular time of the year. Maha Shivratri celebrations are pitched as a 'secular' festival meant to reap the benefits of a rare astronomical phenomenon.

Spirituality also recognizes that religion opposed science only to its own detriment.

Telling people that prayers at a temple work better than medical treatment is an obsolete idea in a world where even the janam-kundalis are computer-generated. We may still choose the middle path and pray at the temple with all the proper rituals while a loved one is admitted to the hospital, but a divorce from science due to reasons of faith is quite impossible for Millennials. Unless, of course, science itself is used to discredit its 'mainstream' version.

In most flavours of spirituality, regardless of the demographics for which they have been customized, scientific or quasi-scientific terms are common enough. The more vague, exotic, and broader a scientific term, the better it is for getting co-opted by spirituality.

For example, 'energy' is used by spiritualists of all sorts to explain everything from 'auras' to 'vibes', 'chi', 'ki', 'zen', etc. Similarly, in recent years, Quantum Physics (sometimes shortened to just 'quantum') has become a blanket concept that can be thrown over almost any sort of quackery by godmen and YouTube podcasters. In a variation of this approach, spiritual concepts or practices are named using scientific-sounding words. 'Inner Engineering', for example, or 'Transcendental Meditation'. This respectability or legitimacy gained by co-opting scientific vocabulary is so effective because it allows our irrational beliefs the pretension of being rational.

Moreover, the scientific veneer helps satisfy the need for self-improvement in our self-obsessed culture.

Religion may hold promises of an ideal afterlife, but spirituality pitches us more productivity, better health, great sleep, and sophisticated conversation fillers for social interactions. All of this is blissful instant gratification and the afterlife sounds way too far in the future—certainly not the kind of thing one wants to think about in their twenties or thirties, or even in their early forties.

However, pointing out spirituality's various advantages over religion can be misleading because it makes it sound like they are two completely distinct competitors for our faith.

The reality is close to Hedstorm's definition. We create our gods in our image, if we were to slightly alter Genesis 1:27.

Hence, the existence of white Jesus, black Jesus, and Hispanic Jesus; hence the meat-friendly Durga Puja in Bengal and the nine-day strict vegetarian diet to worship the same goddess in Uttar Pradesh. Hence also the fact that Ganesha speaks Tamil in Tamil Nadu, Marathi in Maharashtra, and is fluent in Hindi in Delhi.

Neil Gaiman's *American Gods* plays around with this idea and takes it further to suggest that gods are only as powerful as people's faith in them. As old religions become obsolete, their gods grow weak and are replaced by new gods that suit the new world. In the novel, these new gods reflect the things to which we are now truly devoted. For example, there is Technical Boy, the god of computers and the internet, Mr World, the god of conspiracy theories, and Ms Media, the goddess of social media, fake news, and 'content'. Take out the fantasy and it's clear that in this particular case, fiction doesn't fall far from facts.

Spirituality *is* religion, cast in the image of our times. But, traditional religion has also been catching up with the times.

▪

While neoliberal values and consumerism may now be deeply entrenched in our culture, liberalism is on the back foot in many countries around the world.

In India, the Hinduism of my childhood, which swept problems like Islamophobia, caste discrimination, or gender inequality under the carpet, has been replaced by Hindutva, which proudly wears its ugliest aspects on its sleeve.

This rabid adaptation pays good political dividends, is social-media savvy, and carries powerful elements of nationalistic pride.

On a recent visit to Haridwar, I met up with a priest who doubles up as the teacher of Sanskrit literature for the fifty-odd students who stay at Geeta Mandir, the temple right opposite my house. Pandit Vikram Chaturvedi is older than me by a decade and I ask him how he came into this particular line of work.

'I was a very naughty kid,' he tells me shyly, 'so my uncle suggested that I should be put in a hostel. This was the only kind we could afford.'

In addition to Sanskrit literature and scriptures, students also learn Mathematics, History, and Geography at the temple. Career opportunities have also grown in recent years, Pandit Chaturvedi tells me, with jobs for religious gurus opening up in the army and an increased scope in academia.

'But to really make it in this field, one should be like Dhirendra Shastri,' Panditji says towards the end of our conversation, referring to the twenty-seven-year-old head of a religious sect in Madhya Pradesh who grabs news headlines by combining streetside 'miracle' tricks with calls for a Hindu Rashtra. Shastri's sermons regularly get made into Instagram reels and YouTube shorts, to be shared across social media platforms where he enjoys a large following. In real life too, lakhs of people regularly flock to attend his events, and a great deal of law enforcement is deployed to prevent stampedes.

If we did fashion spirituality in our individualist, consumerism-driven image and called it spirituality, one can only imagine what religion's utterly cynical, vendetta-driven future will look like when people like Shastri mould it in their image.

We can look for an example at the dharm-sansad held in Haridwar in 2021 which openly called for violence against Muslims and asked Hindus to keep swords and knives ready in their homes for the future. It was attended by saints and seers from all over the country.

Pandit Chaturvedi doesn't think the event was a good idea—but only because it failed to give due precedence to the local religious bodies in the city.

Walking through familiar routes, I saw people wearing tilaks on Tuesdays. Unlike, the simple 'orange' I used to know as a kid, I think of the tilak's colour as saffron now. A replacement comparable, perhaps, with that of 'Jai Siya Ram' with 'Jai Shri Ram' in the public imagination. Several houses in our neighbourhood also have saffron flags dangling from the terraces. For some, they may be symbols of active support for Hindutva, for others a way of safely assimilating into the majority.

But my sister, who still lives there, has not taught my ten-year-old nephew to recite Gayatri Mantra while passing by temples as our parents taught us.

Boutique hotels are coming up on the Ganga ghats, meanwhile. For a price, you can get the sanitized, convenient, and Instagramable version of any religious ceremony. You can order in an acharyaji just like you would a pizza and the hotel staff will set up a canopy for you right beside the river. After completing all the rituals—which will include detailed explanations from the acharyaji and his helpers—you can head over to the restaurant and break your fast with a satvik buffet.

Once everything has been wrapped up satisfactorily, you can get the hotel staff to click a family photograph with everyone in their best ethnic wear from Fabindia.

Is this religion or spirituality? Something in between? Are you indulging in it because you can sense your bubble of prosperity shrinking every day, or because it's just another 'experience' on your checklist?

Well, who can tell?

I doubt I can, but I would have a go if someone were to ask me to define spirituality.

'If religion was the opium of the masses,' I would say dramatically, 'then spirituality is crack for individuals.'

10

OUR MONOCHROMATIC TONGUE

At the beginning of time, all the Earth's people spoke a common language, goes a story in the Bible.

Being able to communicate with each other flawlessly, they could collaborate perfectly and achieve miraculous results. Eventually, they decided to build a tower in the city of Babel.

In their hubris, they decided to make this tower as tall as possible, tall enough to reach the heavens, tall enough to take a peek at God himself working at his infallible plans. Only, this was the Old Testament god, with a marked fondness for fire and fury. The people should have known better than to build the tower, but they didn't, probably because they had not read the Bible.

In any case, God was not so pleased when he found out about the Tower of Babel and this is how he reacted to it:

> 'Look!' he said. 'The people are united, and they all speak the same language. After this, nothing they set out to do will be impossible for them! Come, let's go down and confuse the people with different languages. Then they won't be able to understand each other.'

Humanity is thus scattered all around the world and given different languages.

The story is meant to explain the diversity of languages, but it also holds the allure of a common language that everyone spoke before God intervened. This 'Adamic language' has been an interesting subject of speculation for people over the centuries, though all evidence points to it being a myth, albeit an enduring one.

Now, imagine if this myth could come true.

All of humanity communicating in a common tongue, using the same expressions, the same metaphors, and analogies. Everyone laughing at the same jokes, confessing their love with the same words. All the awkwardness of ordering food and asking for routes in a foreign country, gone forever. No need for translators, human or otherwise.

Oh, but all that we could achieve together—build another tower to claim the heavenly throne or migrate to other planets en masse.

Can you imagine all this? Well, I envy your optimism, if you can.

On the other hand, if you prefer realism, you may imagine a global language, a marketing-speak supported by all-invasive technology, gobbling up all other languages, eating up cultural diversity, and then dying of obesity.

Admittedly, someone like me who has worked in IT and marketing for close to a decade may be more likely to have such a vision of the future.

In our Black Mirror-saturated imaginations, personal experiences can often present outsized reflections and dystopia seems to be lurking just over the horizon. Therefore, to follow up on a few ideas I had been developing for some time about technology, mass communication, and their effect on language, I thought it best to talk to an expert in the field.

Ganesh N. Devy, the celebrated linguist and Padma Shri recipient, graciously agreed to have a conversation with me while he was in Bangalore for a series of lectures.

Apart from all his numerous achievements and all the awards conferred on him over the years, Professor Devy is best known for the People's Linguistic Survey of India, a project of enormous ambition and scale that sought to highlight and preserve India's linguistic diversity. As someone concerned with keeping languages alive, Professor Devy has his ear close to the ground when it comes to how language is changing with the times.

While we discussed how the algorithms of social media platforms that use technologies like NLP (Natural Language Processing) and AI are inherently biased toward English, he pointed out that this 'technology that uses language as fodder is actually killing language'.

Even English is suffering, he says.

As an example of how entire sets of words—joy words, pain words, pleasure words—are disappearing, he gives a simple example.

'When my grandfather had pain here,' he points to a spot near his ankle, 'he would use a very specific word to tell the doctor what kind of pain he had at what particular place, whereas I can only say "Doctor! I have a 'cramp' in my leg". Distinctive shades of pain and pleasure are no longer explicit in the language as they were in the past.'

Marketing's impact on language, according to him, is indirect.

'The direct impact is on the society, the thinking process, the values systems, and it's because of these that there's an impact on language.' For Professor Devy, it's the root of the problem that needs addressing. 'Marketing is the method or medium via which technology is impacting language. If the method changes, the impact could also change. During Covid, for example, when there was reduced marketing for food products, some old words that we had almost forgotten came back into usage.'

But such rejuvenations are few and far between.

In the big picture, languages are losing out to a rapidly changing world—out of the world's 7,000-odd languages, about 130 die out each year, by Professor Devy's estimation. In India alone, over 200 languages have been lost in the last fifty years.

He is convinced that there is enough evidence to suggest that a time will come—provided that human beings survive long enough—when there will be no 'visual' languages, which is to say that linguistic sounds may survive, but most else will not.

I point out to him that some would call that fearmongering and he cracks a smile.

'There are subjective views of language, yes, but there are also objective ways of measuring linguistic decline,' he explains. 'For example, the use of the past tense. Most languages had more complex forms of the past tense but over time our handling of the past is becoming lethargic. When a language has fewer ways of dealing with the past, that language makes a slow walk towards its demise.'

Various writers, in recent years, have also raised concerns about our language becoming less 'rich'.

Writer and translator Rakhshanda Jalil, for example, in a panel she shared with the Booker Prize-winning author Geetanjali Shree and other eminent literary personalities at the Jaipur Literary Festival, articulated this 'loss of richness' as the loss of a more idiomatic, flavoursome, and pungent language used by previous generations.

Similarly, in an essay entitled 'Generation Amazing!!! How We're Draining Language of Its Power', journalist and writer Emily McCrary-Ruiz-Esparza talks at length about how we are 'draining language of its power'.

She lays the blame on our tendency to resort to hyperbole at the drop of a hat, and our carelessness about looking up the exact words we need to express ourselves. More and more often, according to her, we find ourselves fighting for people's attention and that is why we submit to the 'maxim of extravagance'.

She gives a rather interesting example about someone who wants to attract people to a stuffed pig they have bought recently:

> You really want people to see the taxidermied pig you just bought, so you tell your friend, 'Man, this thing is **incredible.** It's wearing a lederhosen and everything.' Your friend goes to see the pig and he too is surprised by the thing. He starts telling his friends, 'that thing is **incredible**.' This is called 'conformity.' Word gets around the neighborhood and then the whole block is talking about the **incredible** taxidermied pig. This is called 'frequency.' You're out for a walk one

> day, and you flag down a Door Dasher on a bicycle. 'Have you seen the—' 'The **incredible** taxidermied pig? Yeah man, whatever.' This is called 'predictability.'
>
> Predictability is useful when we want to fit in with the crowd, but it's not useful if we want to attract attention, which you need at this point, because you've started charging admission to see the pig. Now you need to innovate, and you're back to the maxim of extravagance again, so the pig becomes **unbelievable**.

The word 'incredible' may have been justified in reference to the singularly dressed pig, but as a result of the advertising by its owner, it became overused and lost its power. This is why it had to be replaced by 'unbelievable' to attract further attention. Sooner or later, the same thing would happen to 'unbelievable', and then the pig's owner would have to look for an even more dramatic word.

This loss of a word's power, or reduction of its intensity, is a linguistic phenomenon called 'semantic bleaching'. It is easily observable in words that have been used so much that they carry little meaning, except as fillers or weights in sentences. The word 'literally' could be a recent example.

As we market our lives on the internet, we reach higher and higher to convey our superiority, just like smartphone companies, having exhausted all superlative adjectives, refer to their new models as PhonePlus, PhonePro, PhoneProMax, and PhoneUltraProMax. Any offbeat thing we experience is 'surreal', each bowl of ramen is 'AMAZING!', each new step in life is 'a life-transforming experience', and all of us must always 'deep dive' into ideas.

Even away from the digital world, hyperbole catches on fast.

While spit balling ideas for a multi-city marketing campaign at work, I once suggested that we should be looking at 'hyperlocal' ways of communicating with our audiences. All I wanted to say (as part of the idea) was that we should refer to each city's famous landmarks in our ads, and that could've been conveyed by using 'local'.

The 'hyper' was meant to lend some extra weight to my suggestion. What does hyperlocal mean? Relating to, or focusing on, matters concerning a small community or geographical area, according to Google, which is the same thing we usually convey with 'local', in most cases.

Hyperlocal is just more-local, local-plus, local-ultra-pro-max.

Anyway, my colleagues liked the suggestion. Hyperlocal worked. Then, it went the extra mile and stuck to the office vocabulary. Until my last day in that office, the word continued to haunt meetings, briefs, feedback, and every other idea to the point where I doubt if anyone still remembers good, old 'local' any more.

When we take such examples, linguistic phenomena appear contained within the physical boundaries of a certain place.

'Incredible' or 'unbelievable' may go through semantic bleaching in the taxidermied pig's neighbourhood, but that is unlikely to have an effect on their meaning in the world at large. Similarly, my previous workplace may stop using 'local' in marketing discussions, but that's not going to affect how other offices in the same building use the word. A few words like 'literally' may have been bleached of their meaning for a great number of people, but that doesn't seem a great cause for concern. New words are always been added to language, after all, and we can always try to find a good substitute for an overused word.

Yet, the 'physical boundaries' have been made much less concrete by 24/7 digital connectivity and the way we communicate has undergone massive changes in the last thirty to forty years.

We must ask ourselves if these changes have encouraged us to use language that is 'less idiomatic, flavoursome, and pungent'. We must wonder why we feel like our words, and the ideas they convey, are not getting the attention they deserve, so that we need to use hyperbole. We must question if, and how, our ability to reclaim old words and adopt new words can keep up with the pace at which we are chewing through words and rendering them meaningless.

To do all this, it helps to understand the interaction between language, technology, and technology-enabled consumerist mass communication, i.e., digital marketing.

▪

As children, we learn language by imitating what we hear from the people closest to us, our family (or alternatively, the orphanage staff).

Gradually, our vocabulary expands, we begin to understand the nuances of different tones, learn how to derive the meaning of new words from context, and become somewhat adept at clearly articulating our thoughts. The scope of our language extends further once we learn how to engage with media in various forms such as newspapers, books, movies, and music.

It allows us to explore words and ideas that we may never have encountered in our immediate environment. Over time we get better at expressing ourselves, and pick up various linguistic skills (using sarcasm, euphemisms, metaphors, etc.) that can help us achieve our goals (teasing someone, for example, or persuading them).

While we employ our individual creativity to decide exactly *how* we use language, much of *what* we use is picked up from a collective linguistic pool that is filled with the language we are exposed to in our daily lives.

In other words, we speak and write what we hear and read. It begs the question, where do we currently do most of our hearing and reading?

Well, if numbers are anything to go by, Gen Z spend an average of eight hours a day online and one expects Millennials to not be far behind. The majority of this time (about 40 per cent), especially for younger people, is spent on social media platforms.

For the common user, these platforms are free to use and they provide everything from news to entertainment, community, identity, and even career opportunities. Yet, they are run by some of the most powerful corporations in the world, and their annual revenues run in billions of dollars. How does that happen when they are free to use? Well, it happens because the paying customers of social media platforms are the businesses and organizations that vie for the users' attention for successful marketing.

Understandably enough, the platforms are more concerned about their customers than the users.

In case this power dynamic is news to you, imagine social media (or the internet itself, for that matter) as a giant marketplace with lots of fun rides and games. The people (users) who walk into the fare don't have to pay for this fun, but the hawkers and shopkeepers (businesses) who shout over each other to attract potential customers pay rent to the marketplace.

The shouting-over-each-other happens to be a fitting analogy for marketing, and the language it uses reflects that. Much of it has always been true of mass communication's other applications as well.

From propaganda pamphlets used by different ideologies in the last century to TV news, and advertisements played on loudspeaker-carrying rickshaws that went around small towns selling digestive pills, the language shares some basic traits. It is meant to grab the reader's attention, it needs to put across the point—the sales pitch—as quickly as possible, and it must be so simple that anyone can understand it without putting the slightest strain on their mind.

Mass communication, after all, is targeted at the masses and it imagines their ideas to be like lumps of clay. By clever use of language, they can be moulded into any desired shape.

So then, what has changed?

Well, mass communication, and marketing in particular, has never been as ubiquitous and as powerful as it is today, courtesy of the internet.

Marketing's effects on language may fundamentally be the same as before, but its scope has increased exponentially. As the internet has become omnipresent and omniscient, so has marketing.

No one would engage with advertising pamphlets or roadside billboards (or read a newspaper/magazine) for more than a few minutes on any given day, but we come in contact with digital marketing every second of the time we are online, which frankly, translates to all the time.

Going back to my previous analogy, before the internet and social media, you walked into the marketplace, bought what you needed, and returned home.

If the shouting hawkers gave you a headache, you returned home sooner and did not go back for a long time. But now, in our slick new world, you spend the better part of your day, each day, in the marketplace.

Most of what you read, listen to, or watch, is actually the shopkeepers trying to sell you something. You could opt out, sure, and return home, but you would miss out on a lot of important things that now happen exclusively in the marketplace, so you have started living there and you have made it your home. Or, you have made your home a marketplace, depending on what sounds less disturbing.

As a result, the language we come into contact with adheres to the ideal characteristics of marketing-language: algorithm-friendly, simple, brief, and familiar.

Copywriters often judge their writing on metrics like 'Can a five-year-old understand this ad?', and 'Can my grandmother understand what the product is after reading this banner?' Since different people can have grandmothers and five-year-olds who are exceptionally smart or dumb, there are quantitative metrics available for better judgement.

The Flesch–Kincaid readability test, for example, that scores writing based on how easy it is to read and assigns these scores to different reader-maturity levels ranging from '5th Grader' to 'College Graduate' and 'Professional'.

Various SEO (search engine optimization) tools used by marketeers factor in the Flesch–Kincaid test, or its more sophisticated alternatives, to help marketeers optimize their writing for search engines like Google. The simpler a piece of writing is, the more it is divided into neat, little chunks under headings and sub-headings, the better chance it has of showing up high on the results page when someone searches the internet for whatever it is that the business is selling.

The undue importance on brevity follows from the emphasis on keeping language 'easy'.

Marketing copy has to be brief because it needs to deliver its punch fast, and also because each extra alphabet, whether it's on billboards, newspapers, or TV, costs extra money. Major online marketing platforms such as Google, X, Facebook, WhatsApp, etc., all have specific character limits on ads posted on them.

Familiar styles in writing are easy to read, which is why so much of the writing on the internet sounds the same, why most of the sentences are 'padded' alike with phrases such as 'therefore, it's important', 'with respect to', 'having regard to', 'let's deep dive into', 'in order to', 'the fact that', etc. This pretentious style is considered professional, and can be seen in frequent use in blogs and on platforms like LinkedIn.

No one could suggest that any of these qualities—simplicity, brevity, or familiarity—are inherently bad in language. It's the reason behind our current fondness for them that makes them problematic.

Marketing likes brief, easy language because it wants to be understood clearly by the dumbest of prospective customers, who are euphemistically referred to as the 'lowest common denominator' of the 'target audience'. The same is true for news or propaganda published on the internet.

All this writing needs to be alike because all of it is trying its best to be algorithm-friendly or SEO-friendly or platform-friendly.

It is also why there are common modes of expression between entirely different kinds of organizations—political parties make cleverly written memes in the same way as business start-ups who do it in the same way as film production studios who do it in the same way as famous stand-up comedians. Taking this commonality to its extreme logical end, it may even be argued that because of the medium's nature—the rules of 'content' on the internet or social media—all language, regardless of its source and destination is, eventually, a form of marketing-language.

This would not be cause for concern if marketing was only being done by corporations, but that's no longer the case.

▪

If you open a brand's profile (say, Nike) on Instagram and compare it to your own Instagram profile, you will notice that there is not much difference in the capabilities the platform offers you, a mere mortal, and Nike, a business worth billions of dollars.

There may be a few extra bells and whistles, but the basics will be the same. Both profiles (yours and Nike's) will have people they follow, people who follow them, and options for creating different types of content that other people on Instagram can engage with. Like Nike, you can also run marketing campaigns to increase the number of your followers and run sponsored content to make yourself more visible on Instagram.

It's the same story on other platforms.

It's also one of the most profound ways in which the internet has changed how we think about ourselves.

All of us, with our follower counts, our pages or profiles, are now brands unto ourselves. It doesn't matter that most of us don't have any actual products or services to market. We can always market our thoughts, ideas, images, videos, our very selves. We can craft for ourselves a perfect image and believe that's how the world perceives us.

It's referred to as 'personal branding'.

The number of people who actually see us on these platforms may be negligibly small, consisting mostly of those who know us personally, but that doesn't stop us from imagining that if we try well enough, we can have the same kind of audience as an actual brand like Nike.

Some, arguably, have been successful with this and are called 'influencers'. They have followings larger than many businesses and are increasingly used as cheaper and more relatable alternatives to actors and celebrities. It's called 'influencer marketing' and the monetization of content by businesses (or the platforms themselves) forms the 'creator economy'. As entertainers and marketing freelancers, influencers are known for making a good buck for their efforts.

For the majority of content creators, however, becoming an influencer remains an aspiration and, increasingly, a delusion.

When individuals treat themselves as businesses (or influencers), it follows that they will communicate like businesses, and end up using language the way businesses use it. They will try and make sure that everything they write and speak is algorithm-friendly, simple, brief, and familiar so that it can be easily grasped by the (largely imaginary) masses.

On the surface, it is easily seen in the millions of videos that begin with 'Hello friends' and end with 'Please like, subscribe, and share', but it goes deeper, I believe and affects how we think of language.

This flattening of language can be explained by understanding that something that's meant to be understood by everyone *has* to be vanilla. It cannot use the local ticks that make a language belong to a place and people. It cannot be idiomatic because idioms require cultural context and they need to be unravelled with the kind of attention span not exercised while scrolling through social media feeds. It cannot use specific 'joy words, pain words, or pleasure words' that denote subtle differences because it prefers umbrella terms that can convey a generic meaning to a greater number of people. It has to constantly reach out for hyperbole because it keeps overusing all the 'trending words' to a point where they turn 'cringe' and have to be discarded for more impressive alternatives.

Also, since we have started looking at ourselves as brands, we have also inherited the issues faced by brands.

Businesses have always worried about their customers' loyalty to the brand and they plan regular communication to make sure that they are not forgotten. In much the same way, we worry about being forgotten by our followers and getting replaced by a superior content creator, so we have to keep writing, talking, and making videos.

We don't care too much about what we say, or how we say it, because we say so much, and we keep doing that because most social media platforms punish those who don't. People regularly get 'shadow-banned' for not publishing content, and for not engaging with other people's content.

We have to worry about brevity just as much as any business because X allows everyone to use the same number of characters and Instagram captions can only be so long, regardless of whether it is an individual's or an organization's profile. The SEO guidelines that decide whether someone reads what we write on the internet or not, are also much the same whether we are writing a blog about the latest cameras to be purchased on Amazon or writing a personal essay about memories of the first harvest in our village.

Used under such market constraints, language becomes a tool or a currency to please the all-powerful algorithms, and maybe that's the point.

Maybe all our concerns about language point to the fact that we look at it only as a commodity. Our marketing-addled way of life does what it does to language because it thinks of language as a tool, a means to an end.

It does not understand that language is so much more than that.

Language is the way a people live, a culture in itself, the residue left to us after thousands of years of evolution. It's not the light in an electric bulb, billable by units spent, but the sun that illuminates our existence, lets us probe the dark recesses of our mind so that the scary shadows can be captured in cages made out of words, articulated, and turned unscary.

This is, I realize, a rather sentimental view and some would dismiss ideas about technology or late-stage capitalism on language as Luddite rants.

In the interest of taking a fair view, therefore, we must consider that concerns about language, even when expressed by renowned linguists and writers, could be something of an overreaction.

■

The most enduring aspect of counterculture is its cyclical nature.

It is understandable because the edginess that is so attractive in counterculture depends upon it remaining the view of a minority. When the majority does accept this view, a part of counterculture must reverse its position to continue being the minority view.

In the early days of the internet, when people were still wary of it, the cool thing was to talk about its great promise for a free movement of ideas all over the world.

Once it became an indispensable part of our lives and social media platforms became massively popular, the counter-cultural position shifted to talking about the various ways in which computer technology was making our lives less human or less authentic. In the last few years, just as much of this position has been driven by misplaced puritanism and nostalgia as by genuine concerns about the huge amount of control technology has over our lives.

Now, since this criticism of technology itself has become all too common a point of discussion, there is a growing tendency—a counter-counterculture of sorts again—to dismiss it as ineffectual hand-wringing at best and fearmongering at worst.

That's not entirely without reason.

We do tend to put the blame for all things distasteful on new technologies and even the intelligent among us can sometimes exaggerate our reservations about their effect on society. Personally, I try to remember Douglas Adams's three rules that describe our reaction to technology:

1. Anything that is in the world when you're born is normal and ordinary and is just a natural part of the way the world works.

2. Anything that's invented between when you're fifteen and thirty-five is new and exciting and revolutionary and you can probably get a career in it.
3. Anything invented after you're thirty-five is against the natural order of things.

It is indeed idiotic to be afraid of new things simply because they are new, and keep dreaming of some imagined golden past while the world moves on. But, can we avert our eyes from problems simply because we are bored of hearing about them?

The internet and social media *are* extremely powerful forces, their ubiquity (and our dependence on them) as technologies *is* unprecedented, they *do* affect a great many aspects of our lives, we *are* living in a world where our attention is seen as a resource by businesses capitalizing on the 'attention economy'.

Neither cynicism nor smirking indifference will serve us well.

It may feel as if we are resistant to paranoia when we turn a deaf ear to complaints, but we must ask ourselves if it's our cool-headedness behind this or the comfort of giving up on problems that feel too large for us to solve.

The inclination to defend popular new things is not restricted to technology. Those who caution against dangers to language run into similar issues as those who, supposedly, decry 'progress'.

This is apparent in the introduction to George Orwell's 1946 essay, 'Politics and the English Language' which he begins with a disclaimer:

> Most people who bother with the matter at all would admit that the English language is in a bad way, but it is generally assumed that we cannot by conscious action do anything about it. Our civilization is decadent and our language—so the argument runs—must inevitably share in the general collapse. It follows that any struggle against the abuse of language is a sentimental archaism, like preferring candles to electric light or hansom cabs to aeroplanes. Underneath this lies the half-conscious belief that language is a natural

growth and not an instrument which we shape for our own purposes.

The kind of defensive attitudes Orwell is referring to remain active and healthy in our time. Due to the similarity of their arguments, I will pick up an example as representative of the whole.

Writing for *The Guardian*, David Shariatmadari characterizes worry about linguistic decline as an unnecessary glorification of the past.

'Linguistic decline is the cultural equivalent of the boy who cried wolf, except the wolf never turns up,' Shariatmadari writes. 'Perhaps this is why, even though the idea that language is going to the dogs is widespread, nothing much has been done to mitigate it: it's a powerful intuition, but the evidence of its effects has simply never materialized. That is because it is unscientific nonsense.'

Primarily, Shariatmadari uses two arguments to defend his position.

First, while writers (James Beattie, Jonathan Swift, and George Puttenham, are among the many he cites), have always been moaning about a decline in our linguistic prowess, great literature has been produced in all their times and continues to be produced today.

Second, any change in language is only its evolution with time, and those who refer to a decay in language as reflective of a decay in our thoughts are mistaken because we continue to thrive as a species.

Criticizing the concerns of John Humphrys, the award-winning BBC broadcaster, he says, 'John Humphrys was born in 1943. Since then, the English-speaking world has grown more prosperous, better educated and more efficiently governed, despite an increase in population. Most democratic freedoms have been preserved and intellectual achievement intensified.'

These are both interesting positions to take for someone who comes across as calm and composed as Shariatmadari.

The first, because it uses literature as evidence of language's endurance even as it holds that writers—who produce this literature—are overly concerned with preserving language. It would seem absurd then to consider the quality of literature at any given time as representative of the quality of language at large.

The second, because despite Shariatmadari's admirable love for the scientific method and objective evidence, his view of the world's 'growing prosperity' is completely subjective. I do not intend to fault him for the view, because that may very well be how the world looks from Cambridge and London, but I know that many would not agree with it even in 'the English-speaking world'.

Regarding other views similar to Shariatmadari's, most of them seem to mistake discussions about how language is changing with a changing world as a call for exercising puritanical restrictions on it.

Nothing could be further from the truth because being pedantic with language is the least of my priorities, and I doubt it is of others who are concerned about it.

As new, traditionally underprivileged segments of society, like writers of colour, women, and Dalits, find increased representation, language will change, and it must. Translations in literature are enjoying their brightest moment. That may change languages in irreversible ways, and it must. Archaic words, expressions, and idioms will go out of usage, and they must.

No one in their right mind would suggest that language must be preserved in a jar of formaldehyde or captured in a photograph to be kept in museums.

But, a dismissal of concern about the condition of language in our time with something along the lines of 'people have always been saying language is deteriorating, but look it's still fine' feels flippant. Honestly, it sounds quite similar to the 'each generation thinks it's the last generation' defence that has been a favourite of climate-change deniers.

Well, look where that got us.

■

'Can something be done to change this state of things?' I asked Professor Devy towards the end of our conversation.

'Only collective action can stave off the linguistic-cultural disaster, just as in the case of environmental crises,' he replied thoughtfully and told me how, when he organized the People's Linguistic Survey of India, a large number of people participated and recorded their languages so that the country was able to see, actually see and hear, about 700-800 different languages.

'But I don't know if that will happen again, because it was not easy and I could do it only because it was a collective effort.'

Despite everything, there may still be some hope, even if it is of a particularly cynical variety.

'Humans are amazing creatures,' he muses, 'they create a lot of problems for themselves but sometimes they can solve them too. Perhaps this problem will also get solved, and I am only saying "perhaps", because of all the weapons that humans have created—knives, guns, nuclear bombs—language has been the oldest and most effective. No other weapon comes close to achieving its cost-effectiveness, easy accessibility, and mass effect. So, I am not saying that humans will try to save language because they are kind creatures, but they might do it because they are cruel creatures.'

Whatever the ultimate reasons, I hope that's true, that things will turn around in the nick of time—or even better that all our reservations will prove needless.

Meanwhile, even as I write this essay, the latest buzzword around the world is ChatGPT, a large language model that is being touted as the next step in the AI revolution. To put it simply, a large language model (LLM) is a computer program that trains on vast amounts of text with the help of machine learning algorithms and is eventually able to use language in a near-human manner. While the definition of 'near' in 'near-human' is still highly subjective tools like ChatGPT are increasingly being looked at as a replacement, or at least an assistant, for copywriters and journalists. If that happens—and it will happen if it proves to be cost-effective—language will only become more functional, more targeted at achieving 'conversions' in terms of sales and likes, followers and fans.

I am inclined to agree with Noam Chomsky that ChatGPT and its ilk are little things getting disproportionate amounts of attention and money, but I fear that those for whom language has already been flattened out will find these 'little things' enough for their shrunken needs.

What will this do to us?

Well, it's difficult to say for sure but just the other night there was an ad on my Instagram feed, trying to sell me a ChatGPT plugin for WhatsApp.

It showed the screen recording of a conversation in which a woman is telling her husband that she is going to leave him because he pays her no attention. Armed with the miracle plugin, the man instructs ChatGPT to 'write a romantic message to stop the wife from leaving me'. The wife then reads the AI-generated texts, her anger is assuaged, she tells her husband that she is sorry for getting angry at him.

One can imagine how the fictitious couple then proceeds to live happily ever after.

11

ANTI-CAA PROTESTS AND THE THING ABOUT SILENCE

On 15 December 2019, I spent the night reading *The Unbearable Lightness of Being*. Courtesy of Google Photos, and due to my habit of photographing certain pages (as others annotate them), I can recall parts of the book that spoke directly to me:

> Tereza keeps appearing before my eyes. I see her sitting on the stump petting Karenin's head and ruminating on mankind's debacles. Another image also comes to mind: Nietzsche leaving his hotel in Turin. Seeing a horse and a coachman beating it with a whip, Nietzsche went up to the horse and, before the coachman's very eyes, put his arms around the horse's neck and burst into tears....
>
> And that is the Nietzsche I love, just as I love Tereza with the mortally ill dog resting his head in her lap. I see them one next to the other: both stepping down from the road along which mankind, 'the master and proprietor of nature', marches onward.

I could see the onward march of our nation's new masters and proprietors as I read this and I feared that all those who dared to disagree might have to make final breaks of their own.

Four days earlier, the Citizenship Amendment Act (CAA) had been passed in the Indian Parliament.

By then, Amit Shah, the union home minister, had already explained multiple times the chronology of how CAA and NRC, working together, would be used to throw out the people he referred to as 'termites'. In effect, any non-Muslim could identify themself as a refugee under the CAA and claim citizenship without the burden of proof, whereas any Muslim who could not produce the necessary documents could be treated as an 'infiltrator' or illegal immigrant via the NRC. Naturally, comparisons were drawn with the Nuremberg laws that turned Jews into non-citizens in Nazi Germany, making it impossible for them to hold jobs, marry, or stay alive for very long.

Two days earlier, on 13 December, students of Jamia Milia Islamia University in Delhi had marched to the Parliament to protest against the law.

I followed the news during coffee breaks in the office and saw how the students were stopped by the Delhi Police. While having dinner with my mother, who was visiting me in Bangalore, I saw videos in which the policemen dragged students by the hair, lobbed tear gas grenades at them, and charged them with batons. The news channels justified the police action by telling us that the students had first thrown stones at the police.

The protests gained more steam over the 14th.

On the 15th, as I welcomed a Sunday morning by waking up suitably late, thousands of students gathered at Jamia to protest against the CAA.

News channels played videos of burning buses on a loop while we had breakfast and insinuated that the student protest had turned violent, culminating in the destruction of public property. In the coming days, this burning of three empty buses would become an important part of the rhetoric, even after senior Delhi Police officials clarified that the acts of vandalism were perpetrated by some local hoodlums who had mixed with the march.

Later that day, the prime minister, made a flippant remark that painted a target on the back of every Muslim student. Those indulging in arson, he said, 'could be identified by their clothes'.

The dog whistling set the stage for policemen to storm the Jamia university campus that same evening. Grainy videos and photographs were already appearing on social media as I read

Kundera that sleepless night. I was too horrified to go through them immediately.

More videos would emerge over the next couple of days.

I have never been too trusting of authority figures, but it still felt unreal to watch men who operate under the motto of Shanti Seva Nyaya (Peace Service Justice) hunt the people they were sworn to protect. In full riot gear, armed with shields and batons, policemen could be seen breaking into the Jamia library and mercilessly beating up students who were, until seconds ago, busy reading and writing.

Some of the policemen destroyed the CCTV cameras, while others hurled tear gas canisters into a reading room. Students who ran out to escape the toxic gas were again hit with batons by those who had smoked them out like mice.

The horrifying visuals were soon everywhere on social media.

My boss at the office, a self-avowed centrist who discouraged political discussions at the lunch table, remarked on the senselessness of a government using all that state power to beat up a bunch of students. They can do anything they want with that kind of a majority in the parliament, he said, and this is what they choose to do.

I could see why his apolitical stance did not survive the situation's sheer absurdity.

This was happening in 2019, in the national capital, at one of the country's best universities. Maybe all our shock indicated was that we had been too privileged to see, until right then, the broken character of our democracy in all its ugliness. Perhaps we still held naive notions about civil discourse and were outraged to see that no such thing existed without permission from the powerful.

It was not just Jamia, of course. Students at Aligarh Muslim University, where I had sat for an engineering entrance exam only a few years ago, were also brutalized by the police on the 15th.

I had been a college student myself only a year ago and to now see students being treated worse than petty criminals felt like a gross violation of the 'normal' state of things. It looked like the dangers that had been manifest until then in the lynching of poor Muslim men were now knocking at our middle-class doors.

More shocking, however, was the realization that most people continued to go on with their lives as if nothing out of the ordinary was happening around them. Videos from Jamia and AMU alternated with ads for biryani in my Instagram stories, and with a single tap of my finger, I could move to videos of a friend from college taking out his new car for a midnight drive.

When I learned that a protest was going to be held in Bangalore, I applied for leave at the office two days in advance.

Here, finally, was something I could actually, physically do about my opinions.

At the time I was sharing an apartment with two of my oldest friends, Pranav and Dev. In addition to the apartment, we also shared a general distrust of the Hindu nationalist government that came to power in 2014. As the anti-CAA protests spread throughout the country, and Shaheen Bagh emerged as their epicentre, we frequently updated each other about new developments and wondered if the country could still put the brakes on its slide toward authoritarianism.

When I heard about the planned protest in our city, I assumed we would be going together. Pranav, however, refused to come. It wouldn't make any difference, he said, and added something about all sides being the same.

I had been friends with the guy for over a decade at the time and some of our most strongly held convictions were formed together at school. His refusal to come, this newfound apoliticism, was all the more personal because of how much we had in common.

It felt like a betrayal.

Curfew was imposed in Bangalore by dinner time and my manager texted me to check if I wanted to withdraw my leave application.

I asked him to let it remain in place. The absurdity of obeying the government to not protest against the government was laughable. We did not laugh; it was not a funny time and Pranav's words had subdued our excitement of finally being able to do something. Dev and I stayed up late into the night discussing if Section 144 was a licence for the police to do as they pleased.

We talked in hushed voices because my mother was sleeping in the next room and I had no intention of telling her about our plans.

▪

While leaving the house at our usual office timings, we told Pranav to keep his phone with him at all times and he assured us that he would be there in case of any emergency. Ramchandra Guha, the historian and public intellectual, had already been detained in the morning, according to a few posts on Instagram, and other protestors were also being harassed.

It seemed prudent to be prepared for emergencies.

Starting from our house in Marathahalli, we passed hordes of commuters. Regular people going to their jobs—just like we went every morning, and would again the next morning. On that road, however, and on that day, these fellow workers appeared alien to me.

Did they not know what was happening in the country or did they simply not care about it? Did they not have Muslim colleagues who would look subdued at the office? What would they talk about during the lunch and chai breaks? How many were Muslims themselves, people too afraid to show up for a cause that might cost them their jobs or more? How many thought their white-collar jobs would be shields enough against the chasm opening up right beneath their feet?

We passed by an Ashoka Pillar on our way. Its four golden lions stood on a tall greyish column. I would have never noticed it on a regular day. Yet on this particular day, the pillar seemed to be a symbol imbued with the promises of our republic. I pulled the bike to the curb for a moment and clicked a picture of the pillar with my phone. Later, I would tell someone that it was probably the first time I felt patriotic as an adult.

The police presence increased visibly near, the designated protest site, and I quickly photographed a policeman as he made a rude hand gesture at us.

I check the picture now.

A short, dark man with a slightly bulging belly. There is a dark green helmet on his head, its buckle hanging loose, and the camouflage print bulletproof vest around his torso has 'POLICE' emblazoned across it in large yellow letters. The khaki uniform under the vest looks like it was ironed carefully. He might look like any other annoyed middle-aged man on the street without these accessories, but with them, he looks menacing.

He looked more so to us when the images of Delhi Police beating up students were still fresh in our heads.

'Bella Ciao', a folk song used by the Italian Resistance against the Fascists during World War II, was quite popular at the time because a Netflix show called *Money Heist* had featured it extensively.

Looking at the policeman, a specific line from the song came unbidden to my mind:

Una mattina mi son alzato
E ho trovato l'invasor

One morning I woke up
and found the invader

I was so lost in my thoughts that Dev had to tap my shoulder a couple of times to get my attention.

He pointed at a couple of BMTC buses right in front of us at the traffic signal. A-4 size sheets of paper stuck on their windows said 'Police CC'.

'They are probably going there to detain the protestors. Might as well close Google Maps,' Dev ventured. I agreed, and we shook our heads, laughing at the absurdity of following the buses to our destination.

We knew that burning vehicles was a staple of protests in our country, so we parked our bike safely and walked a kilometre to the Town Hall.

We saw policemen ushering people into one of the buses, and it drove off just as we mingled with the remaining crowd of protestors. For the next five hours, it felt as if we had crossed over into TV news footage and become 'news' ourselves.

Old women with covered heads raised chants of 'Azaadi!'. Students moved around with laptop bags on their backs and saw the world through their smartphones' cameras. Young men flitted by, brooding and looking very busy. An uncle asked us to let him know if we felt fatigued or just wanted a bottle of juice.

Dev and I regretted not having made a clever poster, but a girl lent us hers and Dev was overjoyed because it featured a line by Faiz Ahmad Faiz, one of his favourite writers.

> Bol ki lab azaad hain tere, bol zubaan ab tak teri hai.
> Speak, for your lips are free. Speak, for your tongue is still your own.

The policemen stayed on the sidelines this whole while and the buses we had trailed behind stood in wait. Dev looked at them thoughtfully while we had lunch at a nearby darshini.

'Do you think the people being taken away are getting criminal records of some kind?' he wondered.

I told him I couldn't say for sure, but considering the government's distaste for dissent, I wouldn't put it past them.

'I think I'll leave if they start putting people into the buses,' Dev said and I agreed that he should do that.

He was planning to get an overseas job at the time and a police record could ruin his prospects. In any case, I could not see what difference it would make whether he protested for five hours or seven.

Our evening was as uneventful as the afternoon, except for a brief period when everyone started sloganeering loudly and the police began to close in. I asked Dev to stand near a getaway street and gave him the bike's key, in case he needed to move away quickly.

We were thinking of Delhi, I suppose, of water cannons and tear gas grenades, batons, and rubber bullets.

Nothing of the sort happened to us. The police appealed to the protestors to calm down and keep the protest peaceful. Sometime later, when people refused to vacate the protest site, a senior police officer sang the national anthem with them to calm everyone down.

By the time we started on the way back to where we had parked the bike, my heart felt lighter than it had the whole week. I may have continued in a hopeful frame of mind if I had not checked Instagram as Dev pulled out the bike. But I did, and learned that a young Muslim protestor had been shot at and killed by the police in Mangalore.

We reached home only a little later than usual.

When I told my mother where we had been, she said that she suspected my sister was also at Shaheen Bagh (her suspicions were correct, but I did not confirm them). We had dinner in the safety of our home and we laughed about how, in typical middle-class fashion, we had been more worried about the bike's safety than our own. Then, we retired to our warm beds while a young man's family mourned him in Mangalore.

As I thought about this man and Pranav's refusal to come with us, my mind kept going back again and again to Nietzsche's final break with humanity. It was the first time I considered apoliticism seriously and did not dismiss it as an easy choice between being a content pig instead of a thinking, feeling human being.

In the coming days, I would have a number of occasions to think more about it.

▪

In early January, less than a fortnight after attending the protest, I was having ice cream with a colleague when a friend from Delhi forwarded me some videos of masked people entering the JNU campus and beating up students.

Only a month ago in Jamia, the police had seen it fit to barge into the university without so much as a warning, but now they waited patiently at JNU's gates for permission to enter the campus. The visuals, like the visuals from December, were horrifying. We were outraged, as we had been before, and again there did not seem to be a lot we could do except share the visuals with more people on social media and hope for them to be outraged as well.

After reaching home, I sent an email to my former batchmates, seniors, and professors at the Indian Institute of Mass Communication.

Maybe I was thinking about the letter that Tomáš wrote for a newspaper in *The Unbearable Lightness of Being*. Critical of communists, the letter leads to an end of the carefree and essentially apolitical existence prized by Tomáš.

As people who had availed themselves of facilities provided by a government institute, I argued in the mail, we owed it to the country to speak truth to the power. I proposed that we write an open letter expressing our views regarding the recent developments (or, regressions) in the country. Well aware of how much is generally achieved by open letters, I ended with a caveat.

> I am not naive enough to believe that our letter or statement would cause the government or anyone else to change their policies. But I think it is much better to do the right thing, as ineffectual as it may be, rather than sitting quietly and waiting for the lights to go out. Also, I'd rather stand on the right (pun unintended) side of history, I hope you would too.
>
> I look forward to your replies and suggestions.

More people than I had expected replied, including the regional director of IIMC Northeast campus and alumni who had left the country years ago. Everyone agreed that it was necessary to do our part, however insignificant it might be in the larger scheme of things. I volunteered to write the letter and we sent it out, once it had been vetted by some of the seniors and faculty members.

The letter was published in *Mid-Day*, *The Wire,* and

BusinessWorld on 9 January, four days after the JNU students were attacked. Despite all our realism, or cynicism, about the ineffectiveness of the gesture, it still felt good to add our voice to those who were paying the cost of dissent.

We were still exchanging updates on where the letter had appeared and congratulating each other on each new appearance when an alumnus sent us a rather aggressive response.

This is what he wrote:

> Get a job man. Enough of this solidarity bullsh**. Why get into a mess which you can't control? These political goons want you to get involved and create chaos. Concentrate on things that affect you directly. Work for your parents, your family, if not, at least think about them.
>
> Don't create propaganda adding people that don't want to get involved. Get to a position and change things, this will not help in any way.

The conversation went silent as everyone read his mail and tried to make sense of it. I imagined the guy gathering up his rage bit by bit every time he read a new message from us over the last couple of days. Finally, he had exploded and sent this a few minutes past midnight after, I assume, a frustrating Thursday at his office.

It felt important to give him a reply, and I wrote to him that while all of us had a job, he seemed to be missing a spine. I was concerned about my parents and family, but I was also worried about what kind of a country the future generations would inherit from us.

Yet, for some reason that I could not immediately understand, his words had managed to rattle me.

The objection he raised about 'adding people that don't want to get involved' was quite hollow, I knew, because we had repeatedly asked the people who were not interested to mute the thread or mark it as spam. He could have done it with a fraction of the effort it took him to type out his response.

His argument for being apolitical, however, sounded familiar to me.

How different were his 'why get into a mess which you can't control' and 'this will not help in any way' from Pranav's 'everyone is the same and it won't make any difference'? And if there was no difference, if this indeed was the position taken by most of the educated, well-earning, socially privileged young people, then what did it reveal about them? What did it reveal about those, like me, who stood around in protests and wrote open letters after office hours from the comfort of their living rooms?

In any case, conversations in the email thread naturally fizzled out in a day or two.

The offended senior did not sound like someone who would be open to changing his convictions. The justification I wrote in my reply to him, I suspect, was meant more for myself than anyone else.

▪

Horrific visuals and reasons for outrage have not been in short supply, if they ever were, since 2019.

Migrant labourers walking thousands of kilometres during the Covid lockdown, farmers sitting in protest for more than a year and dying by the dozen due to harsh weather conditions, the Hathras rape case and the administration's apathy towards the Dalit victim and her family, followed by the persecution of journalists who covered the case.

I could keep going on about it ad infinitum. I have, for a while. All these things, and so much else besides, have kept me awake at night, made up for a large part of conversations with friends, featured extensively on my social media, and shaped my writing.

Through it all, given my predisposition to keep questioning everything, I have asked myself why I engage in political situations that I know I cannot change for the better.

What is the value in 'being political' that opinionated people, such as myself, seem to take for granted? What did I achieve by adding one more body to the crowd of bodies protesting the CAA on 19 December 2019?

Alternatively, those who chose to be apolitical, should they be condemned for their silence?

I have kept coming back to the boy killed in Mangalore on that same day, and I have wondered obsessively about an alternate world in which the policeman who pulled that trigger was posted in Bangalore. What would Dev have told my mother if I had been present in that boy's place? Maybe that is impossible; the policeman could have been targeting only skullcaps, after all, because his villains *could be identified by their clothes.*

Clearly, the cost of being political is widely different for different people.

So, did others also ask themselves these questions, or was this unbearable lightness of doubt only mine to bear?

Guneet Kaur, a thirty-six-year-old video producer who has worked with various marketing agencies and production companies in Delhi remembers the anti-CAA protests almost longingly during our conversation, and calls it 'a time of hope'. She decided to attend the protests after the events of December 2019 because she felt like a critical point had been crossed in the ruling party's anti-Muslim rhetoric when they passed the CAA.

Her grandparents were among the many immigrants who sought refuge in Delhi in 1947 after the partition of India. Ever since she was a toddler, she heard stories about that horrible time and her family's escape from a place where they were no longer considered legal citizens.

It was due to these stories, she told me, that she could imagine how horrible it may be for someone to lose their homes, or be locked out of the country, they have always called their own. Also, when Jamia, her alma mater, was attacked she felt it a personal duty to stand in solidarity with the university and its students.

From late December to early March, Guneet went to Shaheen Bagh whenever she could get away from work.

Wasn't she afraid? I asked her, especially after a man called

Kapil Gujjar opened fire on the protestors in February and BJP leaders like Anurag Thakur and Kapil Mishra bayed for their blood from public platforms.

We were afraid, yes, she admitted, talking in plural perhaps because she was associating herself with the collective identity of the protest, but the overall atmosphere was still that of cheerful resilience. A library came up at the protest site and so many well-known people came to show their solidarity.

Also, for once she experienced kinship among strangers in a city that is not known for its friendliness.

On a particular day when the Delhi administration had shut down and re-routed parts of the Delhi Metro, Guneet could only leave her office after sundown. The cold was bone-crushing and there was a slight drizzle. As she was wondering if it would be better to drop her plans of going to the protest, an autorickshaw with two young women stopped near the metro station's entrance beside her.

They asked her if she was also heading to the protest at India Gate and offered her a lift when she said yes. Both the girls were Delhi University students, Guneet learned, who had followed the protest on Instagram and decided to join.

She also took her father to Shaheen Bagh one sunny afternoon. 'Everyone was so nice to him. They were all like Sardarji please sit here, Sardarji please have some tea, have some food,' she said, and sent me a photograph that shows a smiling, white-bearded Sikh gentleman with a black turban.

One of his hands is around Guneet and the other one holds tea in a paper cup. Father and daughter are both smiling at the camera. Looking at them and the brightly clothed crowd behind them, I can almost imagine the expression of political views as an exercise in community building rather than a face-off with people who dehumanize others by calling them termites, terrorists, anti-nationals, and God knows what else.

Despite the support from friends, family, and perfect strangers, Guneet was aware that many people around her—especially her colleagues—were against the protests.

She often heard them complain about the traffic problems created by protestors who were usually characterized as directionless youngsters misled by sinister figures. She never confronted those with opposite ideological beliefs, however, because, according to her, it would have been pointless to try and find a middle ground during those emotionally charged months.

It was also a pragmatic choice to not enter into political arguments at the workplace, she said, because she didn't want to lose her job as a result.

At home, she was surprised by her brother who maintained an apolitical position back then and continues to do so now. What baffled her the most about the difference in their outlooks is that it exists despite the fact that they have had a nearly identical upbringing and educational background. When she asked him to accompany her to the CAA protests, he told her bluntly that the kind of government that was in power would not roll back a law just because a bunch of people were sitting on a road somewhere.

Maybe he is right, I think, but people who see a law as a matter of life and death for themselves do not have the luxury of cynicism.

Akanksha Kumar, a journalist who has worked all over the country for various news platforms in the last ten years, discovered as much when she covered the protests in places much more dangerous than Bangalore, or even Delhi.

In the badlands of Uttar Pradesh, especially, she saw first-hand the cost of being politically aware for those the state considers disposable.

'Wherever Muslim women chose to sit in protest, it was followed by some kind of violence by the police,' she told me with a tremor in her voice. 'One of the most horrific videos that came from Lucknow at the time was when Sadaf Jafar was doing a Facebook Live and you could see police personnel pulling her hair. It was a pattern in almost every district I visited. I even met lawyers and activists in Lucknow and areas in western UP, like Muzaffarnagar, who were subjected to torture—given electric shocks—and who had their names added to FIRs simply for following up on cases (on behalf of the protestors) with the police.'

I asked Akanksha about the contrasting ways in which different people, even on the same side, experienced the protest.

On the one hand, for instance, you have a young woman going to a site where there's a library, artists coming in to give music performances, and speeches from eminent intellectuals, while on the other hand, you have conventionally uneducated, poor women going up to face UP police personnel who can shoot at them with zero repercussions.

'There was a mix of hope and fear in both cases. Even in cities like Prayagraj or Kanpur, it was always meant to be a peaceful sit-in. There was a schedule for each day and they would also have certain programmes lined up, like a puppet show or a poem recital taking a dig at the government. But what began as a flash of hope, let's say in the form of a library or cultural events, culminated in violence because that violence was orchestrated by the state.

'In Kanpur, for example, there was this particular site chosen for the protest, and like most cases where people chose empty grounds, this particular site was not causing any public inconvenience, so to say. Yet, one day suddenly these women in Kanpur who went to protest found that the ground had been flooded with water and when they approached the local administration and escalated the matter, there was friction which eventually resulted in violence, and the blame for this was conveniently shifted to the protestors.'

She doesn't think that a great number of people can be apolitical during times such as these.

'I remember having this really charged-up conversation with a guy—the kind that Ravish (Ravish Kumar, former NDTV news anchor and Ramon Magsaysay Awardee) calls a "WhatsApp Uncle"—when I was back in my hometown for a break. He was very inquisitive and he was just going after me like 'are you sure these women are sitting there (at the protest) of their own volition and not because someone is behind them?'.

'Now, we must ask ourselves who has injected this thought

into this gentleman's head. He is no longer apolitical, even though he chooses to stay indoors every single day and tracks news only through Hindi news channels and WhatsApp conversations. So, in our time, and especially in our generation, when we are consuming news on social media and YouTube, there could only be a minuscule fraction of people who are apolitical.'

▪

The Cambridge Dictionary describes apoliticism as 'the fact of having no interest in or connection with politics, or no connection with any political party'.

Going by this definition, I agree with Akanksha in that it is incredibly difficult for anyone to be truly apolitical. If someone does manage the parts about 'having no interest' and 'no connection with any political party', it is practically impossible to have 'no connection with politics'.

Even monks and ascetics in the furthest reaches of the Himalaya cannot be apolitical because their chosen way of life, their isolation, requires tacit political permission. Were those in power suddenly to decide that the monks were a bad influence on society, or that they were ruining some delicate ecological balance, the monks would not be able to continue with their lifestyles, and they might need to protest against the state's decisions, thus becoming 'political'.

This is hardly a theoretical point: one of the first and most famous acts of self-immolation as a form of dissent in modern history was, after all, committed in 1963 by Thich Quang Duc, a Vietnamese monk protesting against the persecution of Buddhists by the South Vietnamese government. Similarly, hundreds of Tibetan monks have died by self-immolation over several years to make a political statement against the Chinese occupation of Tibet.

We can apply the same logic to the apoliticism of the most self-absorbed IT employees, housewives, social media influencers, or any other group of people we care to name.

Whether women can drive or not, whether people can get married to who they want, whether someone can go out for drinks post-midnight, or even whether they can wear what they want and get a haircut of their choice are all, eventually, political decisions. For each one of them, we can easily look up a country that places strict impositions on the same.

Once we accept that true apoliticism is an impossibility, we are well-placed to realize that what is commonly called 'apolitical' is merely a decision to be silent.

This silence, in turn, can be apathetic or cynical.

The apathetically silent are generally those for whom not engaging with politics is either advantageous or unimportant.

Men, for example, may not want to be involved in feminist politics because they are the beneficiaries of existing patriarchal structures and policies. Women from lower-income households may not show an interest in campaigns for period leaves or equal salaries in white-collar jobs. Upper-caste people may scoff at the earnestness of those who take part in caste politics. Straight people may consider gay pride parades a waste of time or frivolous activism that distracts from more urgent issues.

My senior from IIMC, with his advice about focussing on work and family, comes across as someone whose silence is born of apathy. He could not comprehend taking any risk, no matter how small, in protesting a law that targets Muslims simply because he is not a Muslim.

The cynically silent, on the other hand, are people who are perfectly capable of looking beyond their self-interest. But, being aware of the world's ugliness and inherent injustice, they do not believe that their actions can make any real improvement to the state of things. They understand that political parties with opposite ideologies often implement the exact same policies because they are equally affected by lobbying and other obscure factors. Nuance, for them, erases all binaries and paints the world in an even grey colour so that it becomes impossible to take a stand, any stand, with moral certitude. Pranav, or Guneet's brother, are examples of the type.

The categories are not mutually exclusive, of course.

Pooja Manikonda, a twenty-seven-year-old software developer from Telangana, freely admits to being apolitical. Her reasoning sounds simple enough: she feels unable and unwilling to deal with the 'negativity' of political issues.

I asked her to clarify what she meant by political issues.

'There are some things which you feel OK talking about, like women's rights or basic human rights. I can talk about them, discuss them, and even spread awareness around me,' she says. 'But there are a few topics which I feel uncomfortable talking about, or you can say scared to talk about. For example, our car driver in my hometown supports a political party that I hate, but I am scared to discuss it in front of him, because somehow I know that I won't change his thoughts no matter what I tell him, and he might hurt me or my family for opposing something that he likes. I feel the same way about religion, caste, and a few other topics. I hate to admit that I act in this cowardly manner.'

I assured her that I am not passing any judgement about bravery and cowardice over what are, unarguably, her personal choices.

To remain distant from what she refers to as 'negativity', Pooja actively avoids watching the news and reading things that deal directly with political or communal matters.

When she does come across something of the sort on social media or in real-world conversations, it can drive her to tears because she feels helpless about changing anything. Sometimes, she tries to understand more about what's happening and tries to share her opinions on her Instagram stories but usually, if she thinks something can depress her she resolutely avoids engaging with it in any way.

A couple of years ago, I would have taken Pooja at her word and considered her position cowardly, or at least obscenely self-centred.

Recently, however, I have started wondering about the righteousness of being political or vocal without seriously considering the case for silence. International conflicts, like the latest one between Israel and Palestine or the Ukraine–Russia war, and our response to them have also forced me to consider alternate perspectives.

It feels incredibly easy now to believe that the world has shrunk to the size of our smartphone screens, especially for Millennials and younger generations. We consume news about global events on the same social media feeds where we get to know more about local issues, say, the anti-CAA protests. Horrifying visuals can reach us not just from Delhi, Hathras, or Manipur, but from anywhere at all in the world.

This has us placed in a unique position.

We are convinced that we need to, and are qualified to, take firm positions on whatever political issues happen to be trending at any given time.

The participation, conveniently enough, comes in ready-made templates based on our existing political and ideological stances. A right-wing person, for instance, is expected to support Russia and Israel just as a left-wing person is expected to root for Ukraine and Palestine.

What does this mean for apoliticism or silence?

When we say that the internet (or social media platforms, in particular) has polarized us, what we really mean to say is that most of us have lost the ability and humility to be silent. Expressing one's opinion or 'take'—repeatedly, loudly, creatively—is now considered virtuous by the people on every political and ideological side.

Not doing so is considered a clear admittance of ignorance and cowardice.

It follows that people of all political sides consider apolitical people a personal affront to themselves. Efforts are always being made to convince or shame them into picking a side.

Slogans comparing Hindus 'who do not wake up even now' with eunuchs are common on right-wing social media pages. Passionate left-wingers, correspondingly, are more than ready to assume that anyone who remains silent on important matters is either a monster or a sub-human lifeform unable to grasp supposedly simple concepts.

Recently, for example, a book reviewer I follow on Instagram shared stories (in the context of the Israel–Palestine conflict) that said things like 'How you react now is how you would have reacted during the Holocaust' and 'Your silence isn't maturity, blissful ignorance or diplomacy. It is a massacre that's right in front of you.'

Meanwhile, barely any thought is spared in wondering why the issues we are so passionate about keep getting replaced by new issues without ever getting resolved.

It's almost like our political reactions now move on an assembly line run by algorithms and the twenty-four-hour news cycle.

If we were indeed committed to taking a stance on every political issue, then how is it that the brutal violence in Manipur becomes a non-issue almost as soon as Hamas attacks Israel? Why do the people who changed their profile pictures when Russia invaded Ukraine suddenly find Ukraine's plight much less important than that of Gaza? Are there metrics—the number of dead babies, for example—based on which we decide what we will care about on a particular day? Why is the Armenia–Azerbaijan crisis not important enough for us when we profess to be such well-informed and well-intentioned citizens of the world? Why is Sudan's civil war not deserving of our time?

Let's keep aside the matter of our algorithm-driven selective attention, and ask ourselves how exactly our voices matter in the specific issues we care about.

In the anti-CAA protest, for instance, we could hope to influence the decision-makers because, despite everything else, they *are* answerable to us as our elected representatives. While the protests ended unceremoniously because of the Covid-19 pandemic, neither CAA nor nationwide NRC has been implemented to this day. Similarly, in the case of the farmers' protest which started in August 2020, and lasted more than a year, the government had to roll back the three contentious farm acts.

Yet, it feels absurd to believe that the Israeli government will stop bombing Gaza based on how people in India feel about the whole thing.

Hypothetically, even if we were able to influence India's official stance on the matter with countrywide protests, why would the decision-makers care? Israel's government does not depend on our country for financial or military aid, after all, and the very recent precedent in Russia's case shows us that decisions about war are not subject to popular opinion.

For our individualism-obsessed generation that has been promised 'empowerment' by way of digital expression, powerlessness can be a bitter pill to swallow. But we *are* indeed powerless to change most political situations in the world, despite how strongly we may feel about them. Statements about the futility of Internet outrage feel clichéd, but they *are* more true than false.

Increasingly, an exception to our powerlessness is being looked for in our purchasing power. It is a logical thing in the capitalist world order that we are encouraged to turn our buying behaviour into a reflection of our ideological beliefs.

Movements like the Palestinian-led BDS (Boycott, Divestment, Sanctions), for example, aim to lead 'targeted consumer boycotts that can convince retailers across the world to stop selling products from companies profiting through Israel's crimes'. Maybe it can have meaningful impact if its suggestions are adopted by people of the world en masse. One can only hope that it works better than the most stringent economic sanctions placed upon Russia by governments around the world to discourage its invasion of Ukraine in 2022.

Also, bear in mind that while raising the issues of our slippery attention and our delusions of influence where none exists, we have assumed that the positions we take are well-informed.

In reality, that may not usually be the case.

The philosopher Michael Huemer, in his paper 'In Praise of Passivity', asserts that the overwhelming majority of people do not know enough about political issues to contribute anything valuable by speaking.

The sheer amount of time and effort needed to learn about

complex political issues makes it nearly impossible for us to be confident in our convictions. Moreover, Huemer points out that most of the time we are 'instrumentally rational'. That is, we make only those choices for which the benefits exceed the costs. Acquisition of practical political knowledge, however, would need careful cultivation of 'epistemic rationality' habits, which, in turn, require the kind of commitment to truth that most of us don't possess. Instead of being confident in our convictions, we will have to doubt them constantly and engage as much as possible with opposite views.

But those who most passionately guilt others about being apolitical are, in Huemer's words, 'chiefly moved, not by a desire for some noble ideal, but by a desire to *perceive themselves as working for* the noble ideal—not, for example, by a desire for justice, but by a desire to see themselves as promoting justice.'

Given the inability to be suitably informed about most issues, all they do when airing their 'strong' or 'unshakeable' opinions is create cacophony in their respective echo chambers.

Some silence, one should think, would be welcome some of the time.

Those who have the humility to accept it could be referred to as the 'realistically silent', distinct from their apathetic and cynical counterparts.

In any case, the arguments for realistic silence are not all-encompassing.

We do know that it is wrong for the police to beat up students in libraries, for militants to butcher people in their homes, for military superpowers to carpet bomb civilians, for narcissistic rulers to live out their dreams of glory by putting millions of lives at risk, for anyone to rape or murder someone.

We do not need any ideology's dogma to tell us that these things are wrong, and under no circumstances can we allow any ideology's dogma to justify them.

Moreover, we are generally better informed about situations

closer to us. There doesn't need to be any embarrassment about it even if other situations are touted as more important on X and similar platforms.

During the anti-CAA protests, for instance, I had my lived experience in India as the basis of my convictions. The intent of our leaders could be estimated from their past actions. I may not understand legal subtleties, but I could still condemn the brutalization of unarmed students. There was nothing that could justify the treatment of protestors by the police in BJP-ruled states such as Uttar Pradesh, or the excesses of power in full display elsewhere in the country.

Even so, I would like to believe that the last few years have made me less self-righteous and more humble.

I have given a fair amount of thought to the way I felt 'betrayed' by Pranav's refusal to join us, or how I felt alienated from the commuters we passed on our way to the protest. Back then, I could not comprehend how people stayed silent on something that I cared about deeply, but I understand now that I knew nothing about their personal lives and risk capacities.

Compared to me, dissenting against CAA was immeasurably more risky for the Muslim boy who died in Mangalore, as it was for the women in Uttar Pradesh, and for Guneet or Akanksha. I do not know if I could have been as brave as they were, and therefore I have no right to judge Pranav's cynicism or Pooja's refusal to be politically aware.

All of us are apolitical on some issues because it is impossible to care meaningfully or practically about all issues. To try the latter would, in fact, mean an existence of 24/7 performative outrage, that no one should expect from anyone else.

12

RUSKIN BOND: YOUNG BOY, OLD AUTHOR

At school, I was the kind of kid who finished reading his English and Hindi textbooks cover to cover a day before the new grade began. At the time in CBSE Board schools, these books used to be thin collections of celebrated short stories and for me they were like boxes of assorted sweets. I made short work of wolfing them down.

Over time I have forgotten many of these stories, but a few still flutter around like butterflies with faded wings in my memory.

A man climbs down the stairs to a railway platform and walks into the past, in one of them. In another one, that could have been a poem I now remember as a story, the narrator tells his tale from inside the belly of a lion who has, somehow, swallowed him whole. There were a couple of O. Henry stories with their fateful twist endings and the one I remember the best among them is 'The Gift of the Magi'.

But why do we forget some stories and remember others forever?

It has a lot to do with the literary merit of the stories, I am sure, but it also depends on a mix of factors quite beyond articulation. At what point in life one reads a story, for example, and what they are thinking while reading it, what they were thinking just before reading it, whether they relate with the story by way of familiarity or curiosity (or both), what was the weather like at the time they were reading it, and was there a particularly memorable song playing in the background while they read?

Quite inarticulable, like I said.

The story from my school years and textbooks I remember the

best, with all its details intact (for example, the word 'sweetmeat', which confused me at the time) is the one about a young boy who is boarding the night train to his school all by himself.

Do you also remember it? Is the title already on the tip of your tongue? No? Well, let me help you.

At the railway station, our boy Arun meets a kindly lady who asks after him, buys him food, and keeps him company until he boards the train. It is a very short story, with less than 2,000 words to it, but the relationship between the woman and Arun is fully realized. It begins when the stranger introduces herself as Arun's mother to one of his classmate's mothers and it concludes as the train starts moving and Arun calls her 'Mother' while saying goodbye.

I remember wondering what Arun's parents were like that they had sent him all alone to take a midnight train. My family would not even send me out of the house after 9 p.m. at the time.

Used to the sugary endings that characterize so much of children's fiction in our country, I also distinctly remember the climax's bittersweet implication that Arun and the woman would never see each other again as 'she was lost in the milling crowd'.

In case you haven't read it or don't remember it yet, the story was Ruskin Bond's 'The Woman on Platform 8'.

I have no way of knowing whether my classmates also found it as incredible as I did. Maybe they didn't (to be fair, I don't remember most of them being too interested in *any* stories), but I still hope that it warmed up their hearts, the way it did mine, at least for the few days our English teacher spent on it. Heartwarming is, in any case, the first word that comes to mind with regards to Ruskin Bond's work and it seems fitting considering that he lives in Landour, Mussoorie's colder 'sister-town' where some extra warmth can only be welcome.

As I huffed and puffed my way from Landour Market to his house, I thought about the man.

I was a little nervous, I must admit, what with the adage about never meeting your heroes, and the fact that there is a sixty-year age gap between us. He belongs to the Silent Generation and I am a Millennial. Sure, we are both writers, but it's kind of like saying that Rolls-Royce Phantom and Maruti Suzuki Alto are both automobiles.

What if the conversation petered out before I could turn it to the many things I wanted to ask him? I worried, and had to remind myself why I had been camping in Mussoorie for over two weeks to try and arrange this conversation when I could have, much more easily, talked to a younger writer.

Part of the reason certainly lay in how familiar and well-loved Ruskin Bond is among the Millennials. He has an unmatched, totemic significance in culture and an association with all things mountains, quaint hill stations, nostalgia-addled memories of childhood, and a wholesome embrace of indulgence (he loves jalebis!). Moreover, the life-decisions that enabled him to become the writer he is, for example the rejection of the nine-to-five grind in favour of full-time writing, moving away from his family in Delhi to live alone in Mussoorie, then adopting a family instead of settling for a more conventional lifestyle, are all things that point to an essentially Millennial worldview. Or at least, to what we try to make of our worldview, and the image of it that we curate on Instagram.

It was with these thoughts that I reached Ivy Cottage after an hour's walk from Mall Road and climbed up its narrow staircase.

Rakesh Bond, Ruskin Bond's son, opened the door. I introduced myself, we shook hands, and he led me to a room right next to the entrance where his father sat in a comfortable chair next to an electric heater.

Here I reproduce excerpts from the conversation that followed.

▪

Ruskin Bond: So, you're writing a non-fiction book?

A. M.: Yeah, I'm writing an essay collection on Millennial culture—

Ruskin Bond: Talk loudly because my hearing is not so good. You can shout at me if you like (laughs).

A. M.: (laughs) Right. I'm sorry. So I was saying that I'm doing these essays on different aspects of culture. Food, religion, films, the way we use technology, things like that, and you are someone whom so many in my generation have read, irrespective of whether they read many books or not, because your work is in the syllabus and it's very easily accessible. Almost everyone I've met in my age group knows something about your writing.

Ruskin Bond: Yes, that's true, that's true. The small kids are reading me very often in school, but also their fathers and grandfathers. Makes me feel very old—but I *am* very old (laughs).

A. M.: But you're a young boy and an old author, as you have said before.

Ruskin Bond: And do you also do something else? A job?

A. M.: From time to time. Whenever the need for money arises I get a job, and then I do it for eight months or a year, and then I have to sit and write again. I'm bad at multitasking.

Ruskin Bond: Well, that's what I did too. I had jobs occasionally, but soon as I could throw them up, I used to. So, your home is in Bangalore?

A. M.: My home is in Haridwar, but I have lived in Bangalore for years now.

Ruskin Bond: Oh, so your college was in Bangalore?

A. M.: My college was in Chennai, and after that, I went to Bangalore. Then to Mizoram for my postgrad, and back to Bangalore once it was done.

Ruskin Bond: Oh, Mizoram. So you've been all over the country?

A. M.: Yeah, but I kept returning to Bangalore like you always returned to Mussoorie. So Bangalore is my Mussoorie.

Ruskin Bond: (chuckles) Bangalore has changed so much, too. I first saw it in 1960 and it was just bungalows. They didn't have any high-rise buildings and there were lots of gardens. I walked all over.

A. M.: Yeah, and on your birthday, I met this couple who had come all the way from Bangalore to see you because they had met you twelve years ago and now they have a son who loves your books so they wanted him to see you too.

Ruskin Bond: Oh. But I am not able to meet everyone. So many tourists nowadays and without warning they're banging on the door or getting inside at all hours of the day. So I usually ask my family members to tell them I'm not here. If they ask, they'll say I'm in Bangalore or Bombay. (Laughs like a mischievous schoolboy)

A. M.: I've seen that. I hang out frequently at Doma's Inn (a hotel and restaurant right beside Ivy Cottage) and every time I am there, some tourists are talking about wanting to meet you.

Ruskin Bond: Hmm. So did you stay there at Doma's last night?

A. M.: No, no. My sister lives here so I stayed with her. Actually, I have been here since your birthday. I didn't get a picture clicked (at the celebration) because I only wanted to observe and I also thought you must be getting tired. Anyway, I was reading your essays and it seems like you wanted to be a writer right from the beginning. Is that right?

Ruskin Bond: Yes, that's true. By the time I'd finished school, I wanted to be a writer. It wasn't as fashionable then as it is now—

A. M.: Even now it's not.

Ruskin Bond: Now every...every youngster is writing a book; self-publishing is a big thing. Young, old, everybody wants to write a book. In those days, nobody did. There was no glamour attached to it because you didn't become a visible person or a public figure. You didn't become like a movie star or a cricketer. Even if you were successful, you were known only by your name. So, you could even pass a famous writer on the street without knowing who he was—

A. M.: Like Graham Greene.

Ruskin Bond: Yes, I mentioned that somewhere.

A. M.: You met him in London, right?

Ruskin Bond: That's right and I didn't know till afterwards that it was Graham Greene. Writers were known for their work and by their name but they didn't become celebrities like they do today. Today, even a writer gets recognized if he gets well-known. I get recognized, and others, I suppose, Shobhaa De and Chetan Bhagat. They are all sorts of visible. In our time, my earlier days, the only writer who was always visible was Ernest Hemingway because he liked publicity. He even crashed a plane once so that he could get into the papers.

A. M.: Maybe he liked that whole glamour thing....

Ruskin Bond: Yes, to be the centre of attention, and writers still do because writers are usually quite egotistic, I think, just like artists or actors.

A. M.: True. So for me, there were a few writers who made me want to be a writer when I was a kid, like J. K. Rowling was one and so were you. For you was there someone like that, someone you read and thought that I also want to do this thing?

Ruskin Bond: Yes, certainly. When I was twelve, I read David Copperfield, complete and unabridged, and sort of identified with young David who as a small boy, runs away from home and from the factory where he was working, and he grows up and becomes a writer. I sort of identified with him to the extent that I even ran away from home for a couple of days. So from a very early age, I used to fill my exercise books with odd things that I wrote, not for publication, of course, but just like that.

By the time I finished school, it was clear in my mind that I wanted to be a writer and a full-time writer, much to the dismay of my mother, you know, who preferred that I should join the army or something. So even before I went off to England, I was writing stories and had published a few in that year when I was sixteen.

In Indian papers and the *Illustrated Weekly of India* and one or two other papers and a magazine that was published from Madras—from Chennai—called *My Magazine of India*. I used to send them all my rejects and they used to publish them and send me five-rupee money orders. I used to keep cuttings and clippings; over the years, so much accumulates and some of them are still lying around.... Most of what I've written has been published over the years and is still in print. Maybe a few odd stories got lost, but it's hard to trace them going back to the 1950s and 1960s. The age of the magazines is gone, I think, for all those literary magazines and family magazines.

But it was all those early stories that I wrote in the 1950s, 1960s, and 1970s that have come into collections and keep getting reprinted now. So I was lucky I had that backlog. Although I keep writing new things, the old ones have stood the test of time. Many of them have, anyway.

A. M.: Yeah, and you mentioned that you didn't like children's writers like Enid Blyton and others?

Ruskin Bond: Not much. I'd read two or three of her books, but I preferred other children's writers. Like Richmal Crompton, who wrote the William books.

A. M.: Oh, William, I love that too.

Ruskin Bond: Yes, because he was a young rebel and I identified with him. He believed school was a bad place and so did I.

A. M.: That's a very delightful series. My mother actually thought that I had gone crazy when I was reading those books because I used to laugh out loud so much.

Ruskin Bond: Yes, so I liked that. Then I liked adventure stories and, well, I was reading adult books too by the time I was twelve or thirteen. So I read all the early Agatha Christies and P. G. Wodehouse and then some Somerset Maugham and J. B. Priestley. Short stories by H. E. Bates influenced me, I think. So many writers of that of that period.

A. M.: Did you read a lot of horror?

Ruskin Bond: I read not so much horror, but ghost stories. I read M. R. James's *Ghost Stories of an Antiquary* and I liked that, and then, of course, I've written a few ghost stories myself too.

A. M.: Yeah, so my first introduction to you was via ghost stories. You had compiled an anthology called *Stories from the Raj* and I got it from my school's library.

Ruskin Bond: Oh, that's right, yes, for Rupa (who published that anthology). So, I've read a lot of ghost stories and written some—but I don't believe in ghosts because I haven't met any. I have only conjured them in my mind.

A. M.: But I like your ghosts. They are very, I should say, comfortable. They don't creep up on you at night and scare you.

Ruskin Bond: Safe fear. Yes, safe fear. I don't care for horror stories much, because they don't actually horrify me. I suppose a certain type of individual might be affected by them. For instance, a lot of people read H. P. Lovecraft because he writes fantasies and dreams, but I find them boring because I mean other people's dreams are always boring. It's only your own dreams that are interesting to you.

A. M.: Yeah, I have never connected with his work; he writes about Elder Gods and things.

Ruskin Bond: Yes, some people love that kind of fantasy or mythology, but it doesn't come to life for me.

A. M.: How about Stephen King, have you read him?

Ruskin Bond: Read him. Yes, well he's quite effective. Especially, some of his shorter work, shorter stories.

A. M.: I was reading one by him last night called 'The Boogeyman'. It was also quite 'effective', as you say.

Ruskin Bond: Yes, but I do prefer a ghost story to a horror story. Ghost stories are a little more intellectual. They don't frighten you.

A. M.: Yeah, that's true. I just was in that kind of a mood last night, so I also read one of yours where this professor meets a boy who has no face, and then the professor runs back to the school but the watchman there also doesn't have a face.

Ruskin Bond: Yes, I've been thinking recently I should continue that story a little further. So when he sees the watchman who has no eyes, no mouth, no face, Mr Oliver gets scared and wonders what his own face looks like. So he runs into his room and puts on the light and looks in the mirror. And there's nothing there! Yes, so I must finish the story now.

A. M.: It's a great campfire story, right? When Mr Oliver goes back to the watchman, that's the moment when someone screams 'Boo!' and you get scared. I sent it to my girlfriend, and she's living alone right now because I'm here, and it scared her.

Ruskin Bond: (laughs)

A. M.: So, you have pets, right?

Ruskin Bond: Yes, I have two cats. They're up on the roof somewhere, fighting. They're not mine, actually. Siddharth, Rakesh's son, my grandson, he brought them. He was living in Bombay and a few months ago he brought a cat, a beautiful Persian, and then later on another one. But they don't get on with each other. The first one resents the second kid.

A. M.: Yes, yes. That's why I only have one cat, back home.

Ruskin Bond: But, you know, it's never easy. I can't keep a dog because we're right on the road. Twice we've had dogs, but they run on the road and cars come in. Both of them were killed by cars. The cats stay in the house, they don't rush off, you know, here and there. They look after themselves better than dogs and I think dogs are more dependent on humans because they need walks and everything constantly.

A. M.: I was reading about the first cat you had, Susie, who used to sit next to your typewriter. Now, I have a cat in Bangalore called Woolf and she does the exact same thing with my laptop. Whenever I am writing at night she'll just sit quietly there behind the laptop. So I don't know, maybe cats are conducive to writing.

Ruskin Bond: (agrees and nods, then asks his son to bring his cats) So have you been to David's office (he is referring to David Davidar, the writer and publisher, who helped set up our conversation)?

A. M.: No, not yet. I met him in Bangalore where he came for a lit fest.

Ruskin Bond: Oh OK. Well, I have not been to a lit fest for three years now, not since Covid started. I used to go to a few, not many. That's another phenomenon that was not there when I started writing through the 1950s, 60s, 70s, and 80s. It is only in the last twenty years that this phenomenon of lit fests has taken root in India. Also, the book launches—every now and then, every week somebody comes here with a book, wants me to hold it up, and be photographed launching it from my room. (laughs)

A. M.: Do you oblige them?

Ruskin Bond: I don't mind, it's all right. But I mean, back in my earlier days of writing, you wrote a book, you found a publisher. If you were lucky he brought it out and sent out a few review copies. Then you would go to the bookshops and see if they were keeping it. But that was it, you didn't have all the marketing which is there now.

A. M.: Marketing is everywhere now.

Ruskin Bond: Everywhere, yes. Last week I had a new book brought out by HarperCollins, and every now and then I'm supposed to give an interview, or see someone, or do a video.

A. M.: Who runs your Instagram? Or other social media pages?

Ruskin Bond: Yes, well, I don't. Siddhartha, my grandson, has put out a couple of posts and there's a Facebook page in my name and all that.

A. M.: Do you ever use these platforms?

Ruskin Bond: No, well I just occasionally say something, but I don't have much to do with them.

A. M.: I was reading something you had written about Donald Trump during the pandemic.

Ruskin Bond: Yes, maybe in that journal I kept. What did I call him? (laughs)

A. M.: It was pretty clear that you really don't like him, but I guess most people don't.

Ruskin Bond: Yes. Well, he is more of a cartoon than an actual person. He's a business tycoon with megalomania, and he might become president again. You never know with the Americans.

A. M.: Oh yes, their elections are coming up.

Ruskin Bond: Yes, he'll probably get the Republican nomination. So he and Biden will have another round and both of them are getting senile. The Chinese will be happy, I think.

A. M.: Have you visited the US?

Ruskin Bond: No, I haven't been to America. I don't wish to go either because I'm not very good with a gun.

A. M.: (laughs) Yeah, same here.

Ruskin Bond: So no, I only went as a boy to England and then Europe.

A. M.: From my generation, a lot of people are excited about going to America. I did my bachelor's in computer science engineering and many of my batchmates have moved there for education and jobs.

Ruskin Bond: Yes, everybody goes to America. It's the first choice usually, and well, from a career point of view it would be advantageous no doubt, but I don't know...so many who do go there and settle, they're not always happy.

I know a boy I helped bring up and he's a doctor in Baltimore. He's been there now for twenty-thirty years, making a good living, but he keeps saying he wants to be back in India, he wants to be back. He can never do that though because he can't give up his profession there and he's got a family. They've got to be sent to college, so he can't escape. He can, at the most, come to India for a week or so.

A. M.: Most of my friends have gone there with education loans, so they have to pay the bank first before they can come back, which is difficult to do without living there for a long while.

Ruskin Bond: Yes, that's terrible. All my life I've never taken a loan. At least I've never had that load sitting on my head of having to pay back money to the bank.

A. M.: If you take a loan, then you have to take a job, and that may be difficult as a writer.

Ruskin Bond: Yes, you'll have to have a job. Then you have to worry about giving it (the loan) back. I have taken jobs when the going has been difficult. When I lived in Delhi in the early 1960s, I worked for CARE for two to three years, actually. Then I finally got fed up with Delhi and said I am going to write full-time in the hills and I threw up a good job. Even in London, I had to take several jobs but they were temporary.

A. M.: So, how was the experience working with CARE?

Ruskin Bond: It was all right, it wasn't bad. Again, working with Americans, one or two were crazy and one or two were nice. We had different directors coming and going, and they were all very different from each other. I had a travelling job for a good deal of the time, especially when the Tibetan refugees came with the Dalai Lama and the refugees. They put me in charge of the Tibetan relief program.

A. M.: That must have been interesting, right?

Ruskin Bond: Yes. So I did a lot of travel and went to every centre where there were Tibetans. Darjeeling, Shimla, Dalhousie, Dharamsala, and Mussoorie. They (the refugees) made a good go of it, I think. I mean, they've done quite well.

A. M.: You know, Kurt Vonnegut also worked with CARE.

Ruskin Bond: Oh, I haven't read him but I know he is a good novelist.

A. M.: He's very funny. I think you will like him. He wrote very short things, generally, not big tomes or anything.

Ruskin Bond: Yes? I think I must try him then because that's why I like William Saroyan. Short and witty. I read a lot, but sometimes just for relaxation, I'll read crime novels or detective stories and I like reading biographies and history too.

A. M.: Are there any new Indian authors that you really like reading?

Ruskin Bond: Umm, no, nobody specific because there are so many now. So many are coming up. So many young writers also. Again, you see, we didn't have publishers in India back in the day until the 70s and 80s, so you had to publish abroad if you were any good. Now things have changed so that there are foreign publishers in India as well as our own publishers like Rupa and all other family firms.

Fortunately, the book trade is quite buoyant at the moment, and that's benefited writers too. More and more writers get published and even sell books fairly well.

A. M.: Well, yeah, but there is a contradiction here, right? That, on one hand, you have lit fests and everything, but then on the other hand, you have this belief that people are reading less now because of our phones or whatever. Do you think this is true or has it always been like that?

Ruskin Bond: People have always been reading less. It's always been a minority, right? I always tell people that when I was at school, and I finished school in 1950, we had a class of about twenty to twenty-five boys. We had a good library. But there were just, I think, two of us in the class, myself and a German boy, who actually read the books that we had to take out from the library. Others also had to take books out because it was the rule, but then they would be put back unread. In those days there was no television, no internet, there was no technology, all the things we blame today. You could go to a cinema once a month and you could read comics. Everyone read comics, but actual book readers were very few.

What's happened is that today in a class of twenty-five to thirty boys or girls if just two are reading, then in terms of numbers that is vast because education has spread so much and the ability to read in English as well as other languages has spread. So even that very small minority in terms of actual numbers is hundreds of thousands, which is why there are publishers, and books are selling.

So, numerically it's increased—the number of readers—although again it's still a very small minority, I know.

I have three grandchildren and they've all got their mobiles and apps. One of them makes an effort to read, she keeps asking me now and then 'Tell me which book I should read' and she does read some of them but the other two don't bother. You can't force them either.

A. M.: Availability is a bit of an issue in India, I guess. Haridwar didn't even have a bookstore while I was growing up, only shops that sold religious books.

Ruskin Bond: I grew up on borrowed books. I couldn't afford books, so I read borrowed books, or just whatever you came across, you know.

A. M.: Have you read that one yet? *Klara and the Sun*. It's right behind you. (Points at a copy of *Klara and the Sun* lying on a shelf behind Mr Bond)

Ruskin Bond: Yes, I read that one. The Japanese–British author. A lot of Japanese authors are also writing crime fiction and detective stories these days. I had some of my stories published in Japan, but they prefer to buy the eBook rights usually, not so much the printed ones. They seem to be more into reading on devices.

A. M.: They buy a lot of manga comics in hard copies I've heard, that's kind of a thing there.

Ruskin Bond: Oh yes? And yet, comics seem to have gone out now, I think, because you can get everything online. Popeye or Blondie or Beetle Bailey or Donald Duck you know. Except graphic novels, which seem to be doing all right.

A. M.: Yeah, but they are really expensive. Must be a small market in India because most of them cost 2,000 rupees or more, which is not what people in India want to pay for reading.

Ruskin Bond: Very expensive, yes. A popular children's books publisher turned one of my stories, 'The Blue Umbrella', into a comic book once, but they forgot to send any royalties. After ten years, I woke up, and Siddharth sent them a notice saying they never sent my royalties. They checked and found they owed me four to five lakhs, so they finally sent it.

A. M.: It was a very profitable forgetfulness.

Ruskin Bond: Yes, sometimes you have to be alert and I have, you know, I've published with about ten publishers over the years. Penguin, Rupa, Aleph, HarperCollins, National Book Trust, Speaking Tiger, Westland, Scholastic, and so on. Maybe two or three books with each, but with Rupa nearly 100 titles, and the same number with Puffin.

A. M.: Woah, that's really something. And among all these publishers, who have been your favourite editors?

Ruskin Bond: Editors are important, yes. Over the years I've had all sorts. My first editor in London, Diana Athill, she was the editor for André Deutsch and a partner in the company, and she was very helpful. She would make suggestions and we had a personal friendship, in fact, to go to the pictures together or the theatre. She lived to be over 100 and died only a year or two back.

A. M.: Yeah, 2017, I think.

Ruskin Bond: In India, we have had good editors and David Davidar has been great. Thinking of when I started writing, the *Illustrated Weekly* was edited by an Irishman called C. R. Mandy. He encouraged me a lot. I never met him, but he would write to me. If he liked this story, he would tell me why. Nowadays editors don't have the time, they don't get into correspondence. Or you know, they won't discuss your work with you. Either they take it or they reject it.

A. M.: That's true. You say that you have been very open to suggestions from your publishers?

Ruskin Bond: Always have been, yes, and I get along well with editors. I might not always do what they tell me, but it is good to always listen, you know.

A. M.: Have there been any absurd suggestions?

Ruskin Bond: Well, I did a small children's book, *The Cherry Tree*, and an American publisher was bringing it out. In my original story, the one that's published here, it's a boy growing the cherry tree. Well, the editor from America wrote and said Mr Bond it's the year of the girl child and the book will sell better if you turned the boy into a girl.

Also when I wrote stories about my grandfather keeping different animals and birds, he kept a cassowary. You won't get a cassowary in India, so I had to have him bring it from Singapore in the story.

A. M.: Is this the grandfather you invented?

Ruskin Bond: Not really. I did have a grandfather who kept animals, but he died when I was only a few months old, and I don't have any recollection of him. Some of the stories, the early ones, were told to me by my mother. So I put myself in them as a boy of six or seven and imagined what my grandfather was like. When the stories became popular, I invented a few more pets and animals for later stories.

A. M.: What about Uncle Ken?

Ruskin Bond: Again, with Uncle Ken, the early stories were actually almost true. But when they became popular and an editor or somebody said give us more Uncle Ken stories, then I invented a few.

A. M.: But they're really fun, those stories about Uncle Ken.

Ruskin Bond: Yes, I think kids like reading about a grown-up who is more stupid than they are, especially when they are at school.

A.M: So, when did you realize that you're really good with

children's books? Was there an epiphany of sorts?

Ruskin Bond: You see some of my early stories, though they were not written specifically for children, but they got into children's magazines, and some of them got into the school curriculum. It was only when I was about forty that I started writing stories specifically aimed at children or young readers, and those were stories like 'The Angry River' and 'The Blue Umbrella'.

A. M.: I know that you struggled a lot with *The Room on the Roof*, but other than that what has been the most difficult thing for you to write?

Ruskin Bond: Other than *The Room on the Roof*? Yes, that was too much difficult, but nothing very difficult after that. Well, maybe I got a little bogged down then in that autobiography, *Lone Fox Dancing*. I slowed down a bit, you know, and took a little time finishing it, but usually with a short story, I have already written it in my head, visualized it. The characters, the dialogue, whatever is going to happen. It's only a question of putting it down in words and sentences. So I don't get writer's block. I think if you start off without a very clear plan, say for a longer work, you might well get bogged down.

A. M.: Which one took you the longest to finish? *The Room on the Roof*?

Ruskin Bond: No, that didn't take long to write, but since I had to do two or three drafts and I had to change the story and rewrite a lot, so it took a long period of time.

A. M.: Many people believe that hard times make for good writers. Do you agree with that?

Ruskin Bond: Difficult times...well, yes. Certainly, I think that a difficult childhood gave me something to write about too because I've written a lot about childhood and growing up, which perhaps I wouldn't have done if it hadn't been at times lonely or difficult for me. Just as we can see for Dickens—as a small boy his father is in jail for debt and his mother sends him to work in a factory where they have to stick labels on bottles when he was about twelve. So all this did, I think, help him (Dickens) identify with children in similar situations in a way and helped him write about children and their problems or difficulties.

A. M.: Yeah, I think about childhood in that context a lot, probably because my father passed away when I was in the 6th standard.

Ruskin Bond: Same with me, yes, when I was about ten.

A. M.: But I have not been able to write about that till now...so, when was the first time you wrote about it, and I mean how did you deal with it in your writing?

Ruskin Bond: Oh, it wasn't easy. I wrote about my father only when I was about forty. Not when I was writing *The Room on the Roof* and all those early stories. Only when I was forty, in one or two stories, and then in that first autobiographical book I wrote, *Scenes from a Writer's Life*, which Penguin published. It covers my life up to the time when *The Room on the Roof* was published and I was twenty.

A. M.: I love your autobiographical works. Generally, it takes me very long to read non-fiction, but I breezed through *Lone Fox Dancing* in just a couple of days, last week.

Ruskin Bond: Well, Ravi Singh, my editor at Speaking Tiger, got me to write it and prodded me to finish it. Recently, David has also suggested I write something again, something about my writing life, which would be of interest to writers. About the early days of writing and publishing, and how the literary scene has changed specifically in India, so we'll see.

A. M.: I hope we'll see it soon. So, since you don't use the internet much, as a Millennial I am curious as to where you get your news these days.

Ruskin Bond: Well, I read a bunch of newspapers (laughs). I get the *Times of India*, *Hindustan Times*, *Indian Express*, and the local paper. So that gives me plenty, in fact, more than the TV channels.

A. M.: Yeah, and TV doesn't have a lot of news these days anyway.

Ruskin Bond: Yes, this gives you more detail and the editorial pages are usually balanced. I watch sports on TV. Football, cricket, anything, and I follow sporting events.

A. M.: Do you think it's possible, especially now, for writers to be apolitical?

Ruskin Bond: Well, I've always just written about human relationships which are very often unaffected by politics because, I mean, most people don't have strong political views. The average person is interested in his bread and butter, and the cost of living, and how to survive.

A. M.: Did you hear about Salman Rushdie getting attacked last year?

Ruskin Bond: Well, for so many years he was well protected by the British, and now everyone thought nothing was going to happen since nothing had happened for thirty years or so. I think they did not take enough precautions because it was an open hall with people moving around. All he (the attacker) had to do was run up to the stage and stab him.

A. M.: Yes, it was quite unfortunate. You have written a lot about the environment, about nature and our relationship with it, right?

Ruskin Bond: Yes, right, I have. More and more over the years.

A. M.: So a lot of people posit that my generation is going to be the last one in which the majority has access to clean air and water. Are you optimistic about humans going forward with respect to the environment, or do you see it all going downwards, pretty much?

Ruskin Bond: Oh it's hard to foresee the future, but well someday some other planet will collide with us, no doubt. (laughs)

A. M.: But there are people who are dreaming of going to other planets and setting up there.

Ruskin Bond: Right, right. Well, they've made a mess over here, they might as well go and make a mess over there.

A. M.: Yeah, and anyway it will be like five or six billionaires who will go there. Not us. We only have the Earth.

Ruskin Bond: They'll take their entourage and then they'll open factories there.

A. M.: Yeah, yeah, but they won't need writers on Mars. Writers are only going to be needed on Earth, I think.

▪

The conversation ended over another cup of tea and Mr Bond asked me to visit him again when I was done with my book.

We were supposed to meet for thirty minutes, but ended up chatting for close to two hours. Needless to say, my misgivings before the conversation had all been for nothing and talking to Ruskin Bond turned out to be as pleasurable as reading him.

And what about that old question—why do we remember some stories and forget others?

Well, perhaps we remember those stories that listen to us even as we are listening to them, and Ruskin Bond has always written such stories. True to his own assertion, he may be an old author but he is still a young boy, eternally curious about the world, never tired of it, always ready to provide the sort of practical hope that goes beyond platitudes and moral preaching.

Everything we talked about, from the state of publishing in India to horror stories, cats, the environment, and apoliticism reassured me about a message that lies at the heart of Ruskin Bond's oeuvre. Millennials like me, who worry constantly about everything under the sun, would do better to remind themselves of it from time to time:

When all the wars are over, a butterfly will still be beautiful.

13

EVERYONE KILLED SUSHANT SINGH RAJPUT

More than 10,000 farmers and agricultural labourers died by suicide in 2020.

Also in 2020, 8,000-odd people died along railway tracks. Many of them were migrants travelling to their native places, hungry and penniless because of a suddenly announced lockdown.

Also in 2020, a Dalit girl was gang-raped in Hathras. She died two weeks later and was cremated by the Uttar Pradesh police without her family's permission. Three years later, three of the four accused were acquitted by a district court.

All these, and many other outrageous news stories, are now dead and forgotten.

Why?

Perhaps because we live in a fast-paced world, because nobody cares about justice, because of the 24-hour news cycle, because people don't like to engage with 'negative issues' on social media, because the youth have better things to care about, like their education, relationships, and careers.

There are the generally offered refrains and they sound perfectly reasonable.

Yet, there is an incident that still lives on in the public imagination and shows no sign of giving way in the near future: the death of actor Sushant Singh Rajput on 14 June 2020.

It is no longer given much attention by political and media personalities, but a good number of people care enough to keep the conversation going—something that we fail to do with almost every other cause. They diligently devote hours upon hours of their time to boost X trends, they create and watch YouTube videos describing each new non-development in the case as if it were a world-shattering event, they litter venomous paragraphs in the comment sections of Instagram posts featuring the people they blame, which can be anyone, everyone.

The conspiracy theory about SSR's death could be *the* conspiracy theory of our time. It shows how a rumour, repeated and boosted by politicians, celebrities, and media personalities can take a life of its own in the digital world, propagating through it like a virus, providing a sick sense of purpose and perverted opportunity to those who buy into it.

For the longest time, I had wondered about them, mostly internet-savvy young men by the look of things, but I would come to learn that for all their insistence on wanting to be heard, conspiracy theorists can be incredibly shy when it comes to one-on-one conversations.

While doomscrolling X late one night, a phrase caught my attention in the list of trending topics and I decided to take a chance by tweeting about it before going to bed.

This is what I wrote:

> SSR is trending again with something called 'Sushant Man Of Value'.
>
> I'm going to write about the unprecedented endurance of this...thing soon. Please connect if you have any useful insights.

I had not expected anyone to respond but the tweet still got decent visibility. It was reposted twenty-seven times by complete strangers, and some of them took the time to comment on it as well. The general tone and intent of these replies can be aptly conveyed by this one from a user called Pankhi:ComeBackSush.

> SSR trends everyday
>
> May be some day up in the list so, many, like you notice; someday little down, needs to scroll down the trendlist
>
> But His fans (who He fondly calls His friends) make

sure to keep this Friendship alive and trend Him everyday
Bcz, Sushant Man Of Value, indeed

Satwaik Sarkar, one of those who replied in the comments, also sent me a direct message with links to some threads about SSR.

Over the next couple of months, I kept a casual eye on the accounts that had engaged with my tweet. Apart from helping me justify the time I spent on X, this helped me keep track of how much time various 'SSR Warriors' were spending on their holy crusade. It opened up my eyes to factions within the community which bickered regularly about who was more committed to the cause and who was in it only for attention. I also saw the well-organized effort that continues to exist despite this factionalism. The manipulation of X (Twitter) algorithms on a regular basis, after all, is a result of this concerted effort and its success rate can put to shame a few professional marketing teams I have worked with.

One of the people I observed to be the most active in this community was Satwaik Sarkar.

He had already taken the initiative of opening up a dialogue, but I knew that a straightforward approach could be risky. In the Warriors' communication, I had observed a general distrust of journalists, 'liberals', and anyone else they deemed to be sceptical of their beliefs. Instead of jumping the gun, therefore, I engaged with Satwaik in subtle ways. A like here, a comment there. Little things to assure him that my interest in SSR was genuine.

Generally, he responded in kind.

Once I felt confident enough—a few weeks after our first interaction—I messaged him. Reiterating the fact that I was writing an essay about SSR, I asked Satwaik if he would be willing to talk to me.

He responded within minutes and asked me to connect with him after 6 p.m. the next day.

My reminder rang at 5.57 the following evening and I messaged Satwaik on Twitter. 'Are you free?' I asked. 'Not now,' he replied and postponed the call to 9 p.m. At 9 p.m., I messaged him again.

He said, 'Sorry today i cant.'

When I asked him if it would be possible the next day, he said that we could text on Twitter itself because his 'schedule is busy'.

I suggested that instead of using Google Meet, as we had planned earlier, we could get on a simple phone call if that was more convenient for him. I also asked him more questions about himself—what he worked at, where was he living—things that might establish a personal rapport. I told him that 'for my essay, I need the perspective of an actual SSR fan, rather than that of journalists who covered the case'.

He went offline for a few minutes and then sent a flurry of messages:

> Yeah i can
> will share all things
> ok lets shedule tomorrow i will join
> Time will tell you tomorrow

I shared my WhatsApp number with him and told him to message me at his convenience. Later that night, he again sent me the first Twitter thread he had shared with me and I assured him that I would check it out before our call.

Satwaik strung me along for two more days during which my girlfriend teased me about being 'ghosted' and I wondered if it would be better to start nurturing a few other leads on Twitter. I told Satwaik that my deadline was in two days and a few articles I was reading had confused me about the whole thing. Specifically, I mentioned an article that had profiled Nilotpal Mrinal, a key player in the 'Justice for SSR' movement, because I knew it had rattled many SSR Justice Warriors.

Like most groups that believe themselves to be marginalized and oppressed, there is a strong urge among conspiracy theorists to set the record straight. I hoped Satwaik would give in to that urge.

He told me that he was ready to talk as soon as the Twitter Space event he was attending wrapped up. He shared the link with me as well.

I joined the Space and listened to a Warrior, who went by the handle @itshsk015, expand upon the comparative advantages of retweeting and replying to make something trend higher on Twitter. He finished a few minutes later with a pep talk asking the attendees to do their absolute best on the 14th of each month so that people don't forget the date's significance (SSR died on 14 June).

I exited the Space once it went silent and texted Satwaik. The message remained undelivered and my call went unanswered. Then, about fifteen minutes later, the phone rang.

Satwaik had finally made up his mind about talking to me.

▪

There is nothing altogether novel about people taking an outsized interest in the death of a celebrity. Especially, when the celebrity happens to be young, and the death unnatural.

But some things set apart Sushant Singh Rajput's case.

Timing is important, of course.

By June 2020, the country had already been under the Covid-19 lockdown for about three months. That is an incredibly long time for people to stay cooped up, and the lockdown would continue for months after SSR's death on 14 June.

I was living alone at the time and I remember how all the days felt like Xerox copies of each other. Life revolved around a routine of cooking, eating, writing, drinking, and sleeping. It was impossible not to feel paranoid as we sanitized our hands dozens of times a day, rinsed the groceries and Amazon's parcels with urgency, and tried not to be worried all the time about family and friends living elsewhere.

We may also gauge the peculiarly disturbing nature of this particular time by considering that 3.17 lakh people died by suicide in 2020–21. In fact, the year 2021 has the dubious distinction of the highest recorded suicide rate since the beginning of this century.

To make matters worse, a 360-degree post-truth bubble formed around many of us during this time. Confined to our homes, we were completely dependent on the media to stay in touch with reality.

The screens of our TVs, phones, and laptops became our only windows into the outside world.

The flow of wishful facts and rumours was already thriving on social media and messaging apps by 2020, but its consumers as well as producers had more time on their hands. Our confirmation bias could flourish unrestrained. Similarly, by then TV news channels had already dropped all pretence of operating within journalistic principles or caring about the objective truth, but now they had a wider, more willing audience hungry for distractions from the world's bleak reality.

Anyone who could take advantage of the situation did.

In their study 'Anatomy of a Rumour: Social Media and the Suicide of Sushant Singh Rajput', researchers (Syeda Zainab Akbar, Ankur Sharma, Himani Negi, Anmol Panda, and Joyojeet Pal) analysed data from platforms like Twitter and YouTube as well as traditional news media channels to conclude that journalists, politicians, and influencers were key in shifting the narrative. The word 'suicide', for instance, was used the most in the first week after SSR's death, but its appearance in the discourse sharply declined as the 'murder' theory was endorsed by influential personalities.

Politicians from various parties weighed in on the issue in a bid to score petty points over their rivals and appease the electorate. Those associated with the BJP were twice as vocal (61,196 tweets) as those with the INC (32,406 tweets), their closest rival. Among news anchors, Arnab Goswami led the charge and his name became the second most used term besides 'Sushant Singh' and 'suicide'.

It also helped that the controversy's contours fit neatly into the narratives used for political polarization since at least 2014.

The story of SSR as the outsider-underdog struggling against elite benefactors of nepotism in an exclusionary film industry was not so different from that of Prime Minister Modi championing the cause of common men against Lutyens' Delhi or the Khan

Market Gang. Aditya Thackeray, son of Shiv Sena supremo Uddhav Thackeray and a minister in the Maharashtra government, became a stand-in for Rahul Gandhi and was relentlessly targeted by the media and internet trolls. In a nod to 'Pappu', he even got an infantilizing nickname of his own: Baby Penguin.

A uniquely dismal time, a climate of misinformation, and strong feelings of anti-elitism in the country's conservative majority made for a heady cocktail.

Some of us are still partaking.

■

On the phone, Satwaik's voice was at odds with his rather strongly worded tweets and messages. He talked slowly, as if he were labouring at every word, and his volume dropped so low at times that I had to repeatedly ask him to speak louder.

As soon as we were done with the pleasantries, he asked me if I had gone through the Twitter thread he shared. I assured him that I had given it a thorough reading.

The thread he was talking about is a compilation of his various other threads.

The first one is called 'Achievements of @itsSSR in life'. It contains pictures of Sushant Singh Rajput's telescope, an award called 'Techy Celeb of the Year 2018', a boarding pass for a future Mars Mission, and a moon crater named after him.

Another thread, called 'Books of #SushantSinghRajput' is, predictably enough, a compilation of SSR's books, gathered painstakingly from his posts on different social media platforms. Yet another contains all the publicly available photographs of the actor's house in Mumbai, including one of a doorway with the legend 'Cogito Ergo Sum' painted over it.

There are about thirty such sub-threads listed in the original one and each of them has dozens of its own branch-offs. Some, like award compilations, books, or apartment pictures, suggest garden-variety fan-worshipping but others are stranger.

For instance, there is one called 'Cryptic T Shirt of Sushant' with photographs of various t-shirts that the late actor wore at different times.

In another, called 'Handwritten note of @itsSSR', a Twitter user writes that 'he (SSR) was openly telling us that AI, exponential technologies will be 100 times more catastrophic in future. But very few people read "between the lines", for rest it was just an insta post'.

It took Satwaik a month to compile the entire thread and a lot of effort went into trawling the internet for titbits about SSR, he told me proudly. Teenage fans of boy bands and starlets may be expected to invest that kind of time and effort, but it sits oddly on a final-year biotech student who would soon need to worry about his job prospects.

I asked him when he had become such a dedicated fan and he told me that as a school kid he used to watch *Pavitra Rishta* (a soap opera in which SSR acted as the male lead) with his mother, and that's how long he has 'known' SSR.

But he didn't watch most of the actor's movies until after June 2020.

His college had shut down at the time and online classes were yet to begin. The news about SSR came as a shock to the entire family and no one could have dinner properly that evening, he remembered. Initially, he had believed it to be a suicide but the media reports changed his mind. When I ask him if he remembers any media reports in particular that 'opened his eyes', as he puts it, he says that he can't recall clearly but knows that it was the coverage by *Times Now* that first made him aware about the possibility of a conspiracy around SSR's death.

Are you a big fan of movies, I asked, and Satwaik demurred with a low chuckle. When I probed further, he said he doesn't watch movies because he doesn't have the time. What about the time spent on Twitter? He ignored the question when I repeated it.

The last Bollywood movie he watched was *Dil Bechaara* which also happens to be SSR's last film, released posthumously. He considered watching *Kashmir Files* but did not eventually because he doesn't like the things Vivek Agnihotri says on Twitter.

What about Hollywood? Yes, he still watches 'English' films. Which one did he watch recently? *Avengers* Part 2, he said, referring to a movie that released in 2015. What was his favourite SSR film? He took a long pause and I wondered if he was trying to remember the names of a few movies.

Chhichhore? I suggested. No, no my favourite is *Dhoni*, he said.

For someone who has not watched a movie in a long time, and very few movies even before that, Satwaik seemed strangely sure about the fact that SSR was the best actor in the Hindi film industry. The threat he posed to the careers of many superstars may have played a part in the conspiracy against SSR, according to him.

What is his particular take on SSR's death? I asked him after circling the subject for a fair bit of time.

What can I say, bro? It's pretty clear to everyone that she did it.

Rhea? I clarified and Satwaik confirmed. He was referring to SSR's ex-girlfriend, who was vilified by the entirety of our TV news media for months and interrogated by three central agencies—NCB, CBI, and ED—besides the Mumbai Police. She was eventually let off the hook because there was no evidence linking her to any conspiracy and the news cycle had moved on by then.

But how did she get away with it then, even after getting arrested? I asked Satwaik.

She was just a 'small fish', bro. There are a lot of people involved. Big and powerful people. *Everyone* got him killed, then covered it up.

Satwaik's voice was a whisper when he talked about these 'big and powerful people', almost as if he imagined someone listening in on our conversation. When I pressed him about who he thinks is at the heart of the conspiracy, he started talking about suspicious suicides in the South Indian film industry. Are these connected to SSR's death? I asked him, knowing what his answer would be, and he repeated the favourite slogan of conspiracy theorists everywhere: everything is connected.

But still, if he could name some names, who would he hold responsible for the injustice against which he and the other SSR Justice Warriors are fighting?

He mentions two people who were among the media's favourite punching bags in 2020: veteran film director Mahesh Bhatt and Aditya Thackeray.

Does he have any solid reasons to believe that they are guilty? Satwaik drops his voice so low as to be almost inaudible and tells me that he has 'all the proof'. Before ending the call, I asked him if he might consider sharing this proof with me and he assured me that he definitely would.

A few hours after our call, Satwaik sent me the link to a Google Drive folder. By his own admission, he spent months compiling this repository of 'proofs'.

▪

Samiksha, a psychotherapist who runs her practice in Noida, remembers that a lot of people, including some of her patients, were badly triggered by the news of SSR's death.

'Most people were at home and not able to meet any other people (at the time). The news was all they could see to connect with the outside world. They were consuming a lot of social media, but that was also showing similar content. So, they were acutely affected. They were feeling depressed and negative, and some of them went to the extent that they reached out for (therapy) sessions because they were panicking or feeling that anxious due to this news.'

Like Satwaik, Samiksha also recalls a distinct point when the media began reporting that there may be something more to the tragic incident than suicide.

'Initial conversations were focussing on mental health issues and the importance of staying in touch with loved ones during the lockdown,' she said, 'but the whole thing about murder and drugs derailed all that.'

I told Samiksha about Satwaik and the amount of time he has

spent—and continues to spend daily—on this case and asked her if there is a particular kind of person who would be attracted to conspiracy theories like these.

'There are certainly many indications of obsessive behaviour,' she said. 'This boy (Satwaik) looks at Sushant as a hero and when someone says that he was depressed and he may have died by suicide then that feels wrong because how can his hero be depressed? Loneliness due to an inactive social life or an emotionally distant family can also drive people into such theories.'

She also explained that entertaining the possibility of mental health issues during the pandemic would have been difficult for people who were trying their best to ignore issues of their own.

Believing outlandish claims of SSR's Bengali girlfriend controlling him with 'black' magic or siphoning money off of him after making him a drug addict seems much more comfortable, in comparison. It didn't hurt, of course, that such theories supported misogynist tropes loved by a large part of our society, and their discussion provided sleazy entertainment on news channels.

Samiksha also pointed out that on a basic level, murder, as a concept, is easier for us to accept than suicide.

'When we get to know that someone has killed themselves, it's like the person gave up on their life and everything in it. It's an extremely sad thing to accept for anyone, and especially for those who may be experiencing loneliness or a lack of direction and prospects in their own life.'

Suicide is self-annihilation. An internal kill switch of sorts that anyone can consider flipping off. Murder, on the other hand, has external causation and it is out of the victim's control. Understandably enough, in addition to the grief that accompanies any death, suicide also engenders despair towards life.

To avoid this existential despair, some people may embrace disbelief or alternative explanations against the fact of suicide itself.

For example, consider this anonymous comment on an article reporting the Mumbai Police's assertion that no evidence of abetment to suicide was found against Rhea Chakraborty.

> A jolly good natured human being, a celebrity at that, suddenly commits suicide and the police says 'nothing suspicious'...i believe that our mumbai police is one of the best but it is under some pressure to either cover-up something or protect someone

Like Satwaik, the commentator here assumes that he knew the actor (a jolly good natured human being and a celebrity) from his on-screen personas, public interactions, and social media platforms. As Samiksha theorized, this imaginary SSR just cannot give up on life or even have mental health issues, because to do so would be a betrayal of everything—money, fame, intelligence, etc.—that he represents for his fans.

It explains why even perfectly rational and otherwise logical people were so ready to be credulous about the speculations floating around in the second half of 2020.

At this point, however, the incident is more than three years in the past.

The world has nearly returned to pre-pandemic conditions. Educational institutes and offices are demanding physical attendance and there are scores of things that have been deemed more important by TV news anchors. Celebrities and politicians who were all so vocal—or rabid, rather—regarding 'justice' for SSR have also moved on to other ways of grabbing headlines.

For young people like Satwaik Sarkar, however, Sushant Singh Rajput's death still remains the most important thing to have happened to them.

■

Even as news anchors outshone each other in being vicious and absurd, a few journalists were rooting for truth amidst media trials and political games.

Nidhi Suresh was one of them and in September 2020 she interacted with several young men involved with the #JusticeforSSR campaign. I asked her to share her experiences with the people she had profiled in a report called 'Inside the online cult of #JusticeforSSR'. An engineering student from Faridabad, a YouTuber, and a member of the Karni Sena (a far-right Hindu organization based out of Rajasthan) featured prominently in it.

'The sense I got from my research was that for everyone who attached themselves to the "cause", it was more about them than the cause itself,' she told me during our conversation. 'There were very personal motivations that propagated this whole phenomenon.'

As an example, she pointed out Saahil Choudhary, a YouTuber who wanted to be an actor or a model.

Choudhary had already tried his luck in Mumbai and could not quite understand why he had been unable to make it despite taking dance training and being good-looking (by his own estimation). The only explanation he could accept was a lack of contacts in the film industry. When SSR died, it confirmed this idea for him.

SSR was one of the few who had made it big in Bollywood without prior connections in the industry, after all, and now there were reports that this ideal 'outsider' had been killed by his ex at the behest of shadowy 'insiders'. The unfairness of it was personal for Choudhary. It made him angry and motivated him to embark on a crusade for justice.

It also gave him a way to boost his fledgling career.

When things did not work out for him in Bollywood, Choudhary had returned home to become a gym instructor. He also began making YouTube videos on the side and experimented with different kinds of content such as cooking videos and gym training videos. None of this did much for his aspirations of becoming a YouTuber until he started making videos about Sushant Singh Rajput, some of which have garnered millions of views by now.

Dheeraj Singh, an engineering student, was a much more interesting character, according to Nidhi Suresh.

As an administrator of a Facebook group called 'Justice for Sushant Singh Rajput', Dheeraj got some female attention for the first time when the controversy ballooned up.

'He kept coming back to that and it stood out because even in our conversation he didn't want to hang up,' Nidhi Suresh said. 'He just wanted to keep talking about different things. In between, he said things like how nobody in his family talked to him and he felt alone. Basically, he had just started this Facebook group that became huge and then he wanted to keep feeling important.'

Dheeraj was largely unconcerned about his career prospects.

'He didn't really come across as someone who was particularly interested in what he was studying. He was bored, he was lonely, and he wanted some attention from women. Beyond that most of his conversation was about how women have become like this like that.'

Nidhi Suresh found Surjeet Singh Rathore, the Karni Sena member, to be much less forthcoming than Choudhary and Dheeraj. His investment in the conspiracy theory had its roots in the rather simple motives of gaining political and ideological mileage.

All three men, she realized, were less interested in discussing SSR's death than in discussing how men were at a disadvantage in a world where women had been empowered by feminism. They were more inclined to talk about Rhea Chakraborty because they could project their own failed relationships onto her and indict all the women they didn't like in one fell swoop.

Is there any way to reach out to these men through the fog of petty opportunism, social apathy, and misinformation that surrounds them, I wondered while thinking about them and Satwaik.

Nidhi sent the published article to all three men. Two of them did not respond and she doubts if they ever read it.

Dheeraj, who did read it, was expectedly upset at seeing his unsparing portrayal in the article. He said his words had been taken out of context and asked if he could change certain quotes. When Nidhi explained to him that editing the article would not be possible unless there were some factual errors or he had been misquoted somewhere, Dheeraj was unable to understand.

Eventually, it became clear that he wanted to prolong the

conversations to keep talking to a woman for as long as possible, and Nidhi stopped engaging with him.

▪

Material motivations like Saahil Choudhary's YouTube channel and Surjeet's ideological career are certainly common among many SSR Warriors.

This is Trickle-Down Theory for the post-truth reality.

In the New India, politicians, news anchors, and celebrities sit at the top of the misinformation pyramid, but there is no dearth of those willing to follow their lead at the grassroot level. There is no reason for restraint: if the bigwigs are banking on wild conspiracy theories to gain success and popularity, why shouldn't the common man?

In her 2018 book *Dreamers: How Young Indians Are Changing the World*, Snigdha Poonam captures this perfectly while profiling a Radio Jockey who hosts a programme that is '40% information and 60% entertainment'. He explains his guiding principle to her: 'Take. Take is the most important. You have to take 90-degree news and spin it 360-degree.'

'Shanky (the RJ) doesn't offer his audience—nearly a million listeners—news,' Poonam writes, 'but the emotions with which to react to it: pride, relief, shame, outrage.'

In principle, Saahil Choudhary's YouTube channel on which he uploaded videos discussing Rhea Chakraborty's dating life is not very different from the news channels broadcasting her pictures in swimsuits and sportswear during panel discussions. Both present their unique 'takes' without much care for facts.

Surjeet's political aspirations are also fundamentally similar to those of political leaders who twist and turn the truth for electoral advantage on a routine basis.

Further motivations lie in the Indian youth's desperate need for a sense of identity and purpose.

Millions of young Indians, raised on the promise of bright futures with comfortable jobs, have been getting frustrated with the job market for quite a while now. They have reason to be. According to a 2018 report by the National Statistical Office (NSO), the unemployment rate was the highest among young urban jobseekers. In 2019, just 20 per cent of employed people were under thirty years of age.

At the same time, their personal lives cannot be expected to provide them much respite.

Without job prospects, they carry little value in the transactional set-up of arranged marriages. Dating apps, insofar as they have penetrated the non-metropolitan market, are also fiercely competitive—recent estimates put the male-female ratio at 1:10 on Tinder, the oldest and most popular of these platforms.

While talking to Satwaik, and getting to know about people like Dheeraj, it is possible to discern bitter resentment against socio-economic gatekeeping. They feel that for some incomprehensible reason, they have been denied access to the good things they were entitled to in life, whether it's money, respect, or companionship. There is a lot of frustration and anxiety because they can see—even if they can't admit it to themselves just yet—how bleak their future looks. Much is wrong with the world, that is clear to everyone, but they cannot suddenly start questioning the blind faith they have placed in their political leaders (the BJP is by far the most popular party among Millennials in India) and the society.

When the conspiracy theories about SSR's death came along, they moulded together all this anxiety, frustration, and resentment into self-righteous activism. It became a way to indulge in much-needed escapism, provided them with an identity ('Justice Warriors'), and a community of others who shared that identity.

Organizing Tweet-storms every day with his peers gives Satwaik the same kind of fulfilment that someone else his age may get after pulling off a particularly difficult project at work. The dopamine hit is the same, after all, even if the former has become invested in his beliefs to the point of being delusional.

The folder Satwaik shared with me contains heaps of evidence about SSR's murder, according to him. In reality, it's half a gigabyte worth of screenshots from the case's news coverage and images downloaded from the social media handles of various celebrities.

One of the most incriminating pieces of 'evidence' is a picture posted by Mahesh Bhatt on his Instagram handle.

I stared at it nonplussed when Satwaik pointed it out to me and I asked him to explain what he meant. The picture shows a Mickey Mouse figurine lying down on a street. It looks like a bomb exploded on the street sometime before the picture was taken.

'The leg,' Satwaik said, 'it's bent.'

Indeed, one of Mickey Mouse's legs is bent at an odd angle. 'I see it yes, but so what?' I asked, genuinely wondering if I had missed something.

'Just like legs of SSR,' Satwaik explained.

I did not ask him where and when SSR had been lying with his legs bent unnaturally, or why—everything else aside—does he think that Mahesh Bhatt would leave cryptic clues about his (imagined) crimes on public platforms where bright young minds like Satwaik's could pick on them. To ask these, or any other questions, I felt would be to indulge him in fantasies that could hardly be good for him.

Our communication winded down after that, though Satwaik asked me how the book was coming along a few times on Twitter.

The last time we talked, he told me he was working as an editor of the Bangla desk at a recently started news portal. The site is headed by one Sai Ram, who has a picture of Arnab Goswami as the banner of his Twitter profile and holds the dubious honour of appearing on one of Republic TV's panel discussions. I wished Satwaik the best of luck with his future in journalism, or whatever passes for it in our times.

There is a toxic cyclicity at work here that is as absurd as it is terrifying.

The more we slide towards precarity, it appears, the more inclined we are to put stock in conspiracy theories. The more we do that, the less likely we are to care about the things that could actually take us out of our precarity. Similarly, the young men who call themselves SSR Justice Warriors can abuse Rhea Chakraborty all they want, and trade as many misogynist tropes as they can, but it can hardly be expected to make them more attractive to women. It is a zero-sum game, a dead end, but it remains to be seen for how long it will still go on.

14

THAT'S SO CRINGE!

Amit, a senior software developer from Chandauli (a small district in Uttar Pradesh) who currently lives in Bangalore and works from home for a US based company, usually spends his work breaks watching YouTube Shorts.

The 'Shorts' are fifteen- to sixty-second-long videos presented to Amit in an Infinite Scroll feed, a web-designing technique that delivers exactly what it sounds like, i.e., 'as the user scrolls down a page, more content automatically and continuously loads at the bottom'. Amit can scroll his way to eternity without running out of videos. So, what are these short videos about? About anything, really. Most popular YouTube channels, from news outlets to entertainment companies, now create Shorts from snippets of their longer videos, but more than anything else it's 'cringe content' that Amit likes to watch during his breaks, he said. 'It's quick and funny. I don't really want to commit to a good movie or show during weekdays.'

He thought for a couple of minutes when I asked him why cringe felt so funny to him. 'It's a bit like watching Mr Bean, you know?' he said, referring to the TV show, a staple of Millennial childhoods, that showed the eponymous protagonist make a fool of himself as he went through the motions of daily life.

So, what is cringe? That's easier to wonder than answer.

According to the Oxford English Language Dictionary definition, cringe is something that causes 'feelings of acute embarrassment or awkwardness'. Kate Ryan, writing for the *New York Times*, says that 'cringe is not any one thing, but you know it when you see it'. Vox describes it as 'a shortened form of "cringey," which itself is a shortened form of "cringeworthy", referring to the embarrassment (often the second-hand kind) of witnessing something that is awkward, uncomfortable, passé, or cliché'. As should be apparent from these definitions, recognizing something as cringe is highly subjective. I may cringe, for example, when I see a popular YouTuber talk earnestly about black magic and yetis in his podcasts, or when I encounter fellow Indians trying to be cool by using words like 'nigga' or 'y'all'. Someone else may do so when they see a couple from Patna dancing with abandon.

This subjectivity makes it difficult to ascertain exactly how much entertainment we derive from cringe content. Some statistics are available, however, to help us form an estimate.

For instance, as of 2023, the time average Indians spend on social media was more than four times of what they spend on OTT apps like Netflix and Amazon Prime. Among these social media users, as many as 250 million are users of short-form video (SFV) platforms such as Reels, Shorts, Moj, etc., and 98 per cent of daily mobile video engagement is taken up by Millennials and Gen Z. Before TikTok was banned by the government of India in June 2020, our country of 1.3 billion people had already spent 5.5 billion hours on the app in 2019. While we may not talk about the Reels and Shorts we watch the same way we talk about attending a popular concert or going out to a movie, it is clear that in the last few years our idea of entertaining ourselves has come to mean watching under-a-minute videos on our smartphones. They fit most neatly in the grooves of our 24/7 work lives, they do not ask for active engagement, and nobody ever runs out of new videos to watch. For many of us, like Amit, it's how we end and begin a typical day.

What makes this particular form of entertainment unique is the blurred line between creators and consumers. Most of what we consume is created by people just as amateur as us, which means that it is nowhere as professional or polished as the fare usually served on-screen. Some amount of embarrassment and contempt is to be expected.

Not that SFV platforms, or even the internet, have a monopoly on cringe entertainment, of course.

Bollywood has always delivered a steady supply of the same with its attempts at fantasy (*Aabra Ka Daabra*, an attempt to tap into the magic-school genre, or *Jaani Dushman*, a 2002 supernatural-thriller), sex-comedies (the Masti franchise which began in 2004 and may continue long after the last Millennial is dead of natural causes), hypermasculine cop-dramas (*Sooryavanshi*, *Singham*, et al.), not to forget the filmographies of great actors like Himesh Reshammiya, KRK, and many others. Other fields of art such as music (a fedora tip to Himesh Reshammiya again, and to various songs from the 80s) and writing are also not far behind. Then, of course, reality shows like *Roadies* and *Big Boss* have been around for decades and continue to dish out cringe to their audiences season after season.

But the internet culture with its constantly shifting definitions of cool and uncool, as well as the general tone of mockery is perfectly suited to things being recognized as cringe. It provides entertainment and the ability to comment on it at the same place—how could anyone resist, especially when the comment will also be visible to everyone and able to get 'likes' just like the content itself?

One might even go so far as to say that the popularity of SFV platforms has led to the democratization of cringe: why should only the wealthy filmmakers and television executives be able to inflict their terrible self-expression on us, huh?

But the image of Millennials in R&R, scrolling their infinite feeds to play videos that they purportedly find embarrassing or contemptuous, while others produce more and more of that content, brings us to the central question:

What is the appeal of cringe content for our generation, and what does that appeal imply?

▪

When Amit compares his favourite shorts with *Mr Bean*, he is referring to the element of schadenfreude that's common between them.

The pleasure derived from the misery of others was also a major part of the appeal in many Charlie Chaplin movies, as it was in the Tom and Jerry cartoon show where we chortled as the cat persistently went through unfortunate (and often very painful) situations in its pursuit of the mouse. Yet, even if judged under present-day internet sensibilities, would anyone refer to Mr Bean, Charlie Chaplin, or Tom and Jerry, as cringe? Seems hard to believe, and it tells us that schadenfreude—which is as commonplace as the small chuckle that escapes us when we see someone stumble—can only be a part of why cringe content appeals to us.

When I asked people around me why they watch the Instagram Reels and YouTube Shorts they share with friends with disclaimers like 'I watched it, so you must watch it too', their answers were mostly variations on the theme that they engage with such content just to 'see that type of people'. Implicit in this explanation is an other-ing of a particular 'type' of people, which makes sense because identifying something as cringe is essentially an act of gatekeeping. By laughing at people whose antics we call cringe, we want to reassure ourselves and others that we are better than those people, that we fit in within the aesthetics of what is considered cool or, at least, normal on the internet.

According to Natalie Wynn, an award-winning YouTuber and cultural critic, what makes cringe irresistible to us is the combination of schadenfreude and a boost in our self-esteem. When we see someone act with a lack of self-awareness (regardless of whether this is intentional or not) we feel repulsed, i.e., we cringe, because we imagine ourselves in their shoes for a moment. We laugh at them and keep going back to watch them, because we want to treat ourselves to the comfortable realization that there is someone worse, more embarrassing than us, out there.

The self-validating voyeurism of cringe has its own categories, its own language.

'Nibba-Nibbi' videos, for example, are videos of teenage

couples whose public displays of affection are deemed too sappy and immature, their subjects are trolled and often asked to finish their homework before making promises of everlasting love. A 'lolcow' is someone who can be milked for laughs or LOL moments. Their content can be shared, dissected, and then reposted to make fun of it. 'Humilitainment' or 'hatewatching' are terms used to describe the act of seeking entertainment in content that shows, or hints at the possibility of, someone's humiliation and which you already know you will despise. Certain types of videos—things like bad lip-syncs, skits in rural settings, or experimental recipes—are also broadly considered to be cringe mines.

Evidence of our fascination with such content for entertainment is also apparent in the immense popularity of cringe-reaction videos.

YouTubers like Nischay Malhan (21.4 million subscribers on YouTube) get millions upon millions of views on videos in which they 'roast' cringe content creators after having mined social media to find the most awkward videos possible. His videos with titles like 'TikTok Try Not To Laugh/Cringe Challenge vs My Sister' and 'These Viral Jokers Need to Be Stopped!!!' have 52 million and 41 million views respectively. A compilation video he released on Valentine's Day in 2024 was titled 'So Much Nibba Nibbi Love will Make You Jealous (Valentines Roast)' and had gained more than 6 million views by 8 March, which just so happens to be the day when he was awarded a National Creators Award by Prime Minister Modi himself.

Most reaction videos, like Malhan's, are juvenile jeering and rants pretending to be more clever and better than the objects of their ridicule. They are the online equivalent of schoolyard bullying, and the millions who watch them take pleasure in caustic humour. It may or may not be true elsewhere in the world, but it is easy to observe in our country that the identification and consumption of cringe is undeniably associated with punching down in the established social hierarchy.

To understand this better, I talked to Yashraj Sharma, an FPA

London awardee journalist, who met several content creators and consumers from rural and semi-urban areas in the aftermath of TikTok's demise and Instagram Reels' rise in 2021.

'This idea or trend of sharing so much of so-called cringe content has really grown in the last few years,' he said. A big reason behind our obsession, Sharma reckons, is that calling some content—generally the stuff produced on cheaper phones, without an awareness of the acceptable aesthetics or etiquette on social media platforms—cringe is our reaction to the light that this content shines on the caste-class divide around us.

For example, one can consider the reels of a vlogger called Raja that went viral across SFV platforms in early 2024. The complete lack of self-awareness with which Raja had documented each and every ceremony of his wedding made the videos instantly identifiable as cringe. The unplastered walls of his house, the haldi ceremony where he sits topless with a bulging belly, or the songs he chose for his lip-syncing were a world apart from the plush wedding videos with well-choreographed dance performances and pre-wedding shoots that people generally share on Instagram. The comment sections under Raja's reels are full of people trolling him and his family, the mildest of these call him poor, jobless, and ugly. To be relatable to us, the oh-so-better viewers, even brands like Tinder India have left comments like 'arranged marriage is scary, what if he—' on his videos. Evidently, there is something about the videos made by the guy that makes us recoil even as we can't get enough of him. It is as if we are shocked that people from Samastipur, Bihar, can do something other than being quietly poor, that they can also take joy in getting married and sharing the event on social media. We express our shock through laughter and we want to share it with as many like-minded people as possible.

An easy way to ascertain whether something has been identified as cringe entertainment or not is to compare the number of likes it has with the number of times it has been shared, according to Sharma. If the latter is higher, it generally means that people took more pleasure in laughing at it with their friends than in watching it.

While interacting with former TikTok stars like Savitri and Sanatan Mahto from rural Jharkhand, Sharma realized that it is the entire ecosystem of platforms, consumers, and creators that reinforces existing social divisions.

It is no coincidence that TikTok was the platform that brought 'cringe culture' to the fore because unlike Instagram and YouTube the majority of TikTok's creators were from villages and Tier III cities. With fourteen regional languages available to them on the platform, TikTokers could set the aesthetic however they wanted, and it worked for them: at the time TikTok was banned in India, four out of the world's fifteen highest-paid TikTokers were Indian. In contrast, when Reels was launched in India it carried the baggage of Instagram's aspirational aesthetic with it. The TikTokers, expectedly found it difficult to make the transition, with Sanatan Mahto telling Sharma 'I'm not able to connect with the songs in the trends on Instagram. Samaj hi nahi aata hai (I cannot understand it).' It is precisely this inability to connect, or fit, on their end of the camera, that looks so cringey from our end of the screen.

Incidentally, a look at the search and usage of the terms 'cringe' and 'cringey' via Google Trends (in India) and Ngram (globally) reveals a definite rise starting in 2016, the year when TikTok mobile app launched in India. Web searching for 'cringe' peaked in May 2020, a month before the ban in TikTok was announced, and has remained higher than March 2020 ever since. Similar trends are available from YouTube search data.

▪

Savitri from Ongole, a small city in Andhra Pradesh, is twenty-nine and has 2,363 followers on her public Instagram account, where she regularly posts new reels. The videos feature her lip-syncing to trending songs or film dialogues, spending time with her husband and kids, and using various beauty products and accessories. Her 'acting' videos, according to her, are more successful than her dance videos.

Based on my personal experience with the internet, it was apparent to me that on any given day social media could turn its collective gaze on her account, deem her a cringeworthy lolcow, and bestow upon her the curse-boon of virality. At the time of our conversation, her best-performing reels were getting 20,000 to 30,000 views, which is not great by Indian standards, but also not altogether bad considering that she started taking it seriously only a year ago. Eventually, Savitri hopes to turn her content creation into a full-time career, and while she doesn't have any paid partnerships yet, she has done a few 'barter deals' in which she received free beauty products as the payment for featuring them in her videos.

'My goal was to become popular and who don't want money, first preference is popularity then next money,' she said while talking to me about her aspirations. And what about her 'haters', or people who might leave discouraging comments on her content?

Well, she doesn't care. 'I don't have any haters right now, but if I have I simply ignore them. I like acting so I will make good acting videos as a content creator.'

Savitri doesn't know what 'cringe' means and she had never encountered the term until I asked her about it. When I showed her the viral wedding Reels from Raja's account, she was a bit taken aback, and asked me 'is this account comes under comedy?' Despite not understanding Hindi very well, and not sticking to the Instagram aesthetic herself, it was clear that she found Raja's content contemptible. I told her to check out his massive follower count and asked her if she might ever consider making similar content to get more followers.

'No I won't do that type reels if I also get many followers,' she said, 'I don't like if people make fun on me, I will do only decent comedy reels.'

Only time will tell whether 'decent' comedy reels bring her the success she needs to make them her full-time profession.

Meanwhile, businesses have also observed where we go for our regular bite-sized doses of entertainment and what we watch there. From the Google-KPMG 2021 and Redseer reports, for example, it is known that 60 per cent short-video format users are from Tier II cities, and in 2020 over 95 per cent of video consumption on Meta, Instagram, and YouTube was in the local language, with 75 percent of all Indians browsing the internet in Hindi, Bengali, and Marathi. According to Redseer, the short-video app economy is expected to generate sales of as much as $19 billion by 2030.

The so-called cringe creators and their content would definitely get part of the pie, which is probably why a lot of intentional cringe has been flooding social media lately. It's ridiculous get-ups, strange moral lessons, and inedible food galore for everyone and its most fanatic naysayers are probably being served the largest portions by social media algorithms.

Funnily enough, as Millennials slowly age out of internet dominance, various traits of our generation are being identified as cringeworthy by the younger folks out there.

A popular example of our supposedly embarrassing online behaviour is the 'Millennial pause', i.e., the moment we take before speaking in a video recording. Mentions of Millennials and 'cringiness' actually saw a 119 per cent increase between November 2022 and October 2023, according to Meltwater. There is even a TikTok trend in the US called Millennial Core dedicated to making fun of Millennial clichès and cultural mainstays like *F.R.I.E.N.D.S* and Harry Potter. It can only be so long until we import the trend to India.

I am sure there is an opportunity for an earnest take in this ironical twist of cringe culture, but I will refrain from expressing it because—you guessed it—'takes' are so clearly cringe in 2024!

EPILOGUE

While working on this book, I have wondered several times if I was being too hard on my generation. Especially when they have already been stereotyped as Starbucks-sipping, sanctimony-spouting, spiritually-confused yuppies in so much of popular culture. In the end, though, I like to believe that in most cases I was able to take a balanced view, even though our times make it difficult to resist the cynical pleasure of occasional doomsaying.

To our credit, I do believe that Millennials really did want to make the world a better place. More than any previous generation, perhaps.

From climate change to wage equity, body-image issues, sexual liberty, and much else, we have shaped important conversations in significant ways. Courtesy of the internet and social media, we have been connected with people and ideas that would have remained invisible to us in a previous era. The anti-elitism that characterizes so much of what we consider cool or uncool is also a result of the righteous-rebellion vibe that marked our moral and ethical value systems growing up. That we have suffered sometimes from tunnel vision in our attempts to bring about meaningful change, that the internet's evolution was taken over completely by a handful of businesses, or that our anti-elitism devolved quickly into widespread anti-intellectual sentiments is unfortunate, but it is not entirely our fault. We exist, after all, within systems that are fully understood by just about no one. Our individualism may have led us to overestimate our impact and importance in the world, but that's more naivete than idiocy or malice.

As we inch slowly towards our thirties and forties, it is to be expected that the world's problems will start appearing less important to us than our back aches, home loans, and ageing parents. We may find ourselves more invested in the homework of our kids than the hottest ideological battle on X. Marketing departments, politicians, and media outlets too will gradually shift their focus to younger generations and we will have to get used to not being the centre of attention. It happened to every generation; it will happen to us.

Meanwhile, the social, financial, and ideological divides within our generation appear set to grow only deeper with time.

Luxury apartments in Gurugram sell within days of launch and millions languish without any prospect of upward economic mobility as India goes through a time of 'jobless growth'. Caste-based crimes rise while X trends call for abolishing affirmative action in education. Precarity becomes so acceptable to us that elections are increasingly won on promises of freebies rather than new jobs and development. Who is to blame? It's either the government or the Mughals, depending on who you ask.

Soothsaying has been a dangerous vocation historically, and predicting what our generation, or the world at large, will look like in five years or ten seems downright impossible. By the time you read this, the 2024 General Elections will already be over with significant participation (or lack thereof) from the Millennials. The BJP would either be on the way to its third term in power, a decade of its rule validated by the electorate, or not. Dramatic inferences aside, the results of this election would clearly inform us about the priorities of our peers and those who come to power will decide much about the religions we practise, the language we speak, the food we eat, the movies we watch, the way we protest, the things we write, and the people we can love.

What about Gen Z, our successors to the limelight?

Well, it's too early to judge, but since they are the first 'digital-native' generation, we have reason to expect that in time they will come to use the internet with more responsibility than we ever could. Already, there are signs that they are not as enamoured by digital technology as we were. As information technology permeates deeper into the country, different ideas of India that exist parallel to each other may also find ways to bridge their divide. On the other hand, Gen Z will have to grapple first-hand with the far-reaching consequences of AI development, data privacy, and the regulations that are brought in to control these two, especially in their work lives. For all issues concerning religion, social reform, and ideology where we Millennials found ourselves with a foot each in both the twentieth and twenty-first century, Gen Z may take firm stances for better or worse.

In any case, however, one can always hope from them what one hopes from any generation on the cusp of adulthood: that they will do better than those who came before.

ACKNOWLEDGEMENTS

Keeping up with writers is not easy, to say the least, and I'm grateful to everyone who believed in me, lived with me, and supported me as a friend from the beginning of this book, until its publication.

I owe special thanks to Simran, who has been right beside me for most of the craziness with her incredible support, and to my family that cheered my life choices even when they looked like recipes for certain disaster. As far as mothers are concerned, I won the jackpot, and my sisters gave me a moral compass when none of us understood much about the world. I am also thankful to Devender with whom I first imagined that we would be writers one day; to Harsha, Aakash, and Akhil for always championing my work; Prakhar, Praphul, and Vasanth for consistently believing me to be a much better writer than I am; Husain for being up to celebrate even the smallest of my achievements; and Neha for being the most accommodating boss-friend-mentor that any writer can hope for in their day job.

I am indebted to everyone who agreed to talk to me about the subjects I took up and answered my questions patiently.

The publication of this book also owes a great deal to Aienla Ozukum, my editor at Aleph, who trusted the essays and gave invaluable inputs leading to their final form.

NOTES

WHO ARE THE MILLENNIALS, REALLY?

xii **Well, because generational shifts are 'very real':** Malcom Harris, *Kids These Days: Human Capital and the Making of Millennials*, New York: Little, Brown and Company, 2017, p. 3.

xiii **Most Millennials were between the ages of 5 and 20:** Michael Dimock, 'Defining generations: Where Millennials end and Generation Z begins', *Pew Research Centre*, 17 January 2019.

xiv **The 2008 financial crash left many people disillusioned:** 'Mobile data price in India among cheapest. Where it is less costly than India?', *Live Mint*, 28 July 2022.

xiv **As award-winning author and generational workforce expert:** Tammy Erickson, 'Generational Differences Between India and the U.S.', *Harvard Business Review*, 1 March 2009.

xvii **I love going to McDonald and ordering hamburger and snacks:** sunandashyam65, Post, Mouthshut.com, available at www.mouthshut.com/product-reviews/McDonalds-Ranipur-Haridwar-reviews-925891680.

xix **Consider, for instance, that a majority (about 70 per cent):** Divya Bhati, 'Nearly 70 percent of young Indians wish to work for tech companies despite thousands losing job this year', *India Today*, 21 December 2022.

xix **(10 per cent, according to some estimates) of engineering graduates:** 'Why only 10% of 15 lakh engineers graduating this fiscal year', *Times of India*, 20 December 2023.

xix **The majority of American Millennials hold liberal positions:** 'The Generation Gap in American Politics', *Pew Research Org*, 1 March 2018, available at ww.pewresearch.org/politics/2018/03/01/the-generation-gap-in-american-politics.

xix **and right-wing leaders generally depend on older generations:** Ibid.

xix **In India, on the other hand, right-wing Hindu nationalism:** Nikita Kwatra and Pramit Bhattacharya, 'Which party has the millennial vote in India?', *Mint*, 1 May 2019.; Vivan Marwaha, 'Viewpoint: Why India's millennials support PM Narendra Modi', *BBC*, 4 October 2021.

xx **As Snigdha Poonam wrote in her book:** Snigdha Poonam, *Dreamers: How Young Indians Are Changing Their World*, New Delhi: Viking, 2018, pp. 19–20.

xx **'86 per cent of them have been found to feel anxious':** Ibid.

THE BODIES OF MILLENNIAL MEN

1 **A few months ago, I had given up on formal shirts:** Elaine Pope and Larry Charles, 'The Fix-Up', Sienfieldscripts.com, available atseinfeldscripts.com/TheFixUp.html.

2 **I also know that the fitness-wellness industry:** Global Wellness Institute, 'The Global Wellness Economy Stands at $4.4 Trillion Amidst the Disruptions of COVID-19; Is Forecast to Reach $7 Trillion by 2025', Hospitality.net, 25 January 2022.

3 **According to Baas, these trends finally boiled over:** Michiel Bass, 'The three Khan films that started Indian middle-class men's love for abs, pecs and biceps', *The Print*, 15 September 2020.

9 **Essentially, it means ensuring that 70 per cent of the total calories:** Dawn MacKeen, 'What Is the Keto Diet and Does It Work?', *New York Times*, 2 January 2020.

9 **The Keto diet, the latest in the long tradition of fad diets:** 'History of the Keto Diet', Keto-Mojo.com, 23 March 2021, available at keto-mojo.com/article/history-of-the-keto-diet.

9 **Big money is involved, of course, with some estimates:** M. Shahbandeh, 'Ketogenic diet food market value worldwide in 2022 and 2028', Statista.com, 8 August 2023, available at www.statista.com/statistics/1051384/ketogenic-diet-market-value-global.

10–11 **As Samantha Irby said in an interview:** David Marchese, 'Samantha Irby Says It's OK to Hate Your Body', *New York Time Magazine*, 17 June 2023.

11 **In sixteenth-century Europe, for instance:** Christophe Forth, 'The Lucrative Black Market in Human Fat', *The Atlantic*, 26 May 2019.

11 **You could also buy candles and soaps made with human fat.:** Ibid.

11 **The market for human fat (called 'axungia hominis'):** Ibid.

12 **The Germans were accused of doing so with the corpses:** 'First world war "corpse factory" propaganda revealed', *The Guardian*, 26 October 2015.

12 **Come World War II and the Nazis too were accused:** 'Nuremberg Trial Proceedings Vol. 7 Sixty-second Day', Avalon.law.yale.edu, available at avalon.law.yale.edu/imt/02-19-46.asp.

12 **As recently as 2009, a gang was arrested in Peru:** 'Peru's Police Say Gang Drained Victims' Fat', *New York Times*, 19 November 2009.

12 **Two of the suspects, according to a report:** Ibid.

12 **While the story was later contradicted:** Rory Carroll, 'Peruvian officials express doubt over alleged fat smuggling gang', *The Guardian*, 1 December 2009.

12 **The phenomenologist Aurel Kolnai can be of help:** Aurel Kolnai, *On Disgust*, Barry Smith and Carolyn Korsmeyer (eds.), Chicago: Open Court, 2003, p. 61–62.

13 **Fat, itself, according to Kolnai is a reminder:** Ibid., p. 45.

13 **In his incredibly insightful paper 'Fat and Disgust':** Christopher Forth, 'Fat and Disgust, or, the Problem of "Life in the Wrong Place"', USA: University of Kansas, p. 48.

14 **'Do not judge':** 'Mathew 7:1–2', Bible.com, www.bible.com/bible/111/MAT.7.1-2.NIV.

15 **The anti-obesity gold rush has just begun:** Tressie McMillan Cottom, 'Ozempic Can't Fix What Our Culture Has Broken', *New York Times*, 9 October 2023.

15 **Now, we know how easy it is to get prescriptions:** Chaiti Narula, 'Weight loss drugs making waves: All about Ozempic, Wegovy, and Mounjaro', *India Today*, 18 July 2023.

18 **A 2019 *Reuters* report estimates that 42 million litres:** Simon Scarr, Weiyi Cai, Vinod Kumar and Alasdair Pal, 'The race to save the river Ganges', *Reuters*, 18 January 2019.

18 **Each place it passes through gives the Ganga:** Ibid.

18 **We generally find it difficult to visualize exorbitant statistics:** Ibid.

19 **The Modi government launched the Namami Gange Programme:** 'Namami Gange Programme', Nmcg.nic.in, available at nmcg.nic.in/NamamiGanga.aspx.

19 **Uma Bharati, of Babri Masjid demolition fame, was chosen:** Manraj Grewal Sharma and Dipankar Ghose, 'Meticulously planned, Uma Bharti took onus: Justice Liberhan on Babri Masjid demolition', *Indian Express*, 2 October 2020.

19 **However, when she stepped down from the position in 2017:** Sunetra Choudhury, 'Uma Bharti, Rajiv Rudy Among 3 Who Quit, Cabinet Rejig Likely Tomorrow', *NDTV*, 1 September 2018.

19 **only a fraction of the ₹20,000 crores:** Vishwa Mohan, 'Only 13 of 145 Ganga projects completed under Namami Gange', *Times of India*, 4 April 2017.

19 **They also leak diesel into the waters:** 'GAIL sanctions ₹21cr for replacing motorboat engines', *Times of India*, 28 January 2021.

19 **and the noise produced by their engines:** Shreya Dasgupta, 'Ganga has become so noisy that river dolphins are struggling to talk to each other', *Scroll.in*, 20 November 2019.

20 **The water my companions drank had a 22000 MPN/100ML:** Kenneth John, 'Bacterial pollution in Ganga highest in Kanpur, Varanasi: Report', *Hindustan Times*, 28 May 2019.

20 **The permissible limit is 50 MPN/100ML for drinking water:** Ibid.

20 **500 MPN/100ML for bathing.:** Ibid.

21 **Air Quality Index (AQI) had been above 450:** Nushaiba Iqbal, 'Explained: What Does An Air Quality Index Of 450 Mean?', Indiaspend.com, 10 November 2022.

21 **The main contributor to this air pollution:** Damini Solanki, 'Why Delhi Air Worsens During Winters?', *News18*, 24 October 2022.

22 **So it goes, as Vonnegut said:** Kurt Vonnegut, *Slaughterhouse-Five, or, The Children's Crusade: A Duty-Dance with Death*, New York: Dial Press Trade, 2005, p. 8.

22 **On one hand, there are various reports:** Fred de Sam Lazaro and Sarah Clune Hartman, 'India's effort to clean up sacred but polluted Ganga River', *PBS*, 11 February 2020.

22 **the United Nations put 'Namami Gange':** Yagya Sharma, 'UN ranks 'Namami Gange' among Top 10 World Restoration Flagship programmes', *Hindustan Times*, 17 December 2022.

22 **Various media outlets reported Yogi Adityanath's pronouncement:** 'Ganga clean now, thanks to Namami Gange: UP CM', *Indian Express*, 9 January 2023.

22 **in its December 2022 report to the National Green Tribunal:** 'Report of the Oversight Committee, NGT, U. P. Lucknow', Greentribunal.gov.in., available at greentribunal.gov.in/sites/default/files/news_updates/.pdf.

24 **In the case of earbuds, their need and demand:** William Gallagher, 'Apple launched AirPods seven years ago, and changed the world again', Appleinsider.com, 7 September 2023.

24 **It looks profitable to do so:** 'Airpods Revenue Vs. Top Tech Companies', AcumenFinancial.co.uk, 20 December 2021, available www.acumenfinancial.co.uk/advice/airpods-revenue-vs-top-tech-companies.

24 **Most earbuds come with irreplaceable batteries:** Evan Noronha, 'AirPods Teardown', iFixit.com, 20 December 2016, available at www.ifixit.com/Teardown/AirPods+Teardown/75578.

24 **Since batteries in most units begin to show a decline:** Andrew Kirkcaldy, 'AirPods Pro battery life info – and how to extend it', Pcguide.com, 8 September 2023, available at www.pcguide.com/headset/airpods-pro-battery-life.

24 **Gold used in electronic circuits, for example, is taken out:** Seyed Roham Razavian Tabari and Erfan Salahinejad, 'Selective recovery of gold and silver from electronic wastes through a sequential process of Qalkari and room-temperature hydrometallurgy', *Journal of Environmental Management*, Vol. 351, 2024, available at doi.org/10.1016/j.jenvman.2023.119778.

25 **Only 20 per cent of the world's electronic waste:** 'UN report: Time to seize opportunity, tackle challenge of e-waste', UNEP.org, available at www.unep.org/news-and-stories/press-release/un-report-time-seize-opportunity-tackle-challenge-e-waste.

25 **YouTube's annual CO_2 emissions are the same as that of a city:** Mark Sweeney, 'Streaming's dirty secret: how viewing Netflix top 10 creates vast quantity of CO2', *The Guardian*, 29 October 2021.

25 **Watching a month of Netflix's top 10 global TV hits:** Ibid.

25 **'I'm not saying we don't need to care about it':** Ibid.

26 **Most of the world's cobalt, for example, comes:** Kara Norton, 'Cobalt powers our lives. What is it—and why is it so controversial?', *National Geographic*, 21 December 2023.

27 **Various studies suggest that millennials are more aware:** '2023 Gen Z and Millennial Survey', www2.deloitte.com, available at www2.deloitte.com/in/en/pages/about-deloitte/articles/deloitte-india-2023-gen-z-and-millennial-survey.html.

27 **In a 2021 survey of 10,000 young people:** Caroline Hickman, Elizabeth Marks, Panu Pikhala, Susan Clayton, et al., 'Climate Anxiety in Children and Young People and their Beliefs About Government Responses to Climate Change: A Global Survey', *Lancet Planet Health*, Vol. 5., No. 12, December 2021, available at www.thelancet.com/journals/lanplh/article/PIIS2542-5196(21)00278-3/fulltext.

28 **Kirana store owners who use polythene bags:** Karen McVeigh, 'Coca-Cola, Pepsi and Nestlé named top plastic polluters for third year in a row', *The Guardian*, 7 December 2020.

29 **Well, according to Oxfam International, a billionaire emits:** 'A billionaire emits a million times more greenhouse gases than the average person', press release, Oxfam.org, 7 November 2022, available at www.oxfam.org/en/press-releases/billionaire-emits-million-times-more-greenhouse-gases-average-person.

29 **No problem, because H&M has got a 'sustainable' range:** 'H&M launches new sustainability concept with the debut collection science story', press release, About.hm.com, available at about.hm.com/news/general-news-2021/h-m-launches-new-sustainability-concept-with-the-debut-collectio.html.

29 **No worries because Burger King and McDonald's:** 'McDonald's plant burger

launch late to vegan party', *BBC*, 9 September 2021.

Only, if it's from Oatly, remember that one of their investors: Edward Helmore, 'Activists sour on Oatly vegan milk after stake sold to Trump-linked Blackstone', *The Guardian*, 2 September 2020.

29 **the US President who did not even believe that climate change is real:** Justin Worland, 'Donald Trump Called Climate Change a Hoax. Now He's Awkwardly Boasting About Fighting It', *TIME*, 8 July 2019.

29 **It can be a letdown for many people to know:** Rebecca Solnit, 'Big oil coined 'carbon footprints' to blame us for their greed. Keep them on the hook', *The Guardian*, 23 August 2021.

29–30 **If that sounds like a familiar name:** Mark Kaufman, 'The Carbon Footprint Sham', *Mashable SE Asia*, available at sea.mashable.com/science/11514/the-carbon-footprint-sham.

30 **The calculator and the campaign around it encouraged people to measure:** Ibid.

30 **It is easy to manipulate us into looking at ourselves:** Dr Paul Griffin, 'The Carbon Majors Database CDP Carbon Majors Report 2017', United Kingdom: Climate Accountability Institute, 2017, available at cdn.cdp.net/cdp-production/cms/reports/documents/000/002/327/original/Carbon-Majors-Report-2017.pdf?1501833772.

31 **When a study talks about how we can all start using Kindle:** Joe Hutsko, 'Are E-Readers Greener Than Books?', *New York Times*, 31 August 2019.

31 **Amazon's CO_2 emissions grew by as much as 18 per cent:** Annie Palmer, 'Amazon emissions increased 18% last year as Covid drove online shopping surge', *CNN*, 1 August 2022.

31 **Until we hold our elected representatives accountable:** Kenneth John, 'Bacterial pollution in Ganga highest in Kanpur, Varanasi', *Hindustan Times*, 28 May 2019.

32 **'WE PROBABLY COULD HAVE SAVED OURSELVES':** Kurt Vonnegut, *Fates Worse Than Death: An Autobiographical Collage of the 1980s*, New York: G. P. Putnam and Sons, 2005, p. 116.

ABOUT *THE KASHMIR FILES*

34 **Doodh mangoge toh kheer denge, Kashmir mangoge:** Tinnu Verma, *Ma Tujhe Salaam*, 2002, 2 hr., 42 min.

35 ***Dil Se* (1998) informed me that militants had their own stories:** 'Kashmir "mass rape" survivors fight for justice', *BBC*, 7 October 2017.

37 **References to a 'new India' that is more proactive:** Namrata Joshi, 'Uri: The Surgical Strike' review: Triumph of the Will', *The Hindu*, 11 January 2019.

37 **the film's release only a few months before the 2019 general elections:** 'Uri director Aditya Dhar on why the film released before the general elections', *Hindustan Times*, 11 January 2019.

37 **the lapping up of government endorsements:** Milana Rao, '"The Kashmir Files", "Uri: The Surgical Strike", "Dangal": Films that received government's support', *Times of India*, 22 March 2022.

38 **The former was commissioned by Adolf Hitler:** 'Leni Riefenstahl's "Triumph of the Will"', Museums.nuernberg.de, available at museums.nuernberg.de/documentation-center/nazi-party-rallies/triumph-of-the-will.

38 **and the latter was a retelling of the US Civil War:** '100 Years Later, What's The Legacy Of "Birth Of A Nation"?', *NPR*, 8 February 2015.

38 **Both these 'well-made' movies have long ago been exposed:** Susan Sontag, 'Fascinating Fascism', in Susan Sontag, *Under the Sign of Saturn*, New York: Vintage Books, 1981, pp. 73–109.

38 **In any case, while *URI* may be a little shy:** Jeffrey Gettleman, Kai Schultz, Suhasini Raj, and Hari Kumar, 'Under Modi, a Hindu Nationalist Surge Has Further Divided India', *New York Times*, 11 April 2019.

38 **It has enjoyed immense success at the box office:** Aman Wadhwa, 'Made in ₹20 crore, this film earned ₹340 crore, won two National Film Awards, led to multiple controversies', *DNA India*, 21 April 2024.

39 **a tax-free run in most BJP-ruled states:** 'More BJP-ruled states make "The Kashmir Files" movie tax-free', *Business Standard*, 14 March 2022.

39 **The best political promotion, of course:** Aryan Prakash, 'Conspiracy to discredit "Kashmir Files", PM Modi slams "Jamaat" slamming movie', *Hindustan Times*, 15 May 2022.

39 **There has been some silliness involved:** 'Nikhil Chinapa questions Vivek Agnihotri, asks how The Kashmir Files is an "official contender" at the Oscars 2023', *Indian Express*, 13 January 2023.

39 **Nadav Lapid, an Israeli filmmaker, calling it vulgar:** Vasudha Venugopal, 'Israeli envoy slams Nadav Lapid for calling Kashmir Files 'vulgar propaganda', *Economic Times*, 30 November 2022.

39 **After watching it multiple times:** Sanjay Kak, 'The dangerous 'truth' of The Kashmir Files', *Al Jazeera*, 13 April 2022.

39 **In the world of Vivek Agnihotri, the Muslim is a monster:** Vivek Agnihotri, *The Kashmir Files*, 2022, 170 mins.

39 **The monster is manifest in a Muslim child:** Ibid.

40 **in the women who will throw away:** Ibid.

40 **friends who would sell you to the butcher:** Ibid.

40 **Pandits hang from trees by the dozen:** Ibid.

40 **a woman is made to eat rice soaked in her husband's blood:** Ibid.

40 **Later, she is roughed up by a militant:** Ibid.

40 **As Stephen King theorizes in *Danse Macabre*:** Stephen King, *Danse Macabre*, New York: Everest House Publishers, 1981, p. 27.

42 **Supported and enthusiastically promoted by Joseph Goebbels:** Gary Kidney, 'Jud Suss: The Film That Fueled the Holocaust', Warfare History Network, April 2016, available at arfarehistorynetwork.com/article/jud-suss-the-film-that-fueled-the-holocaust.

43 **As the other Jews leave the state, one of the characters:** Viet Harlan, *Jud Süß*, 1940, 1 hr. 38 mins.

43 **On Himmler's orders, the SS units about to be sent to slaughter:** Kidney, 'Jud Suss: The Film That Fueled the Holocaust'.

43 **Screenings of the film were punctuated by riled-up audiences:** Mohammed Zubair, (@zoo_bear), Post, X.com, 14 March 2022.

43 **In Bijnor, after watching the movie a group of people raised calls:** Kaushik Raj, (@kaushikrj6), Post, X.com, 16 March 2022.

43 **The hate it brought to the fore may have played a part:** Supriya Sharma, 'How 'Kashmir Files' added to communal fires in Khargone that ended with

bulldozer injustice', *Scroll.in*, 29 April 2022.

44 ***The Kerala Story* (2023) has already reused the formula:** Shalmesh More, 'The Kerala Story Box Office: Adah Sharma Starrer Goes Beyond a Monstrous Profit Of 600%', Koimoi.com, 26 May 2023.

44 ***Ajmer 92* (2023), similarly, is a movie about a sexual exploitation:** 'Ajmer 92: The gangrape and blackmail case that shook the city', Firstpost, 17 July 2023.

44 **After the Nazis lost the war, and Veit Harlan was tried:** 'VEIT HARLAN, 64, A FILM DIRECTOR; Creator of Anti-Semitic "Jud Suss" for Nazis Is Dead', *New York Times*, 14 April 1964.

44 **He was acquitted by the court twice and died a free man:** Ibid.

45 **As Rushdie said months before being stabbed in the eye:** Yeshi Seli, '"We must tell better stories than the tyrants": Revisiting Salman Rushdie's speech months before fatal attack on him', *New Indian Express*, 14 August 2022.

TRUTH & LIES. WRITING & IDENTITY

46 **In 2014, Navayana, a publishing house:** 'About', Navayana.org, available at navayana.org/about.

46 **Originally, *AoC* was written by Dr Ambedkar:** G. Sampath, 'BR Ambedkar, Arundhati Roy, and the politics of appropriation', *Mint*, 19 March 2014.

46 **Over the years, *AoC* has been published by numerous small presses:** B. R. Ambedkar, 'The Annihilation of Caste', [online facsimile], available at ccnmtl.columbia.edu/projects/mmt/ambedkar/web/readings/aoc_print_2004.pdf.

47 **When *AoC* was first published, Gandhi expressed:** Muzaffar Ali, 'This book examines how the Gandhi-Ambedkar debate on caste influenced theories on the public sphere', *Scroll.in*, 9 October 2023.

47 **The book's launch in Hyderabad was cancelled:** Gee Imaan Semmalar, 'The Not-So-Intimate Enemy: The Loss and Erasure of the Self Under Casteism', RountableIndia.co.in, 19 March 2014, available at www.roundtableindia.co.in/the-not-so-intimate-enemy-the-loss-and-erasure-of-the-self-under-casteism.

47–48 **'Save Ambedkar writings':** Ibid.

48 **A news website called *Dalit Camera* wrote an open letter:** 'An Open Letter to Arundhati Roy', Dalit Camera: Through Un-touchable Eyes, 14 March 2014, available at https://www.roundtableindia.co.in/an-open-letter-to-ms-arundhati-roy.

48 **Various essays critical of her appeared:** 'About Us', RoundtableIndia.co.in, available at www.roundtableindia.co.in.

48 **In an article published by *The Independent*:** Murali Shanmugavelan, 'Arundhati Roy's book on caste rejected by some anti-caste activists', *The Independent*, 16 December 2014.

48 **Towards the conclusion of his piece:** Ibid.

48 **Shanmugavelan equates Roy's acknowledgment:** Ibid.

49 **In 2021, an essay called 'The Native Scholar Who Wasn't':** Sarah Viren, 'The Native Scholar Who Wasn't', *New York Times*, 25 May 2021.

49 **Described as the kind of person 'who once commented':** Ibid.

49 **By 2008, the University of Michigan had denied tenure:** Ibid.

50 **In 2015, an anonymous Tumblr:** Ibid.

50 **While working on her thoroughly researched essay:** Ibid.

50 **It felt as if both of them were 'beginning to find':** Sarah Viren, 'The Accusations

Were Lies. But Could We Prove It?', *New York Times*, 18 March 2020.

50 **The feeling began to dissipate, however, when Marta:** Ibid.

51 **The investigator at ASU told Marta and Sarah:** Ibid.

51 **Their attacker, or the 'villain' of their story:** Ibid.

51 **Viren's suspicions were confirmed:** Ibid.

51 **This is the timeline Viren provides:** Ibid.

52 **If Viren and Tecedor went ahead with the lawsuit:** Ibid.

53 **G. Sampath, for example, in an article:** G. Sampath, 'BR Ambedkar, Arundhati Roy, and the politics of appropriation', *Mint*, 19 March 2014.

53 **Akshay Pathak, another savarna like G. Sampath:** Akshay Pathak, 'The Judge, the Jury and the Goddess', RoundtableIndia.co.in, 7 March 2014, available at www.roundtableindia.co.in/the-judge-the-jury-and-the-goddess.

53 **He admits to being a Brahmin himself:** Ibid.

53 **Karthik Navayan, in his article:** Karthik Navayan, 'Introducing Arundhati Roy and Friends', RoundtableIndia.co.in, 10 April 2014.

53 **Some critics resorted to pointing snidely:** Murali Shanmugavelan, 'On how Arundhati Roy introduces AoC without losing her upper hand', RoundtableIndia.co.in, 25 April 2014.

54 ***The Print* published an article:** Debalina Dey, 'Arundhati Roy joins Shashi Tharoor, Kangana Ranaut in list of 'casteless' upper-caste Indians', *The Print*, 6 September 2020.

54 **Before that, the conversation had already been weaponized:** 'In Re: Arundhati Roy', GlobalFreedomofExpression.columbia.edu, available at globalfreedomofexpression.columbia.edu/cases/re-arundhati-roy.

54 **In an article published by *The Guardian*:** Pankaj Mishra, 'Pankaj Mishra on Arundhati Roy: Hindu nationalists have many ways to silence writers', *The Guardian*, 2 February 2016.

55 **I was introduced to Andrea Smith:** Robin Greenslade and James Robinson, '14 years old Ex-KGB man Alexander Lebedev buys Independent for £1', *The Guardian*, 26 March 2010.

55 **Lenape scholar Joanne Barker, who signed an:** Viren, 'The Native Scholar Who Wasn't'.

55–56 **'A true story written about Marta and me':** Viren, 'The Accusations Were Lies. But Could We Prove It?'.

61 **In 2020, 153 prominent journalists, authors, and writers:** Elliot Ackerman, Saladin Ambar, Martin Amis, Anne Applebaum, et al., 'A Letter on Justice and Open Debate', *Harper's Magazine*, 7 July 2020.

61 **'We are already paying the price in greater risk':** Ibid.

62 **Three days after its publication:** *The Objective*, 10 July 2020.

62 **Major outlets:** Mary MaCnamara, 'Column: 'Cancel culture' is not the problem. The Harper's letter is', *Los Angeles Times*, 9 July 2020.; Laura Bradley, 'J.K. Rowling and Other Assorted Rich Fools Want to Cancel "Cancel Culture"', *Daily Beast*, 7 July 2020.

62 **The counter-letter began by saying:** Bradley, 'J.K. Rowling and Other Assorted Rich Fools Want to Cancel "Cancel Culture"'.

62 **It also did not matter that the 'rich fools':** Sarah Ellison and Elahe Izadi, 'The Harper's 'Letter,' cancel culture and the summer that drove a lot of smart people mad', *Washington Post*, 23 July 2020.

63 **The writer and their work can be dissected:** Samantha Puc, (@theverbalthing), Post, X.com, 21 February 2023.
63 **'a poverty baron who flies around the world':** Shanmugavelan, 'Arundhati Roy's book on caste rejected by some anti-caste activists'.
63 **Even if someone takes the time to look:** See www.linkedin.com/in/theverbalthing.
63 **In her X bio, she calls herself a 'fat witch':** See twitter.com/theverbalthing.
63–64 **Yet, in none of her introductions on websites like CBR:** See www.cbr.com/author/samantha-puc.
64 **As Sarah Viren found out after going through her ordeal:** Viren, 'The Accusations Were Lies. But Could We Prove It?'.
64 **In a 2022 essay, the Nigerian writer:** Alexander Alter, 'Chimamanda Ngozi Adichie Sparks Controversy in Online Essay', *New York Times*, 16 June 2021.
65 **As the German–American political scientist Yascha Mounk points:** Hugh Breakey, 'How a new identity-focused ideology has trapped the left and undermined social justice', *The Conversation*, 15 November 2023.

EAT YOUR FEARS

66 **'Tell me what you eat':** Jean Anthelme Brillat-Savarin, *The Physiology of Taste*, Anne Drayton (tr.), London: Penguin Classics, 1994, p. 13.
66 **As a result of its religious importance to Hindus:** 'Haridwar man opposes sale of eggs in prohibited area, BJP worker, son attack him', *Hindustan Times*, 16 August 2022.
68 **Sweet, salty, and umami 'evolved to point animals':** Rob Dunn and Monica Sanchez, *Delicious: The Evolution of Flavor and How It Made Us Human*, Princeton: Princeton University Press, 2021, p. 15.
68–69 **A study undertaken by Sodexo to map the eating habits:** 'Sodexo Maps Food Eating Habits Of Millennials', *BW People*, 9 May 2019.
69 **'Millennials are not only ready to taste food from across the world':** Ibid.
69 **Courtesy of a recently added option called 'Intercity Legends':** 'Zomato launches 'Intercity legends': Now order food from other cities, here's how it will work', *Indian Express*, 28 September 2022.
69 **In her 2015 book, *A Taste of Generation*:** Eve Turow, *Taste of Generation Yum: How the Millennial Generation's Love for Organic Fare, Celebrity Chefs and Microbrews Will Make or Break the Future of Food*, independently published, 2015, p. 10.
70 **87 per cent of them said that will indulge in a meal:** Ibid.
70 **I really think it comes down to technology:** Joe Pinsker, 'Why Are Millennials So Obsessed With Food?', *The Atlantic*, 14 August 2015.
70 **Soon, every other person started calling themselves a 'foodie':** 'foodie', Google Books Ngram Viewer, available at books.google.com/ngrams/graph?content=foodie&year_start=2000&year_end=2019&corpus=en-2019&smoothing=0.
71 **As per *The Changing Culture of Eating in India*:** Nusra, 'The Changing Culture of Eating in India', Indianretailer.com, 7 June 2013.
73 **Recently, for instance, one of his social media posts:** Krish Ashok, (@_masalab), Post, Instagram.com, 4 March 2023.
74 **First, it can be easy to overlook the fact that the average life expectancy:** 'India Life Expectancy 1950-2024', Macrotrends.net, available at www.macrotrends.

net/global-metrics/countries/IND/india/life-expectancy.

75–76 **The fact that it has a high glycaemic index of 84.4:** 'Is Jaggery Good for Diabetes? Evaluating the Effects on Blood Sugar Levels', reviewed by Dr Rajeev Singh, PharmEasy.net, available at /pharmeasy.in/blog/is-jaggery-good-for-diabetes-evaluating-the-effects-on-blood-sugar-levels.

76 **no significant health advantages over processed sugar:** 'What is Jaggery? Misleading Nutrition Benefits vs. Sugar', Superfoodly.com, 13 February 2019, available at superfoodly.com/what-is-jaggery-nutrition-benefits-vs-sugar.

76 **It is perhaps best summarized by the title of a *Wall Street Journal* article:** Sarah Nassauer, 'When the Box Says 'Protein,' Shoppers Say 'I'll Take It', *Wall Street Journal*, 26 March 2013.

76 **These products are invariably more expensive:** Bee Wilson, 'Protein mania: the rich world's new diet obsession', *The Guardian*, 4 January 2019.

76 **Whey, for example, used to be a useless byproduct:** Ibid.

77 **In India, the market size of whey protein is expected to grow:** 'India Whey Protein Market Size', Mordorintelligence.com, available at www.mordorintelligence.com/industry-reports/india-whey-protein-market/market-size.

77 **As Bee Wilson, a British food writer and journalist, puts it:** Bee Wilson, 'Protein mania: the rich world's new diet obsession', *The Guardian*, 4 January 2019.

77 **Michael Pollan, the celebrated writer:** Michael Pollan, *In Defense of Food: An Eater's Manifesto*, New York: Thorndike Press, 2008, p. 18.

77 **According to Pollan, nutritionism, like most ideologies:** Ibid., p. 43.

77 **The basic assumption, or the ideological premise:** Ibid., p. 44.

77–78 **'the whole point of eating is to maintain and promote bodily health':** Ibid.

78 **In this respect, Pollan and others mention the 'French Paradox':** Emma Wightman, 'The 'French paradox' turned out to be an illusion, but it led to some interesting research', *The Conversation*, 10 July 2017.

78 **In an essay entitled 'Unhappy Meals', Polan quotes:** Michael Pollan, 'Unhappy Meals', *New York Times Magazine*, 28 January 2007.

78 **Well, according to the Vegan Society:** 'Definition of Veganism', Vegansociety.com, available at www.vegansociety.com/go-vegan/definition-veganism.

80 **Beef, the archenemy of vegans, is particularly contentious:** B. R. Ambedkar, 'Read what Ambedkar wrote on why Brahmins started worshipping the cow and gave up eating beef', *Scroll.in*, 2 August 2016.

81 **A little learning is a dangerous thing:** Alexander Pope, *An Essay on Criticism*, [online facsimile], available at www.poetryfoundation.org/articles/69379/an-essay-on-criticism.

82 **'Eat food. Not too much. Mostly plants.':** Pollan, 'Unhappy Meals'.

MILLENNIALS IN THE MOONLIGHT

84 **Currently, millennials make up more than a third:** '7 In 10 Workers Are Millennials In India: Report', *Zee News*, 26 August 2023.

84 **The IT industry, in particular, has been quite partial:** 'Office Buzz. What Gen Z and Millennials want', *Hindu Business Line*, 18 December 2022.

85 **Rishad Premji, Wipro's chairman, has called it:** 'Gone in 10 minutes: Rishad Premji underlines Wipro's 'black and white' approach to ethics violations', *Economic Times*, 20 October 2022.

85 **Ramachandran Sundararajan, chief people officer:** Shreya Bose, 'HCL Opposes Dual-Employment But Doesn't Consider Moonlighting As A 'Big Issue' For Their Company', Trak.in, 17 October 2022.

85 **'My fervent desire and humble desire to youngsters':** Ritu Maria Johny, 'Infosys' Narayana Murthy on India's work culture, favouritism and some advice', *Hindustan Times*, 24 February 2023.

85 **In 2022, Infosys also sent a mail to its employees:** Sneha Saha, 'Infosys may fire employees caught moonlighting, asks everyone to read employment contract', *India Today*, 14 September 2022.

86 **He also fired 50 per cent of Twitter's employees:** Dominic Rushe, Gloria Oladipo, and Johana Bhuiyan, et. al, 'Twitter slashes nearly half its workforce as Musk admits 'massive drop' in revenue', *The Guardian*, 5 November 2022.

86 **In 2022, it was widely reported that Wipro:** Ankita Garg, 'Wipro cuts freshers salary from 6.5 lakh to 3.5 lakh per annum: Full story in 5 points', *India Today*, 21 February 2023.

87 **Consider that Wipro is not a loss-making company:** Raghav Aggarwal, 'Wipro Q3FY24 result: Net profit falls 11% to ₹2,694 cr, dividend declared', *Business Standard*, 12 January 2024.

87 **the Premji family is worth billions of dollars:** 'Premji family', *Forbes*, available at www.forbes.com/profile/premji/?sh=d96137c7c885.

87 **We can also consider that IT CEOs' salaries increased:** Aakanksha Chaturvedi, 'Infosys, Wipro, TCS: IT CEOs' salary increased 1,500% while freshers' salary up only 50% in last 10 years', *Business Today*, 27 December 2022.

87 **Benevolent thoughts of saving youngsters:** 'Narayana Murthy', *Forbes*, available at www.forbes.com/profile/nr-narayana-murthy/?sh=37a92a223e05.

89 **For most Indians, the choice of their career is a family decision:** '82% Indian parents involved in deciding child's career', *Economic Times*, 14 October 2015.

90 **Between 2014 and 2022, for instance, out of the 22.05 crore people:** Harikrishan Sharma, 'Govt job rush: in 8 years, 22 crore applied, only 7.22 lakh were selected', *Indian Express*, 28 July 2022.

90 **only 7.22 lakh were recommended for appointment:** Ibid.

90 **The NASSCOM-Indeed study published in December 2022:** Aakanksha Chaturvedi, '70% young Indians want tech jobs despite mass layoffs says NASSCOM-Indeed study', *Business Today*, 21 December 2022.

90 **The study also provided an explanation for the preference:** Ibid.

90 **In *Kids These Days*, Malcolm Harris defines:** Harris, *Kids These Days*, p. 69.

90 **In an essay published in 2000, Manu Joseph provides a window:** Manu Joseph, 'Great Indian IT Jobs: $20 a Month', *Wired*, 24 November 2000.

91 **'The dream of upward mobility is more like a nightmare':** Ibid.

91 **As of 2022, India has the second-highest number of software engineers:** 'With a Placement Rate of 93.5% Software Engineers have Witnessed 120% Increase in Salary in 2021-2022', *The Hindu*, 2 May 2022.

91 **it is predicted to surpass the USA by 2024:** Ibid.

91 **Yet, as many as 95 per cent of engineers in our country:** '95% engineers in India unfit for software development jobs: Report', *Economic Times*, 20 April 2017.

91 **Even among the remaining 5 per cent, too many would have to settle:** Ibid.

91 **1.4 per cent could write functionally correct and efficient code:** Ibid.

91 **In a 2022, article on the unemployability of engineers in India:** '94% of engineering graduates are not fit for hiring, says this IT stalwart', *Economic Times*, 4 June 2018.

93 **It compares government jobs in Patna where almost 2,000 people:** Alex Travalli and Hari Kumar, 'Want One of India's Best Jobs? You and 1,800 Other Applicants.', *New York Times*, 28 June 2023.

94 **The fate of the planet's biggest generation of workers hangs in the balance:** Ibid.

94 **'Success could mean a more middle-income future':** Ibid.

95 **By the last decades of the twentieth century and into the present:** Jonathan Crary, *24/7: Late Capitalism and the Ends of Sleep*, London: Verso, 2014, pp. 14-15.

96 **'A competitive childhood environment that encourages':** Harris, *Kids These Days*, p. 86.

96 **'In the new work culture, enduring or even merely liking one's job':** Erin Griffith, 'Why Are Young People Pretending to Love Work?', *New York Times*, 26 January 2019.

99 **Shantanu Deshpande, founder of Bombay Shaving Company,:** Shantanu Deshpande, Post, LinkedIn.com, available at www.linkedin.com/feed/update/urn:li:activity:6970213767359946752.

99 **Healthtech unicorn Pristyn Care's co-founder Harsimarbir Singh:** 'Co-founder's post on "interview hacks" his company uses to hire "driven people" triggers debate: 'Interviews at 11 pm, on Sunday', *Indian Express*, 3 September 2022.

100 **In a 2023 interview, Narayana Murthy expressed his belief that young people:** Diksha Madhok, 'Young Indians should work 70 hours a week, says billionaire tech founder', *CNN*, 27 October 2023.

100 **We must assume that Murthy is unaware:** 'Work Hours and Office Timing in India', IndiaLawOffices.com, 6 October 2022, available at www.indialawoffices.com/legal-articles/work-hours-and-office-timing-in-india.

100 **The phenomenon is, in fact, prevalent enough that the Japanese:** Risa, 'Death By Overwork: All About Karoshi', *The True Japan*, 16 July 2021.

100 **Germany, of course, is known worldwide:** David de Jong, 'They Are the Heirs of Nazi Fortunes, and They Aren't Apologizing', *New York Times*, 19 April 2022.

101 **As many as 96 per cent of millennial and Gen Z knowledge workers:** 'Work Relationship Index', HP.com, available at www.hp.com/content/dam/sites/worldwide/apps/work-relationship-index/reports/wri-report/us-en_wri-report.pdf.

101 **75 per cent of all the workers surveyed think it's important to choose:** 'Over 90% of Indian workers prioritise happiness at work over salary, says report', *Mint*, 20 September 2023.

101 **Recent surveys also suggest that Gen Z is not afraid to turn down:** Chloe Kim, 'Pay gap: Will Gen Z salary-sharing on TikTok make a difference?', *BBC*, 29 September 2022.

AT THIRTY, AM I STILL A LIBERAL?

104 **Conservative leaders in the US, for example, so recently sworn:** Khaled A. Beydoun, 'Donald Trump: The Islamophobia president', *Al Jazeera*, 9 November 2016.

105 **The word itself, like liberty, has its root in the Latin liber:** 'What Exactly Is a "Liberal"?', *Merriam-Webster*, availabe at www.merriam-webster.com/wordplay/liberal-meaning-origin-history.

109 **My school was no different from many private schools in India:** Annie Montaut, 'But why do you write in Hindi', *Études Anglaises*, Vol. 62, No. 3, 2009, pp. 332-44.

110 **It can be astonishingly easy to harbour such resentment:** Arundhati Roy, 'The Graveyard Talks Back: Arundhati Roy on Fiction in the Time of Fake News', *Literary Hub*, 12 February 2020.

110 **It sounds reasonable enough when someone comes from:** Ibid.

111 **As Dr Ambedkar said, 'Turn in any direction you like':** Ambedkar, 'The Annihilation of Caste'.

111 **Since problems like these can also become invisible or outdated:** '35,493 Dowry Deaths Reported Between 2017-21: Government', *NDTV*, 14 December 2022.

111 **Moreover, there is a ton of research-based evidence:** Manvir Singh, 'How Dowries Are Fuelling a Femicide Epidemic', *New Yorker*, 12 June 2023.

112 **Neither of them should express any horror when a Muslim is lynched:** 'Dalit Woman Raped, Set On Fire In Rajasthan's Barmer, Dies Of Burn Injures', *NDTV*, 9 April 2023.

112 **To give a recent example, it feels ironic in 2023:** 'We will fight it': AAP after Delhi services bill passed in Rajya Sabha', *India Today*, 8 August 2023.; 'Article 370 revoked: Which political parties supported the bill, which opposed it', *India Today*, 6 August 2019.

113 **Incidentally, the Mayawati-led Bahujan Samaj Party:** 'Article 370 revoked: Which political parties supported the bill, which opposed it', *India Today*, 6 August 2019.

114 **'There is room for debate on how far the supposedly universal principles':** Shashi Tharoor, 'Civilization States Are Profoundly Illiberal', *Noema*, 2 February 2023.

115 **He frequently referred to ideas of thinkers:** Ambedkar, 'The Annihilation of Caste'.

THE AWAARAGARDI OF MILLENNIAL HEARTS

119 **In *The God of Small Things*, Arundhati Roy defines Love Laws:** Arundhati Roy, *God of Small Things*, New York: Random House, 1997, p. 33.

120 **It found that only 19 per cent and 9 per cent of young men and women:** International Institute for Population Sciences (IIPS) and Population Council, 'Youth in India: Situation and Needs', Mumbai: IIPS, 2006–2007.

Moreover, just 8 per cent of young men and 7 per cent of young women: Ibid.

120 **Also from 2007, the Face of Global Sex report published:** 'Indians hang on to lose virginity', The *Economic Times*, 2 June 2023.

121 **Love marriages are on the rise, we are informed by recent surveys:** 'Love Marriages On Rise In India As Arranged Marriages Witness 24% Decline: Survey', *Outlook Business*, 26 April 2023.

121 **Our ideas about sex may also be evolving:** '29% Indians from tier-3 cities are open to the idea of premarital sex, says study', *Times of India*, 11 February 2020.

122 **Major publications have expressed beliefs that we are in the grip:** Rosamund

Hutt, 'The millennial friendship crisis', Weforum.org, 14 August 2019.

122 **A *BBC* article about love and marriage in India:** 'What the data tells us about love and marriage in India', *BBC*, 8 December 2021.

122 **Just 3% had a love marriage and another 2%:** Ibid.

127 **Despite her ample qualifications, Deborah worries:** Joy Buchanan, 'The Part I Remember from Eat, Pray, Love', *Economist Writing Every Day*, 1 July 2023.

127 **It was all: I met this guy when I was living in the refugee camp:** Ibid.

133 **More than 90 per cent people on Tinder in India:** Apoorva Mittal and Shephali Bhatt, 'Fall in Love: Is Online Dating Getting Outdated?', *Economic Times*, 28 October 2023.

134 **Just as we imported other ideas about dating in the West:** Antoinette Radford, 'Who is Andrew Tate? The self-proclaimed misogynist influencer', *BBC*, 12 March 2024.

134 **A Facebook page called MGTOW India:** Gurpreet Kaur, 'Incel Extremism in India: A View from the Global South', Gnet-Research.org, 23 August 2022, available at gnet-research.org/2022/08/23/incel-extremism-in-india-a-view-from-the-global-south.

SPIRITUAL, NOT RELIGIOUS

139 **According to an analysis published in the *New York Times*:** David Leonhardt, 'The Rise of Young Americans Who Don't Believe in God', *New York Times*, 12 May 2015.

139 **By 2021, the number of US adults with no religious affiliations:** Seema Mody, 'Millennials lead shift away from organized religion as pandemic tests Americans' faith', *CNBC*, 31 December 2021.

139 **By 2021, the number of US adults with no religious affiliations:** 'About Three-in-Ten U.S. Adults Are Now Religiously Unaffiliated', Pew Research Centre, 14 December 2021.

139 **In India, religion has shown similar trends of decline:** Vishnu Padmanabhan, 'Religion and the Indian Millennial: What data shows', *Mint*, 9 April 2019.

140 **I tend to agree with studies on the subject of religiosity:** 'Why do levels of religious observance vary by age and country?', Pew Research Centre, 13 June 2018.

140 **Political scientists like Pippa Norris and Ronald Inglehart suggest:** Ibid.

141 **But what should happen if these younger people:** Samantha Raphelson, 'Getting Some 'Me' Time: Why Millennials Are So Individualistic', *NPR*, 14 October 2024.

141 **which also happens to be the largest adult cohort worldwide?:** Dorothy Neufeld, 'There are 1.8 billion millennials on earth. Here's where they live', Weforum.org, 8 November 2021.

143 **Despite the glamorous and peppy sentiments often:** '2023 Gen Z and Millennial Survey', www2.deloitte.com.

143 **We are so exhausted that we have no time to meet people:** Jessica Grose, 'We're Spending More Time Alone. Maybe It's Because We're Exhausted', *New York Times*, 3 December 2022.

144 **Spirituality, the good professor says:** Caroline Newman, 'Why Millennials Are Leaving Religion But Embracing Spirituality', *UVAToday*, 14 December 2015.

145 **In part, it had something to do with the repetitive routine:** 'Watch: Virat

Kohli with wife Anushka and daughter Vamika in Vrindavan to seek Baba's blessings, video goes viral', *ABP Live*, 7 January 2023.

We create our gods in our image, if we were to slightly alter Genesis 1:27: 'Genesis 1', Biblehub.com, available at biblehub.com/kjv/genesis/1.htm.

148 **'But to really make it in this field':** Anirudha Dhar, '"They may practice Christianity but…": Dhirendra Shastri's 'Hindu Rashtra' claim', *Hindustan Times*, 19 February 2023.

148 **We can look for an example at the dharm-sansad held in Haridwar:** Saurabh Shukla, 'Hate Speech-Givers In Haridwar Tell NDTV "Neither Regrets Nor Fear"', Deepshikha Ghosh (ed.), *NDTV*, 23 December 2021.

OUR MONOCHROMATIC TONGUE

150 **In any case, God was not so pleased:** 'Genesis 11:6-11:7', King James Bible, [online facsimile], available at www.bibleref.com/Genesis/11/Genesis-11-7.html.

153 **Similarly, in an essay called 'Generation Amazing':** Emily McCrary-Ruiz-Esparza, 'Generation Amazing!!! How We're Draining Language of Its Power', *Literary Hub*, 27 September 2022.

153 **She lays the blame on our tendency to resort to hyperbole:** Ibid.

153 **She gives a rather interesting example about someone:** Ibid.

154 **This loss of a word's power, or reduction of its intensity:** 'Literally Everything You'll Ever Need To Know About Semantic Bleaching', *Merriam-Webster*, available at https://www.merriam-webster.com/grammar/very-actually-and-other-examples-of-semantic-bleaching.

156 **Well, if numbers are anything to go:** Pamela Bump, 'Millennials vs. Gen Z: Why Marketers Need to Know the Difference [New Data]', *Hubspot*, 10 July 2023.

156 **Well, if numbers are anything to go by:** 'Indian Gen Z spends an average of 8 hours per day online: Isobar-Ipsos #MeetTheZ Survey', *Advertising and Business Insider*, 26 March 2020.

163 **Personally, I try to remember Douglas Adams's three rules:** Jonathan Becher, 'Douglas Adams' Technology Rules', *Forbes*, 7 July 2014.

164 **This is apparent in the introduction to George Orwell's 1946 essay:** George Orwell, 'Politics and the English Language', [online facsimile], available at www.orwellfoundation.com/the-orwell-foundation/orwell/essays-and-other-works/politics-and-the-english-language.

165 **Writing for *The Guardian*, David Shariatmadari characterizes:** David Shariatmadari, 'Why it's time to stop worrying about the decline of the English language', *The Guardian*, 15 August 2019.

165 **Criticizing the concerns of John Humphrys:** Ibid.

168 **I am inclined to agree with Noam Chomsky:** Noam Chomsky, 'Noam Chomsky: The False Promise of ChatGPT', *New York Times*, 8 March 2023.

ANTI-CAA PROTESTS AND THE THING ABOUT SILENCE

169 **Tereza keeps appearing before my eyes:** Milan Kundera, *The Unbearable of Being*, Michael Henry Heim (tr.), United Kingdom: Faber and Faber, 1984, p. 282.

169 By then Amit Shah, the Union home minister, had already explained: Rohan Venkataramakrishnan, 'Who is linking Citizenship Act to NRC? Here are five times Amit Shah did so', *Scroll.in*, 20 December 2019.

169 would be used to throw out the people he referred to as 'termites': Devjyot Ghoshal, 'Amit Shah vows to throw illegal immigrants into Bay of Bengal', *Reuters*, 13 April 2019.

170 Naturally, comparisons were drawn with the Nuremberg laws: Ali Khan Mahmudabad, 'The Citizenship Amendment Act- India's Nuremberg moment', *Times of India*, 21 December 2019.

170 Two days earlier, on 13 December, students: Md Mustafa, Md Minhajuddin, and Shayaan Mujeeb, 'Four years after CAA protests, why Jamia students have lost faith in the system', *Indian Express*, 15 December 2023.

170 In the coming days, this burning of three empty buses: 'Delhi: Anti-CAA protest turns violent as 3 buses burnt in Jamia Nagar', *Economic Times*, 15 Dec 2019.

170 Later that day the Prime Minister, made a flippant remark: 'Those indulging in arson 'can be identified by their clothes': Narendra Modi on anti-CAA protest', *Times of India*, 15 December 2019.

171 In full riot gear, armed with shields and batons: Meghna Prakash, 'We'll Fix Your Blindness: Jamia Student Recalls Delhi Cops' Attack', *The Quint*, 15 December 2022.

171 Some of the policemen destroyed the CCTV cameras: Ibid.

171 Students at Aligarh Muslim University: Ayush Tiwari, 'Beaten, bruised, pelted with stun grenades: Aligarh students recall a night of horror', *News Laundry*, 18 December 2019.

173 Ramchandra Guha, the historian and public intellectual: 'Noted historian Ramchandra Guha detained during anti-CAA protest in Bengaluru', *Hindustan Times*, 19 December 2019.

175 Bol ki lab azaad hain tere: Faiz Ahmad Faiz, 'Bol', [online facsimile], available at www.rekhta.org/nazms/bol-bol-ki-lab-aazaad-hain-tere-faiz-ahmad-faiz-nazms.

176 But I did and learned that a young Muslim protestor: 'People's Tribunal Holds Mangaluru Police Responsible for Violence During Anti-CAA Protests', *The Wire*, 22 January 2020.

177 Maybe I was thinking about the letter that Tomáš: Kundera, *The Unbearable Lightness of Being*, p. 171–72.

177 The letter was published in *Mid-Day*, *The Wire*, and *BusinessWorld*: Vikram Gopal, 'JNU Violence: IIMC Alumni, Staff Write Open Letter to Modi', *The Wire*, 9 January 2020.; 'IIMC Alumni Write Open Letter Expressing Solidarity With JNU Students', *BusinessWorld*, 9 January 2020.; 'IIMC Alumni Staff Pen Open Letter To Prime Minister Narendra Modi Stand In Solidarity With JNU', *Mid-Day*, 9 January 2020.

179 Migrant labourers walking thousands of kilometres: 'The long walk of India's migrant workers in Covid-hit 2020', *Indian Express*, 25 December 2020.

179 farmers sitting in protest for more than a year and dying: 'Why India farmers are protesting again', *BBC*, 13 February 2024.

179 the Hathras rape case and the administration's apathy: Manjula Pradeep, 'Hathras gang rape: Justice for the Dalit victim and her family is crucial', *Hindustan Times*, 3 April 2023.

179 followed by the persecution of journalists who covered the case: Omar Rashid, 'Journalist and three others, arrested on their way to Hathras, booked for sedition in U.P.', *The Hindu*, 7 October 2020.

180–81 I asked her, especially after a man called Kapil Gujjar: 'Man who opened fire at Shaheen Bagh's anti-CAA protest site joins BJP, expelled hours later', *Deccan Herald*, 31 December 2020.

181 BJP leaders like Anurag Thakur and Kapil Mishra: '2020 Delhi riots: HC issues notice to Gandhis, Anurag Thakur, Kapil Mishra, others for "hate speech"', *Scroll.in*, 28 February 2022.

182 'Wherever Muslim women chose to sit in protest': Manish Sahu, 'Anti-CAA protests: Out on bail, Sadaf Jafar says was tortured and called Pakistani', *Indian Express*, 8 January 2020.

182 'I even met lawyers and activists in Lucknow and areas in western U. P.': Dev Ankur Wadhawan, 'UP Police arrested me, gave electric shocks for legal aid to anti-CAA protestors: Kota lawyer', *India Today*, 14 January 2020.

184 The *Cambridge Dictionary* describes apoliticism: 'apoliticism', *Cambridge Dictionary*, [online facsimile], available at dictionary.cambridge.org/dictionary/english/apoliticism.

184 This is hardly a theoretical point: Solcyre Burga and Simmone Shah, 'The History of Self-Immolation as Political Protest', *TIME*, 6 March 2024.

184 Similarly, hundreds of Tibetan monks have died by self-immolation: Edward Wong, 'In Occupied Tibetan Monastery, a Reason for Fiery Deaths', *New York Times*, 2 June 2012.

189 Movements like the Palestinian-led BDS (Boycott, Divestment, Sanctions): 'Get Involved', BDSmovement.net, available at bdsmovement.net/get-involved/what-to-boycott.

190 Moreover, Huemer points out that most of the time: Michael Huemer, 'In Praise of Passivity', *Studia Humana*, Vol, 1, No. 2, 2012, p. 17.

190 But those who most passionately guilt others about being apolitical: Ibid., p. 19.

EVERYONE KILLED SUSHANT SINGH RAJPUT

212 More than 10,000 farmers and agricultural labourers died: Partha Sarathi Biswas, 'NCRB report shows farm suicides on rise: Why more farm labourers ending lives than farmers after Covid', *Indian Express*, 5 December 2023.

212 Also in 2020, 8,000-odd people died along railway tracks: 'Lockdown 2020: Over 8,700 people died on railway tracks during the year, many of them migrants', *Economic Times*, 2 June 2021.

212 She died two weeks later and was cremated: 'Hathras gang rape: India victim cremated 'without family's consent', BBC, 30 September 2022.

213 This is what I wrote: A. M. Gautam (@AMGautamWrites), Post, X.com, 28 July 2023.

213 The general tone and intent of these replies: Pakhi:waitingtoembraceU (@ppakhii), Post, X.com, 28 July 2023.

216 We may also gauge the peculiarly disturbing nature: Parvathi Benu, 'Afterwaves of Covid-19. Is economic distress causing a spike in suicide deaths in India?', *Hindu Business Line*, 23 March 2023.

216 In fact, the year 2021 has the dubious distinction: 'Deaths by suicide highest ever in India in 2021, domestic problems biggest reason, shows NCRB data', *Scroll.in*, 30 August 2022.

217 **The word 'suicide', for instance, was used the most:** Syeda Zainab Akbar, Ankur Sharma, and Himani Negi, et. Al, 'Anatomy of a Rumour: Social media and the suicide of Sushant Singh Rajput', *arXiv*, 8 October 2022, available at arxiv.org/pdf/2009.11744.

217 **Those associated with BJP were twice as vocal:** Ibid.

217 **as those with INC (32,406 tweets):** Ibid.

217 **Among news anchors, Arnab Goswami led the charge:** Ibid.

218 **In a nod to 'Pappu', he even got an infantilizing nickname:** Sachin Gaad, 'Mumbai: Man booked for calling Aaditya Thackeray 'baby penguin', *Free Press Journal*, 16 July 2020.

222 **For example, consider this anonymous comment:** V. Narayan, 'No evidence of abetment found against Rhea Chakraborty', *Times of India*, 7 August 2020.

223 **A jolly good-natured human being, a celebrity at that, suddenly commits suicide:** Ibid.

226 **In her 2018 book:** Poonam, *Dreamers:*, New Delhi: Viking, p. 23.

226 **'Shanky (the RJ) doesn't offer his audience':** Ibid., p. 24.

226 **In principle, Saahil Choudhary's YouTube:** See www.youtube.com/@SaahilChoudharyvlogs.

227 **According to a 2018 report by the National Statistical Office:** 'NSSO Data Puts Unemployment at 45-Year High in 2017-18: Report', *The Wire*, 31 January 2019.

227 **In 2019, just 20 per cent of employed people:** Yogima Seth Sharma, 'Workers below 30 years of age saw significant job losses during lockdown: CMIE', *Economic Times*, 30 July 2020.

227 **Dating apps, insofar as they have penetrated:** Mittal and Bhatt, 'Fall in Love: Is Online Dating Getting Outdated?'.

MILLENNIALS AT PLAY: THAT'S SO CRINGE!

230 **According to the *Oxford English Language Dictionary*:** 'cringe', Oxford English Dictionary, available at www.oed.com/dictionary/cringe_n?tab=meaning_and_use#7808145.

230 **Kate Ryan, writing for the *New York Times*:** Kate Ryan, 'Welcome to CringeTok, Where Being Insufferable Can Be Lucrative', *New York Times*, 3 June 2023.

230 **Vox describes it as 'a shortened form of "cringey"':** Rebecca Jennings, 'When ordinary people go viral, where's the line between comedy and cruelty?', Vox.com, 20 November 2020.

231 **For instance, as of 2023, the time average Indians spend:** Raghav Aggarwal, 'Average Indian spends 194 minutes daily on social media platforms: Report', *Business Standard*, 16 August 2023.

231 **Among these social media users, as many as 250 million:** 'India now has 25 crore users of short-form video platforms', *ET Telecom*, 8 November 2023.

231 **98 per cent of daily mobile video engagement:** 'Gen Z and millennials take up 98% of daily mobile video engagement', *Economic Times Brand Equity*, 28 September 2023.

231 **Before TikTok was banned by the government of India:** Ankita Chakravarti,

'Indian users spent over 5.5 billion hours on TikTok in 2019, reports reveal', *India Today*, 3 February 2020.

233 **According to Natalie Wynn, an award-winning YouTuber:** Natalie Wynn, (@ ContraPoints), Video, YouTube.com, 10 May 2020.

234 **His videos with titles like 'TikTok Try Not To Laugh/Cringe Challenge vs My Sister':** Nischay Malhan (@Triggered Insaan), Video, YouTube.com, 14 July 2019.

234 **A compilation video he released on Valentine's Day in 2024:** Nischay Malhan (@Triggered Insaan), Video, YouTube.com, 14 February 2024.

235 **when he was awarded a National Creators Award:** Pranav Dixit, 'Gaming getting recognition is a big deal: YouTuber Triggered Insaan after receiving award from PM Modi', *Business Today*, 9 March 2024.

235 **For example, one can consider the reels of a vlogger:** See www.instagram.com/raja_vlogs1123.

235 **To be relatable to us, the oh-so-better viewers:** Ashmita Saha, 'Bihar man's wedding vlog explodes on social media, a reel for every ritual', *India Today*, 19 February 2024.

236 **It is no coincidence that TikTok was the platform:** Pooja Singh, 'In tier-2 and -3 towns, TikTok influencers out of income, validation', *Mint*, 5 July 2020.

236 **With fourteen regional languages available to them:** Ananya Bhattacharya, 'After India's ban on Chinese apps, TikTok stars are looking for a new digital home', *Mint*, 3 July 2020.

236 **four out of the world's fifteen highest-paid TikTokers were Indian:** Shephali Bhatt, 'Four Indian creators among top 15 highest paid TikTokers of 2020', *Economic Times*, 23 October 2020.

236 **Incidentally, a look at the search and usage of the terms 'cringe':** 'cringe', Trends.Google. Com, available at trends.google.com/trends/explore?date=2004-11-02%202024-03-11&geo=IN&q=cringe&hl=en.; 'cringe', Google Books Ngram Viewer, available at https://books.google.com/ngrams/graph?content=cringe&year_start=2004&year_end=2019&corpus=en-2019&smoothing=3.

236 **Savitri from Ongole, a small city in Andhra Pradesh:** See www.instagram.com/lakshmibhavani3024?igsh=OWV3ZmZxMmdtbThu.

238 **From the Google KPMG 2021 and Redseer reports:** Dr Tanvi Gupta and Adishri Guha, 'Digital Heartlands Report 2023', *Consumer Cultura Lab*, Udaipur: IIM Udaipur, 2023.

238 **in 2020 over 95 per cent of video consumption:** Ibid.

238 **75 per cent of all Indians browsing the Internet:** Ibid.

238 **According to Redseer, the short-video app economy:** Ibid.

238 **Mentions of millennials and 'cringiness' actually saw a 119 per cent increase:** Ann-Derrick Gaillot and Elena Tarasova, 'Millennial Cringe: What it is, who's talking about it, and what it tells marketers', *Meltwater*, 22 November 2023, available at www.meltwater.com/en/blog/millennial-cringe.

238 **There is even a TikTok trend in the US called Millennial Core:** Andrew Lloyd, 'Welcome to 'millennial core,' the latest trend pointing out all the ways Gen Z thinks millennials are hilariously cringe', *Business India Insider*, 28 November 2023.

EPILOGUE

240 **Luxury apartments in Gurugram sell within days:** Mohak Mangal, (@Mohak_Mangal), Video, YouTube, 4 March 2024.

240 **as India goes through a time of 'jobless growth':** Ira Dugal, 'Where are the jobs? India's world-beating growth falls short', *Reuters*, 31 May 2023.

240 **Caste-based crimes rise:** Ambika Pandit, 'Crimes against SCs went up 13% and against STs by 14.3% in 2022: NCRB', *Times of India*, 6 December 2023.

240 **Already, there are signs that they are not as enamoured:** Blair Currie, 'Gen Z Finds Stability By Embracing The Past', *Forbes*, 24 May 2022.